# HAL LEONARD GUITAR METHOD

## INCREDIBLE SCALE FINDER

Supplement to Any Guitar Method

Easy-to-Use Guide to Over 1300 Guitar Scales

# CONTENTS



by Adam St. James

ISBN 0-634-02027-7

## HAL•LEONARD® CORPORATION


7777 W. BLUEMOUND RD. P.O. BOX 13819 MILWAUKEE, WI 53213




Visit Hal Leonard Online at
**www.halleonard.com**

# INTRODUCTION

This book was designed with one goal in mind: to help guitarists comprehend and utilize all of the distinct tonal flavors available to them on their fretboards through a working knowledge of the most common and most useful scales and modes. You'll use the *Incredible Scale Finder* as both an in-depth study guide and a quick reference tool for years to come.

## Why are scales so important?

Scales hold the key to understanding almost every element of music. With even the slightest grasp of how scales are constructed, guitarists—all musicians in fact—are better able to comprehend: 1) how melodies and songs are constructed, 2) how chords are built, and 3) how to take flight with more exciting and satisfying solos and instrumental breaks.

Strangely, some musicians regard scales as too confining—possessing an inherently imposing set of rules that stifle artistic expression. Nothing could be further from the truth. Knowledge is truly power, and the knowledge contained within these pages is all about musical power and creative freedom.

## Navigating the Incredible Scale Finder

This book consists primarily of guitar neck diagrams that illustrate precise scale patterns from all twelve root notes: C, C#/Db, D, D#/Eb, F, F#/Gb, G, G#/Ab, A, A#/Bb, and B. For each root, we've shown the exact fingerings to the most important modes and scale forms—from one end of the neck to the other. With this information, you'll no longer be trapped in one spot on the fretboard. Instead, you'll see exactly how to move up and down the neck in any key, using a full palette of colorful scales and modes to create sounds that represent your every musical whim and mood.

There are seventeen different scale forms illustrated in this book. For ease of learning and other reasons we'll explain in the next few pages, they're presented in the following order:

1) Major scale (Ionian mode)
2) Major pentatonic
3) Natural minor scale (Aeolian mode)
4) Minor pentatonic
5) Blues scale
6) Mixo-blues scale
7) Mixolydian mode
8) Dorian mode
9) Melodic minor scale
10) Harmonic minor scale
11) Phrygian mode
12) Locrian mode
13) Lydian mode
14) Diminished scale (half-whole)
15) Diminished scale (whole-half)
16) Chromatic scale
17) Whole tone scale

# THE 17 SCALES AND MODES

Learning these scales and modes will be easier if you understand the fundamentals of how they're built. As you may or may not know, a *scale* is simply a progression of notes in a certain order with fixed intervals. (A *mode* is essentially the same thing.) Every scale type is different. To build scales, or to compare them with one another, we generally use two methods:

**1) Whole and half steps.** On the guitar, a *half step* is the distance from one fret to the next; a *whole step* is the distance of two frets. Every scale type can be seen as a pattern of whole and half steps from a root to its octave. Major scales, for example, always follow this formula: whole-whole-half-whole-whole-whole-half.

**2) Numeric formula.** Every note, or degree, of a scale can also be given a specific number that refers to its distance, or *interval*, from the root. Major scales, for example, have seven notes (excluding the octave): 1–2–3–4–5–6–7.

|   1   |   2   |   3   |   4   |   5   |   6   |   7   |
|-------|-------|-------|-------|-------|-------|-------|
|   C   |   D   |   E   |   F   |   G   |   A   |   B   |

Other scales are referenced similarly. The major pentatonic, for example, is a five-note scale that leaves out the 4th and 7th degrees: 1–2–3–5–6. The natural minor scale has seven notes, but its 3rd, 6th, and 7th degrees are each a half step lower: 1–2–♭3–4–5–♭6–♭7. And so on.

Before you start learning fretboard patterns, let's take a quick look at the scales and modes you'll find in this book.

## Major scale (Ionian mode)
(1–2–3–4–5–6–7)

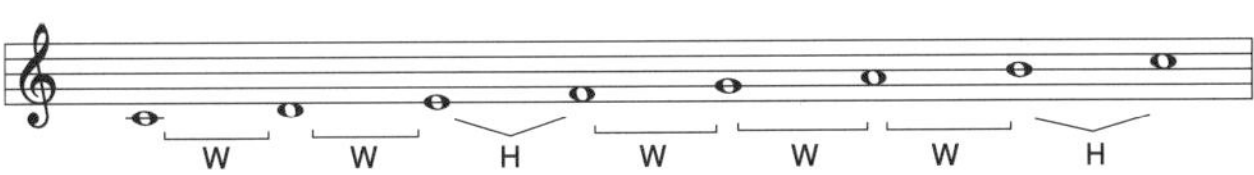

The major scale is probably the most important of all scales to know and understand. During the past several centuries, most Western music has been based on this scale and its modes, which are built by simply rearranging or re-prioritizing its half-step/whole-step formula. This seven-note scale is also referred to as the Ionian mode.

## Major pentatonic
(1–2–3–5–6)

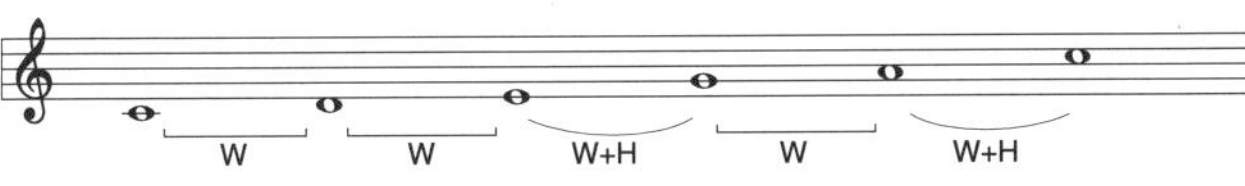

After learning the major scale, it makes sense to learn the five-note major pentatonic scale, which includes all the same notes as the major scale, but leaves out the 4th and 7th scale degrees. This is also a very important and popular scale. Be sure to learn all five positions, as they each facilitate their own cool licks.

## Natural minor scale
## (Aeolian mode)
(1–2–♭3–4–5–♭6–♭7)

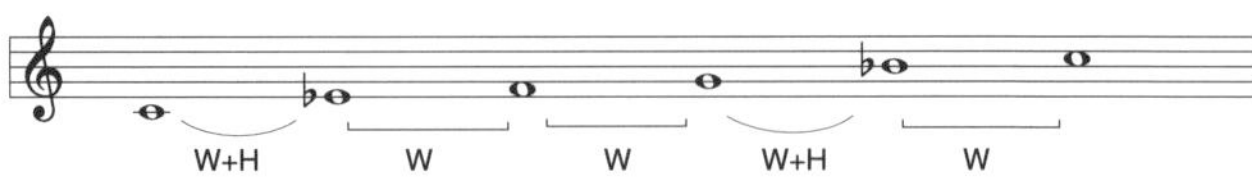


The natural minor scale is probably the second most important scale or mode in the canon of Western music for the past half-millennium. Many guitarists make the seven-note natural minor scale the launch pad for most of their playing, due in part to the easy fingering of its root-position pattern, and partly because the interval from the scale's root note to its minor 3rd just seems to sound so good over most rock- or blues-based chord progressions.

## Minor pentatonic
(1–♭3–4–5–♭7)

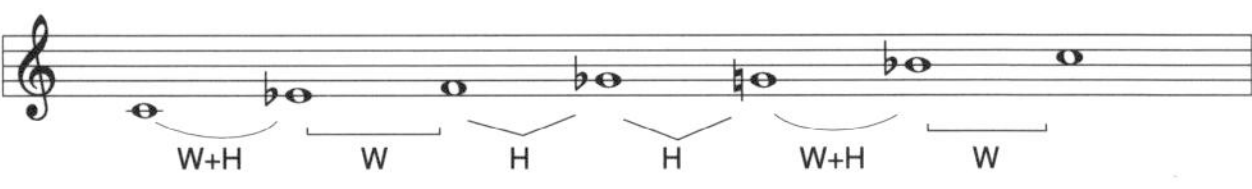


To guitarists, the five-note minor pentatonic scale could be the mother of all scales. This is where many players' knowledge of scales begins and ends. Of course, that approach extremely limits your musical options. It is a very important scale, though, and should be learned in all of its five positions.

## Blues scale
(1–♭3–4–♭5–5–♭7)

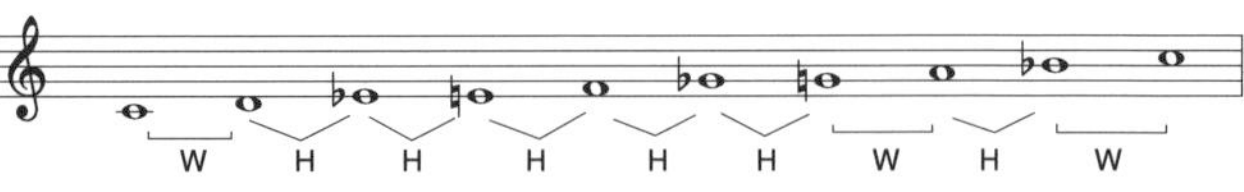


The blues scale is a slight variation on the minor pentatonic. This six-note scale contains all the notes in the minor pentatonic scale plus the diminished-5th interval. It is also a very important scale upon which many great songs are built, though just like the minor pentatonic, many guitarists use the blues scale to the point of musical exhaustion. After the major and minor scales and their corresponding pentatonics, however, the blues scale is probably the next most important.

## Mixo-blues scale
(1–2–♭3–3–4–♭5–5–6–♭7)

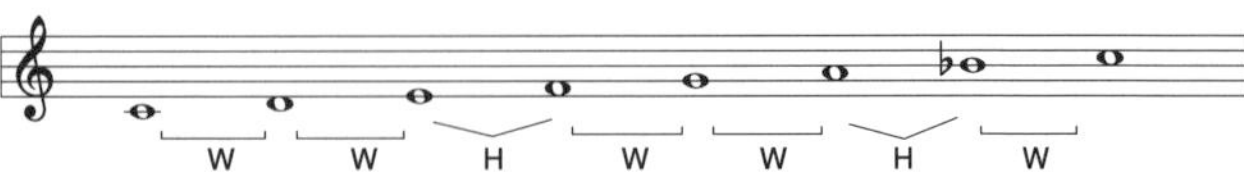


The Mixo-blues scale is a very important tool that many legendary players use almost exclusively. It's a hybrid scale that merges the blues scale with the Mixolydian mode. This nine-note combination scale works extremely well over most blues and many rock songs. The main and most useful feature of this scale is its inclusion of both the minor and major 3rd as well as the minor 7th. Though the Mixo-blues scale might seem complicated at first glance, it can be quite easily memorized by thinking of a major scale with a minor 7th (instead of a major 7th) and an additional minor 3rd and diminished 5th.

## Mixolydian mode
(1–2–3–4–5–6–♭7)



The Mixolydian mode is one of the major modes and is the same as the major scale except that the major 7th is flatted to form a minor 7th. This seven-note pattern is a great scale to use over twelve-bar blues-style chord progressions, though it will often give way to the Mixo-blues scale as the player becomes comfortable with that hybrid scale.

# Dorian mode

(1–2–♭3–4–5–6–♭7)

Dorian is one of the most commonly used modes. This seven-note minor scale is very similar to the natural minor scale (a.k.a. the Aeolian mode), but it contains a major 6th instead of a minor 6th. Try it any time you might otherwise play the natural minor scale and take particular note of how the different 6th intervals affect your music.

# Melodic minor scale

(1–2–♭3–4–5–6–7)

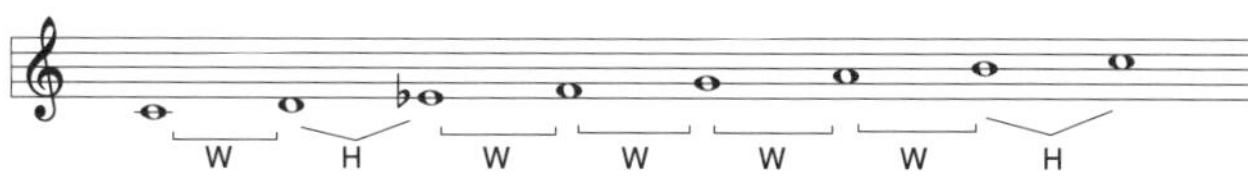


This seven-note minor scale is very unusual in that it can be played differently when ascending than when descending. On the ascent, the melodic minor is identical to a major scale, except for the flatted 3rd degree, which of course makes it a minor scale. On the descent, the 7th and 6th degrees are commonly lowered, making the scale identical to natural minor (refer to the natural minor patterns for this descending form of the melodic minor scale). The reason for this difference is that the raised 6th and 7th degrees tend to pull toward resolution at the octave when ascending. When descending, however, flatting the 6th and 7th degrees creates a downward pull toward the 5th, also a strong resolution note. In practice, the ascending form of the melodic minor is often used exclusively when improvising—particularly in jazz.

# Harmonic minor scale

(1–2–♭3–4–5–♭6–7)

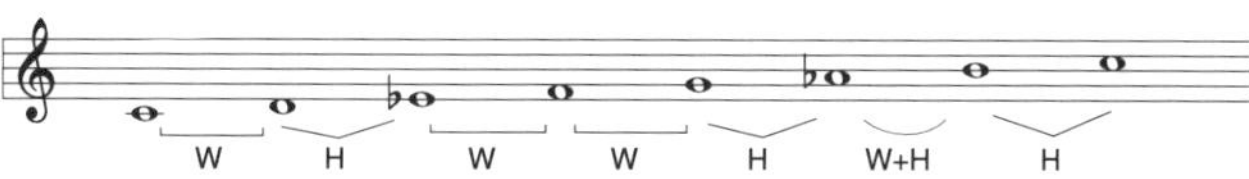


The harmonic minor scale is very exotic sounding for what is otherwise a simple minor scale, albeit with a major 7th instead of the natural minor's flat 7th. The harmonic minor's jump from its minor 6th to its major 7th—an interval of one and a half steps—quickly evokes images of ancient Egypt. While this isn't a true foreign scale, and this book won't explore the vast and intriguing range of scale spellings found in non-Western music, the seven-note harmonic minor is a definite attention-getter.

# Phrygian mode

(1–♭2–♭3–4–5–♭6–♭7)

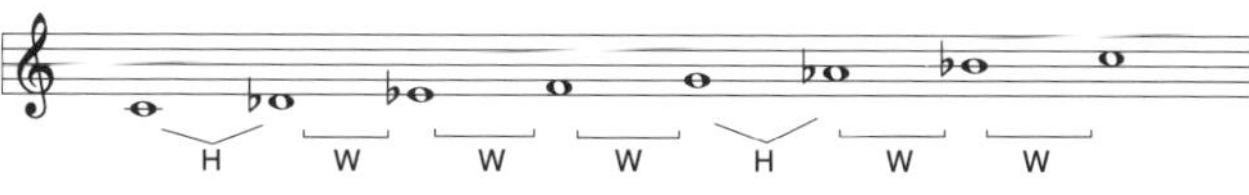


The Phrygian mode is another minor scale with an exotic side. Like the Dorian mode, the seven-note Phrygian is very similar to a natural minor scale, but with one difference: The Phrygian mode includes a very unusual-sounding minor 2nd. This mode is commonly used in flamenco music and works well in any song in which the chords repeatedly resolve to the I (one or tonic) chord from a half-step above (F to Em, for example, with Em as the i chord).

# Locrian mode

(1–♭2–♭3–4–♭5–♭6–♭7)

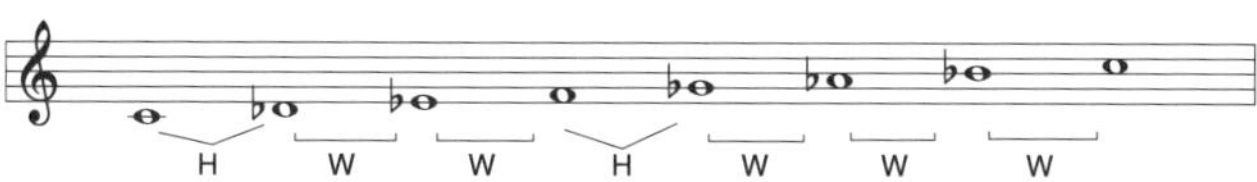


Because the triad built from the root note in the Locrian mode is diminished (the i chord in Locrian consists of scale steps 1, ♭3, and ♭5), the mode is neither major nor minor. The seven-note Locrian mode is sometimes called the "half-diminished" mode and is rarely used outside of jazz fusion or heavy metal. Try using Locrian over a chord progression in the key of E with an F and B♭ chord.

# Lydian mode

(1–2–3–♯4–5–6–7)

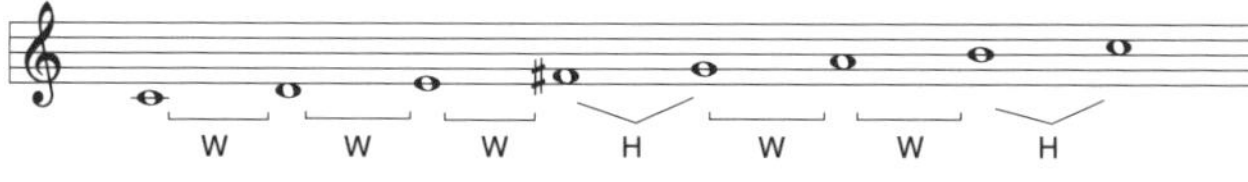


The Lydian mode, a seven-note major scale with an augmented 4th scale degree, is a common jazz tool and was a favorite of many nineteenth-century "Impressionist" composers, particularly Claude Debussy. The raised 4th is the only difference between the Lydian mode and major scale.

## Diminished scale (half-whole)

(1–♭2–♭3–♮4–♭5–5–6–♭7)
Diminished scales are quite fun to throw into solos. These eight-note scales

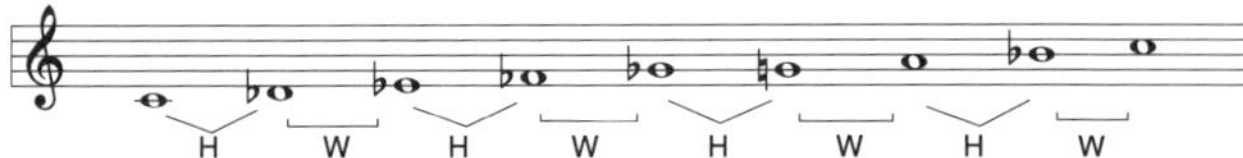

break up the more normal scales and modes that make up the bulk of our playing with a striking, almost cinematic effect. The half-whole diminished scale works well over V7 chords, especially those with flatted 5ths and raised or lowered 9ths. Also, diminished scales (both varieties) can be interpreted enharmonically as several different diminished scales.

In fact, there really are only three different half-whole diminished scales. If you play this scale over a C7 chord, for instance, the diminished scales on C, C♯, and D would be different scales. But by the time you arrived at E♭, you'd be using the same exact scale spelling you used on C, or an enharmonically equivalent group of notes. This is what is known as *symmetrical.* To sum this up:

C diminished = E♭ diminished = F♯ diminished = A diminished
C♯ diminished = E diminished = G diminished = B♭ diminished
D diminished = F diminished = A♭ diminished = C♭ diminished

Even better, there are only two diminished patterns to learn. These two finger patterns alternate consecutively all the way up the neck. The same two patterns work for both the half-whole and the whole-half diminished scales, just in a different order.

## Diminished scale (whole-half)

(1–2–♭3–4–♭5–♯5–6–7)
The eight-note whole-half diminished scale is really the true diminished scale, and

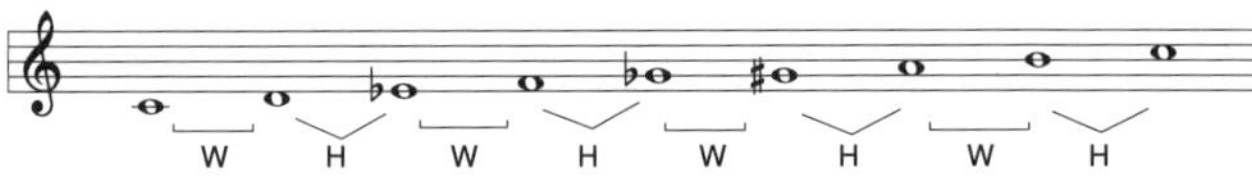

can be used over either diminished chords or half-diminished chords. Again, there are only three different whole-half diminished scales: C, C♯, and D. All others are enharmonically the same as these three.

## Chromatic scale

(1–♭2–2–♭3–3–4–♭5–5–♭6–6–♭7–7)

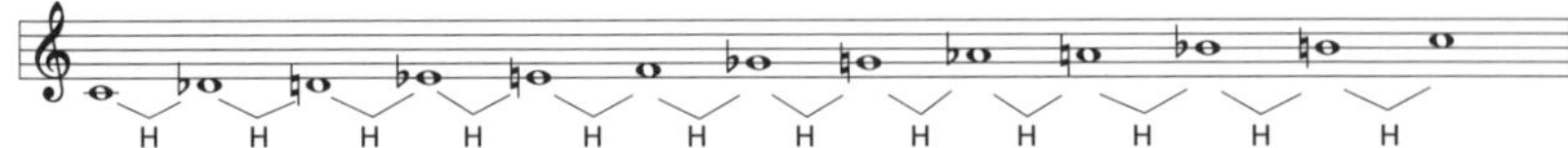

The twelve-note chromatic scale has got to be the easiest of all scales to memorize. It is built entirely of half steps and uses every note on the neck of the guitar. So really, there is only one chromatic scale, and it can begin or end on any note. The chromatic scale also makes for an excellent fret-hand exercise pattern. We show two common chromatic patterns in this book, but you can insert chromatic half-step runs into any other scale, any place on the neck, at any time, without worrying about whether or not you're correctly playing the two patterns illustrated here.

## Whole tone scale

(1–2–3–♯4–♯5–♯6)
The six-note whole tone scale is probably the next easiest to remem-

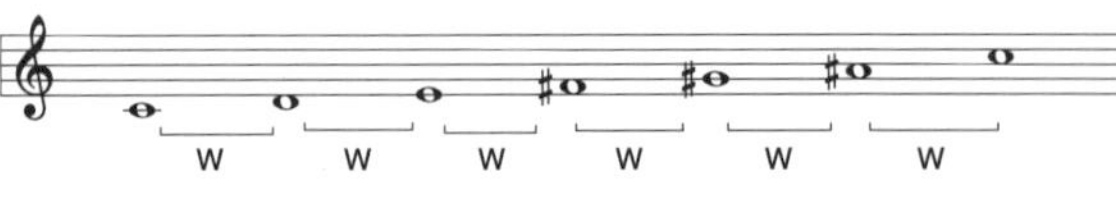

ber, since it is constructed entirely of whole steps. The scale sounds very jazzy—even mysterious—and was used extensively by nineteenth-century composer Claude Debussy as well as many jazz players at the height of the bebop era. Another of the symmetrical scales, there are really only two whole tone scales: one beginning on C and the other on C♯. By the time you get to D, you're playing the same notes as in the C whole tone scale, but starting on D.

# IMPROVISING AND SOLOING

Once you've learned a few of the scales in this book in various positions on the neck, you may start wondering how to apply them to songs. Here are a few tips:

## Major and Minor Keys

Keys are a great way to approach soloing and improvising because they allow you to choose one scale for a whole song (or progression) and stick with it, rather than picking a new scale for every chord. If a song or progression is in a major key, use the corresponding major scale (e.g., C major for the key of C) or its pentatonic version. If a song is in a minor key, use the natural minor scale or the minor pentatonic. To decode a song's key, try plugging its chords into the chart below. All the chords should fit horizontally into one of the rows. If a song is in C major, for example, it will use some or all of the chords in the first row, with an emphasis on the I ("one") chord, C. If a song is in A minor, it will likewise make use of chords in the first row, but with an emphasis on the vi ("six") chord, Am. (NOTE: Some songs go through more than one key, in which case you'll need to use more than one scale in your soloing.)

major keys                                    minor keys

| I | ii | iii | IV | V | vi | vii° |
|---|----|-----|----|----|----|------|
| C | Dm | Em | F | G | Am | B° |
| D♭ | E♭m | Fm | G♭ | A♭ | B♭m | C° |
| D | Em | F#m | G | A | Bm | C#° |
| E♭ | Fm | Gm | A♭ | B♭ | Cm | D° |
| E | F#m | G#m | A | B | C#m | D#° |
| F | Gm | Am | B♭ | C | Dm | E° |
| F# | G#m | A#m | B | C# | D#m | E#° |
| G | Am | Bm | C | D | Em | F#° |
| A♭ | B♭m | Cm | D♭ | E♭ | Fm | G° |
| A | Bm | C#m | D | E | F#m | G#° |
| B♭ | Cm | Dm | E♭ | F | Gm | A° |
| B | C#m | D#m | E | F# | G#m | A#° |
| Ionian | Dorian | Phrygian | Lydian | Mixolydian | Aeolian | Locrian |

## Modes

If a song's chords fit into one of the rows above, but a chord other than the I or vi is emphasized, the song may be in a *mode*. In that case, look along the bottom of the chart above to find the mode that corresponds with the emphasized chord. For example, if a song uses chords from the top row, but Dm is clearly the main, or "tonic," chord (e.g., Dm–G–Am–Dm), try soloing with the D Dorian mode.

## The Chord-by-Chord Approach

If a chord progression moves slowly, or if a song lingers primarily on just one chord, you may want to opt for a chord-by-chord approach to soloing. In that case, simply determine the quality of the chord over which you're playing—major, minor, etc.—and apply whatever scale or mode fits its basic structure. You can even try alternating between different scale types.

| Chord type | Formula | Scale | Mode |
|------------|---------|-------|------|
| Major | 1-3-5 | Major, major pentatonic, blues | Ionian, Lydian, Mixolydian |
| Minor | 1-♭3-5 | Minor, minor pentatonic, blues | Dorian, Phrygian, Aeolian |
| Diminished | 1-♭3-♭5 | Diminished | Locrian |
| Augmented | 1-3-#5 | Whole tone | |
| Major 7th | 1-3-5-7 | Major, major pentatonic | Ionian, Lydian |
| Minor 7th | 1-♭3-5-♭7 | Minor, minor pentatonic | Dorian, Phrygian, Aeolian |
| Dominant 7th | 1-3-5-♭7 | Blues, Mixo-blues | Mixolydian |

Always keep this in mind: Scales and modes aren't usually played from root to root; this is just the way they're demonstrated. The notes of a scale can be played in *any* order, and you don't need to use them all to make music. Experiment and have fun!

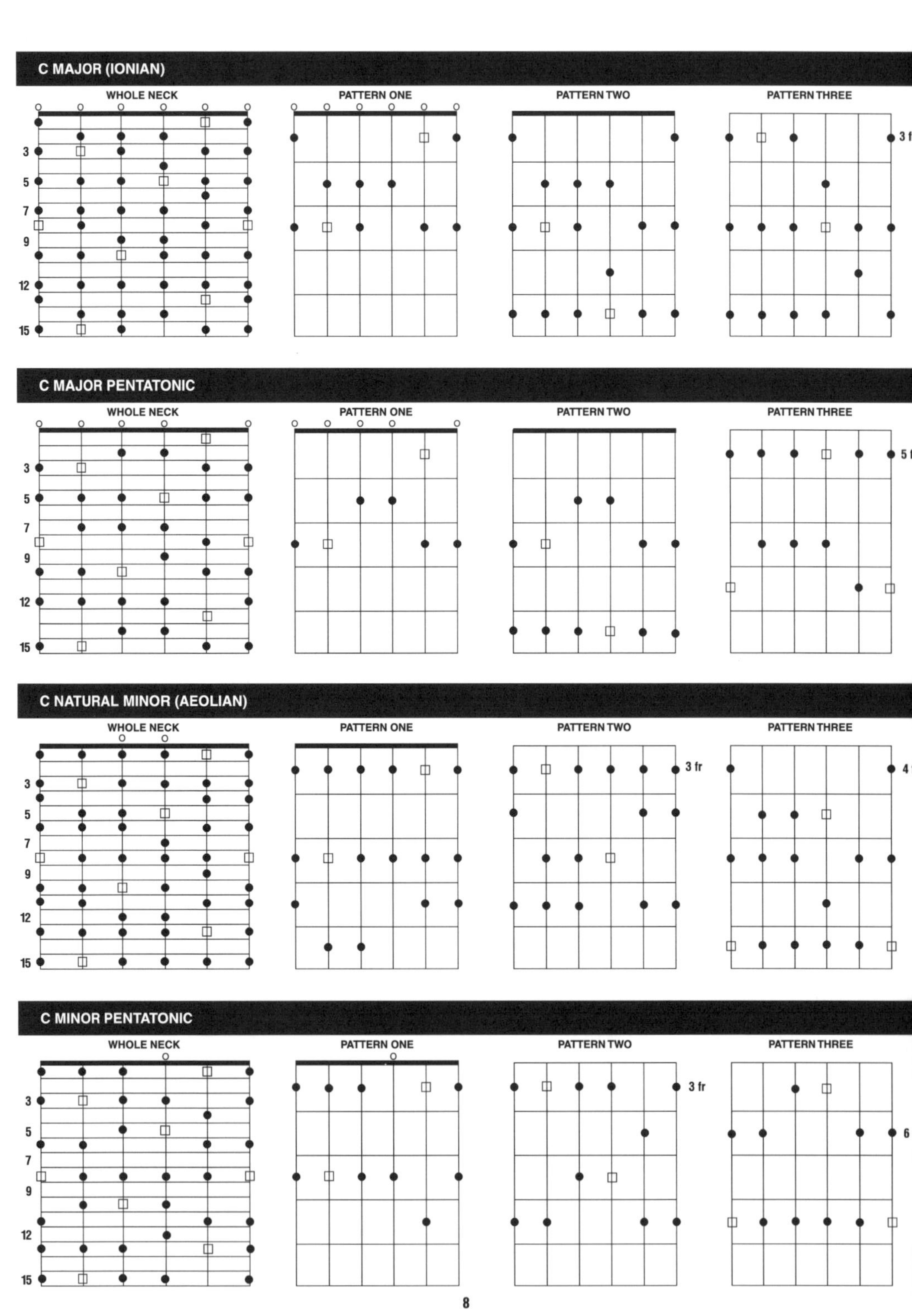

C MAJOR (IONIAN)
WHOLE NECK
PATTERN ONE
PATTERN TWO
PATTERN THREE
3 fr
C MAJOR PENTATONIC
WHOLE NECK
PATTERN ONE
PATTERN TWO
PATTERN THREE
5 fr
C NATURAL MINOR (AEOLIAN)
WHOLE NECK
PATTERN ONE
PATTERN TWO
3 fr
PATTERN THREE
4 fr
C MINOR PENTATONIC
WHOLE NECK
PATTERN ONE
PATTERN TWO
3 fr
PATTERN THREE
6 fr

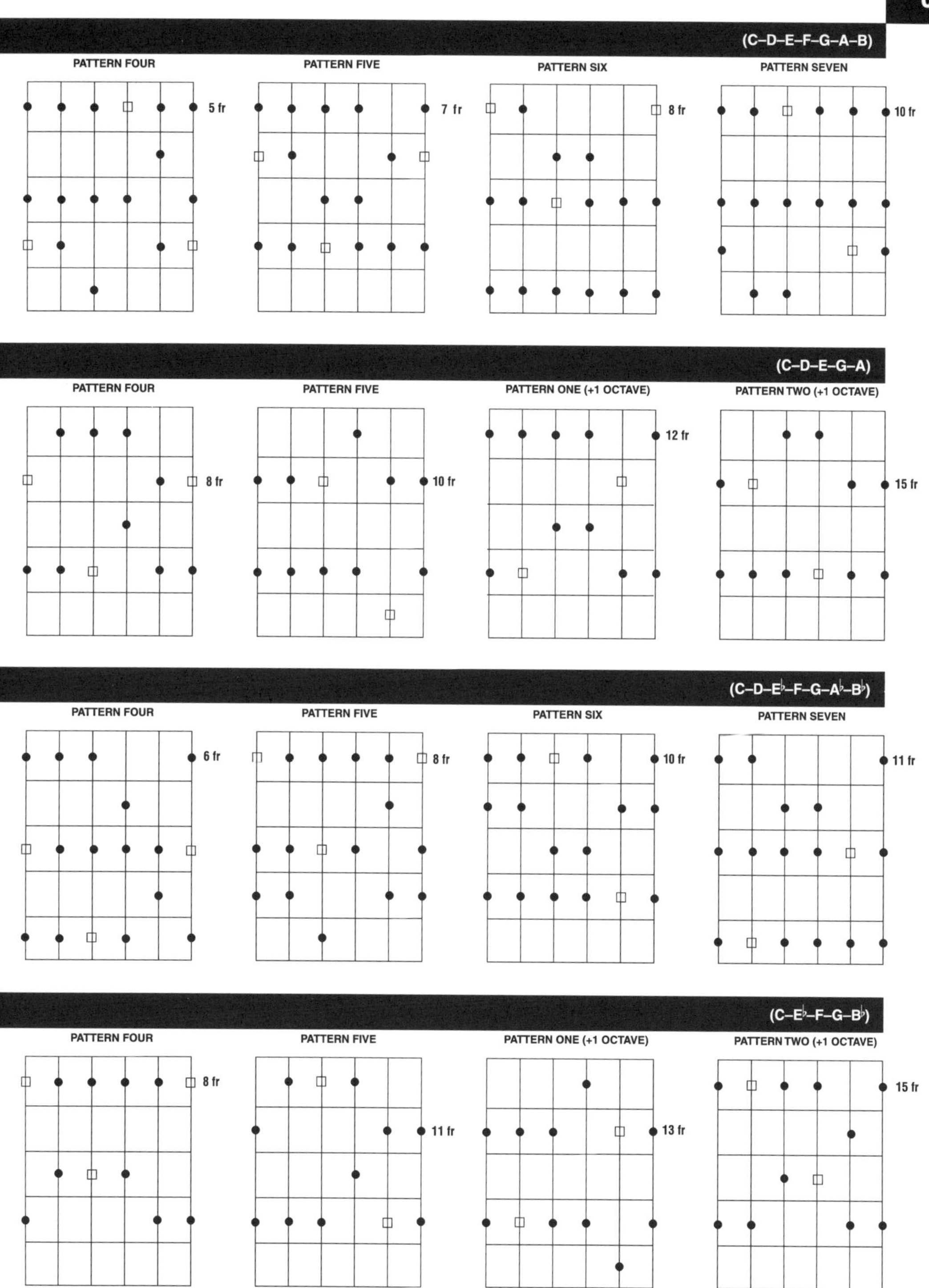

C
(C–D–E–F–G–A–B)
PATTERN FOUR
PATTERN FIVE
PATTERN SIX
PATTERN SEVEN
5 fr
7 fr
8 fr
10 fr
(C–D–E–G–A)
PATTERN FOUR
PATTERN FIVE
PATTERN ONE (+1 OCTAVE)
PATTERN TWO (+1 OCTAVE)
8 fr
10 fr
12 fr
15 fr
(C–D–E♭–F–G–A♭–B♭)
PATTERN FOUR
PATTERN FIVE
PATTERN SIX
PATTERN SEVEN
6 fr
8 fr
10 fr
11 fr
(C–E♭–F–G–B♭)
PATTERN FOUR
PATTERN FIVE
PATTERN ONE (+1 OCTAVE)
PATTERN TWO (+1 OCTAVE)
8 fr
11 fr
13 fr
15 fr

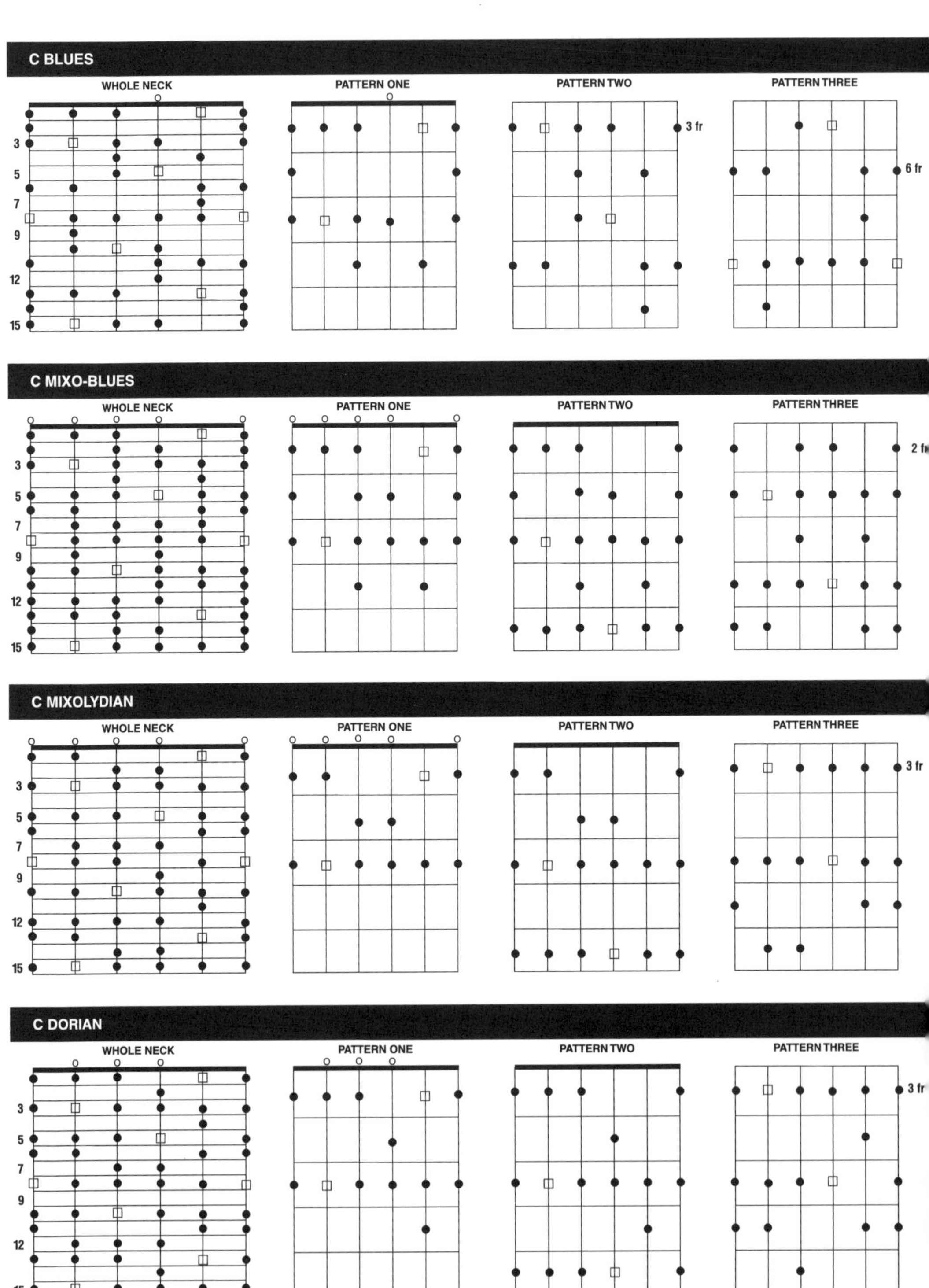


C BLUES
WHOLE NECK
PATTERN ONE
PATTERN TWO
3 fr
PATTERN THREE
6 fr
3
5
7
9
12
15

C MIXO-BLUES
WHOLE NECK
PATTERN ONE
PATTERN TWO
PATTERN THREE
2 fr
3
5
7
9
12
15

C MIXOLYDIAN
WHOLE NECK
PATTERN ONE
PATTERN TWO
PATTERN THREE
3 fr
3
5
7
9
12
15

C DORIAN
WHOLE NECK
PATTERN ONE
PATTERN TWO
PATTERN THREE
3 fr
3
5
7
9
12
15

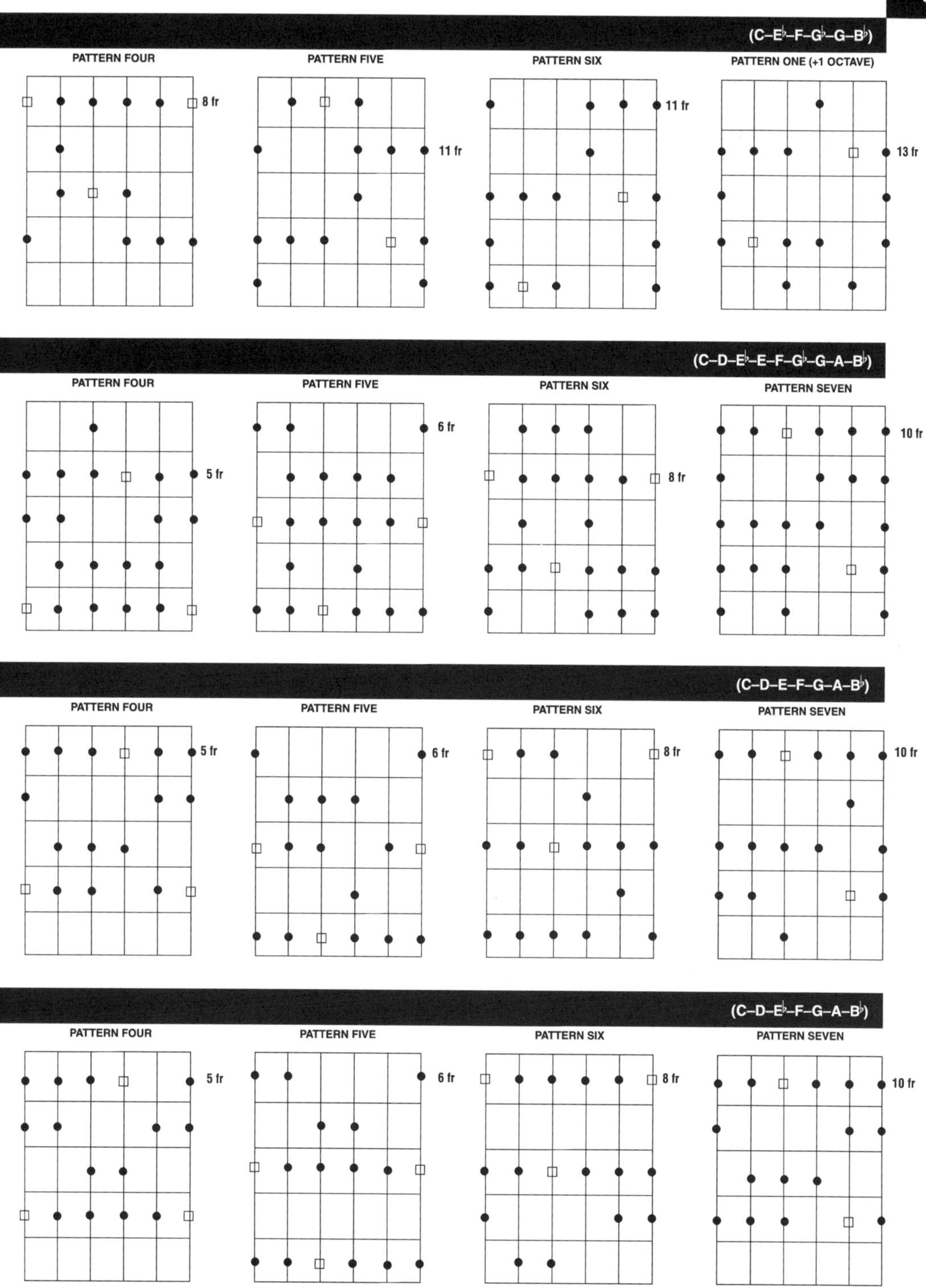
(C–E♭–F–G♭–G–B♭)
PATTERN FOUR
PATTERN FIVE
PATTERN SIX
PATTERN ONE (+1 OCTAVE)
8 fr
11 fr
11 fr
13 fr
(C–D–E♭–E–F–G♭–G–A–B♭)
PATTERN FOUR
PATTERN FIVE
PATTERN SIX
PATTERN SEVEN
5 fr
6 fr
8 fr
10 fr
(C–D–E–F–G–A–B♭)
PATTERN FOUR
PATTERN FIVE
PATTERN SIX
PATTERN SEVEN
5 fr
6 fr
8 fr
10 fr
(C–D–E♭–F–G–A–B♭)
PATTERN FOUR
PATTERN FIVE
PATTERN SIX
PATTERN SEVEN
5 fr
6 fr
8 fr
10 fr

# C MELODIC MINOR

WHOLE NECK    PATTERN ONE    PATTERN TWO    PATTERN THREE

# C HARMONIC MINOR

WHOLE NECK    PATTERN ONE    PATTERN TWO    PATTERN THREE

# C PHRYGIAN

WHOLE NECK    PATTERN ONE    PATTERN TWO    PATTERN THREE

# C LOCRIAN

WHOLE NECK    PATTERN ONE    PATTERN TWO    PATTERN THREE

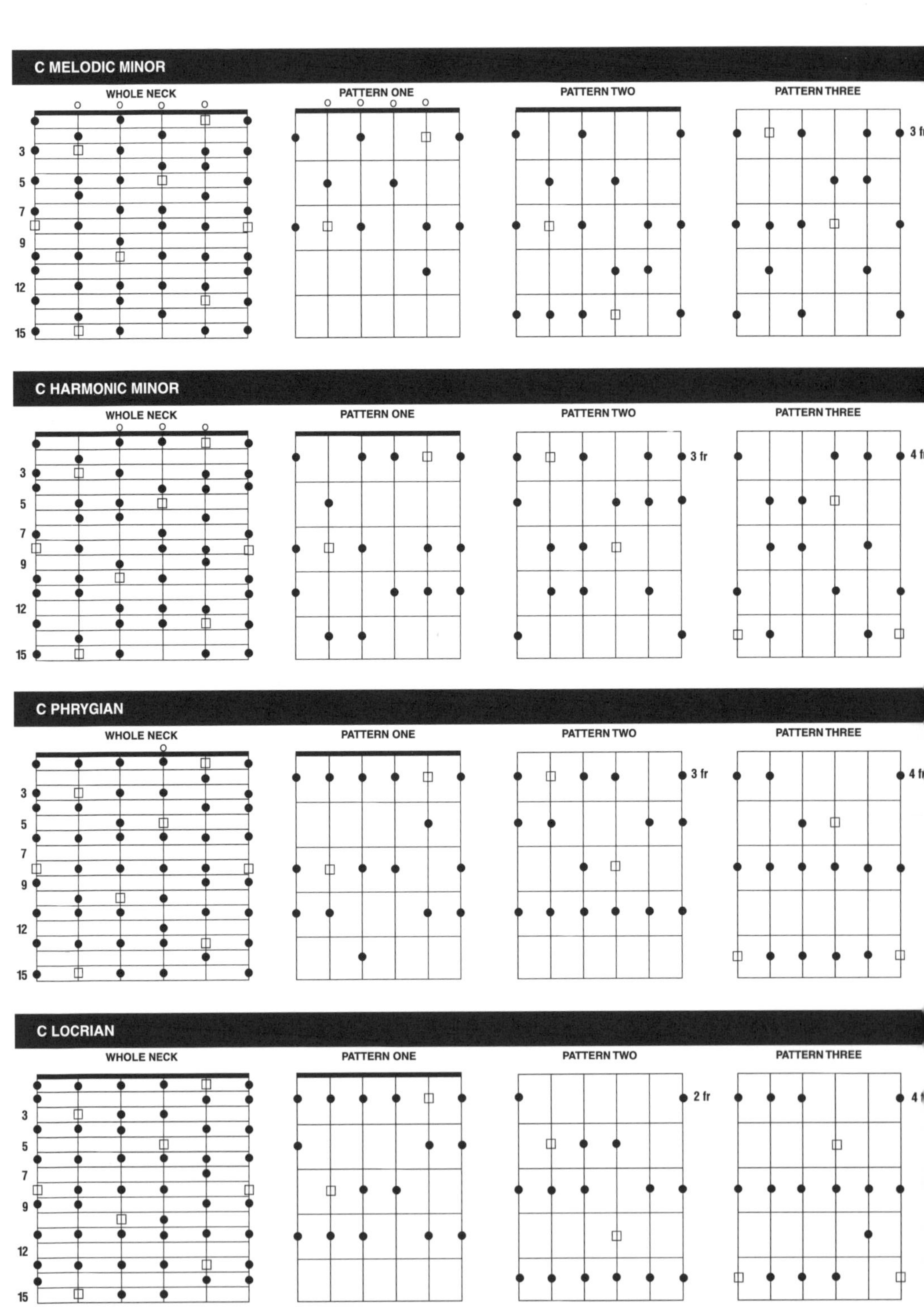

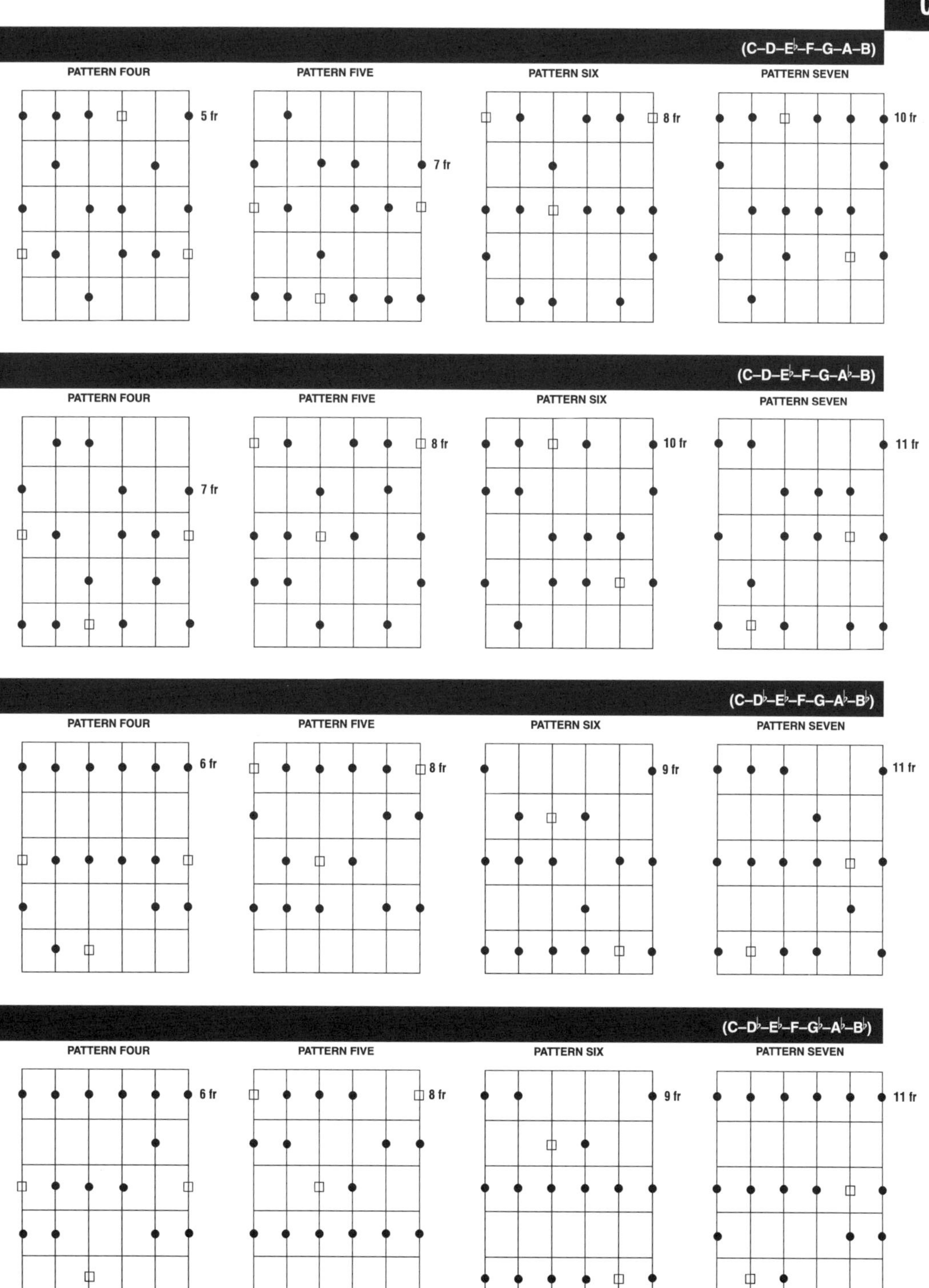
(C–D–E♭–F–G–A–B)
PATTERN FOUR
PATTERN FIVE
PATTERN SIX
PATTERN SEVEN
5 fr
7 fr
8 fr
10 fr
(C–D–E♭–F–G–A♭–B)
PATTERN FOUR
PATTERN FIVE
PATTERN SIX
PATTERN SEVEN
7 fr
8 fr
10 fr
11 fr
(C–D♭–E♭–F–G–A♭–B♭)
PATTERN FOUR
PATTERN FIVE
PATTERN SIX
PATTERN SEVEN
6 fr
8 fr
9 fr
11 fr
(C–D♭–E♭–F–G♭–A♭–B♭)
PATTERN FOUR
PATTERN FIVE
PATTERN SIX
PATTERN SEVEN
6 fr
8 fr
9 fr
11 fr

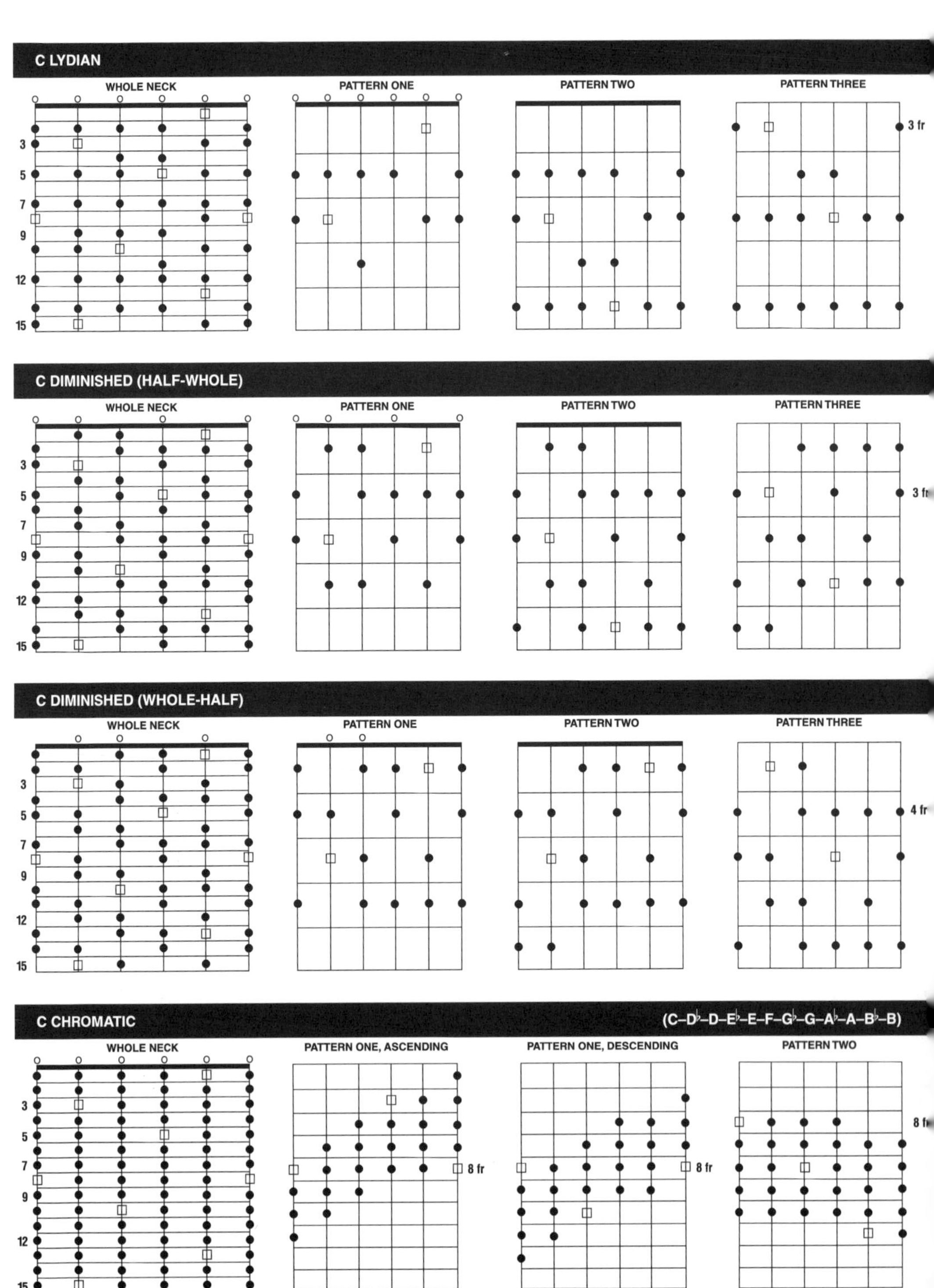


C LYDIAN
WHOLE NECK
PATTERN ONE
PATTERN TWO
PATTERN THREE
3 fr
3
5
7
9
12
15

C DIMINISHED (HALF-WHOLE)
WHOLE NECK
PATTERN ONE
PATTERN TWO
PATTERN THREE
3 fr
3
5
7
9
12
15

C DIMINISHED (WHOLE-HALF)
WHOLE NECK
PATTERN ONE
PATTERN TWO
PATTERN THREE
4 fr
3
5
7
9
12
15

C CHROMATIC
(C–D♭–D–E♭–E–F–G♭–G–A♭–A–B♭–B)
WHOLE NECK
PATTERN ONE, ASCENDING
PATTERN ONE, DESCENDING
PATTERN TWO
8 fr
8 fr
8 fr
3
5
7
9
12
15

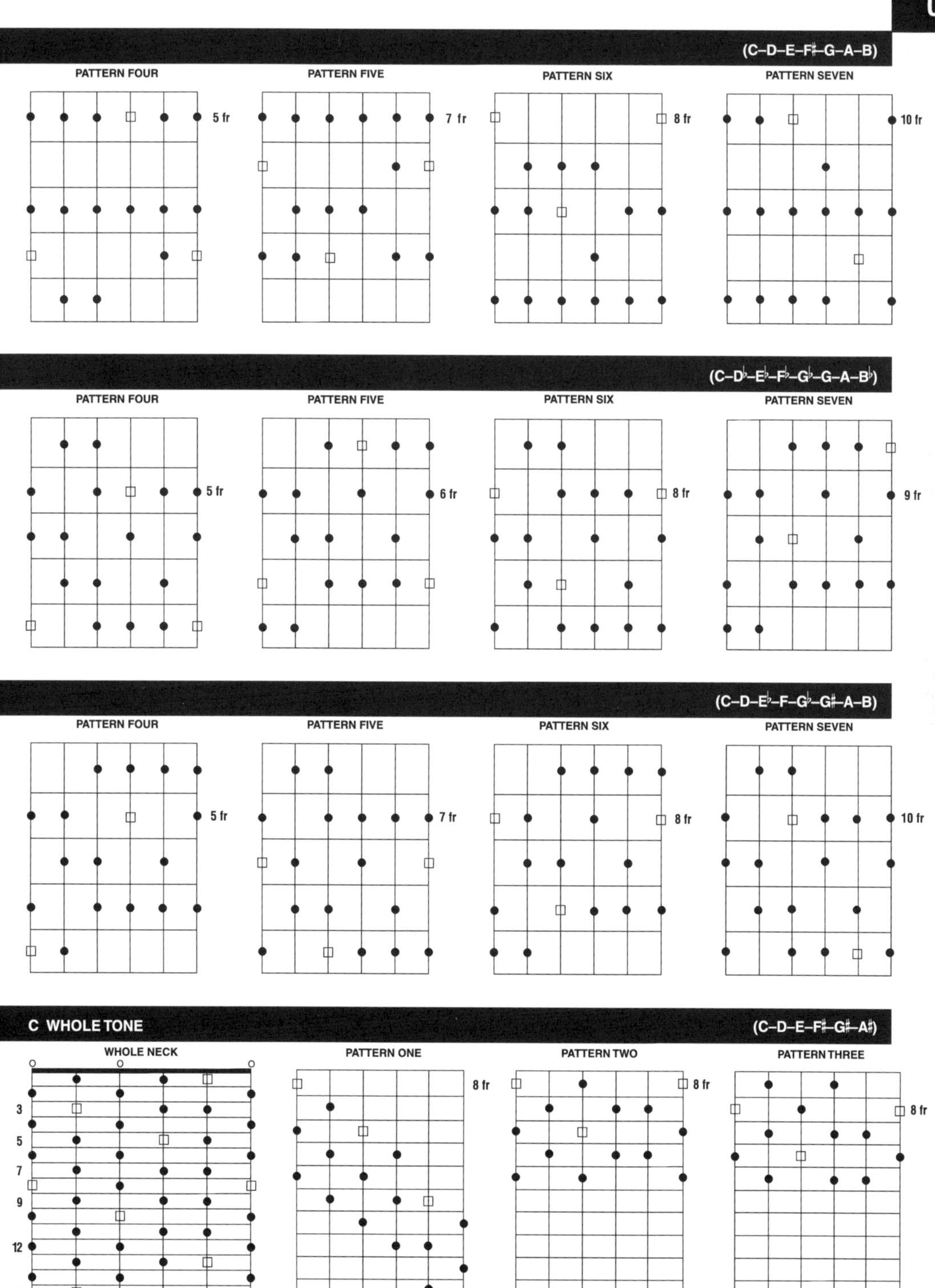

(C–D–E–F♯–G–A–B)
PATTERN FOUR
PATTERN FIVE
PATTERN SIX
PATTERN SEVEN
5 fr
7 fr
8 fr
10 fr
(C–D♭–E♭–F♭–G♭–G–A–B♭)
PATTERN FOUR
PATTERN FIVE
PATTERN SIX
PATTERN SEVEN
5 fr
6 fr
8 fr
9 fr
(C–D–E♭–F–G♭–G♯–A–B)
PATTERN FOUR
PATTERN FIVE
PATTERN SIX
PATTERN SEVEN
5 fr
7 fr
8 fr
10 fr
C WHOLE TONE
(C–D–E–F♯–G♯–A♯)
WHOLE NECK
PATTERN ONE
PATTERN TWO
PATTERN THREE
3
5
7
9
12
15
8 fr
8 fr
8 fr

# C# MAJOR (IONIAN)

# C# MAJOR PENTATONIC

# C# NATURAL MINOR (AEOLIAN)

# C# MINOR PENTATONIC

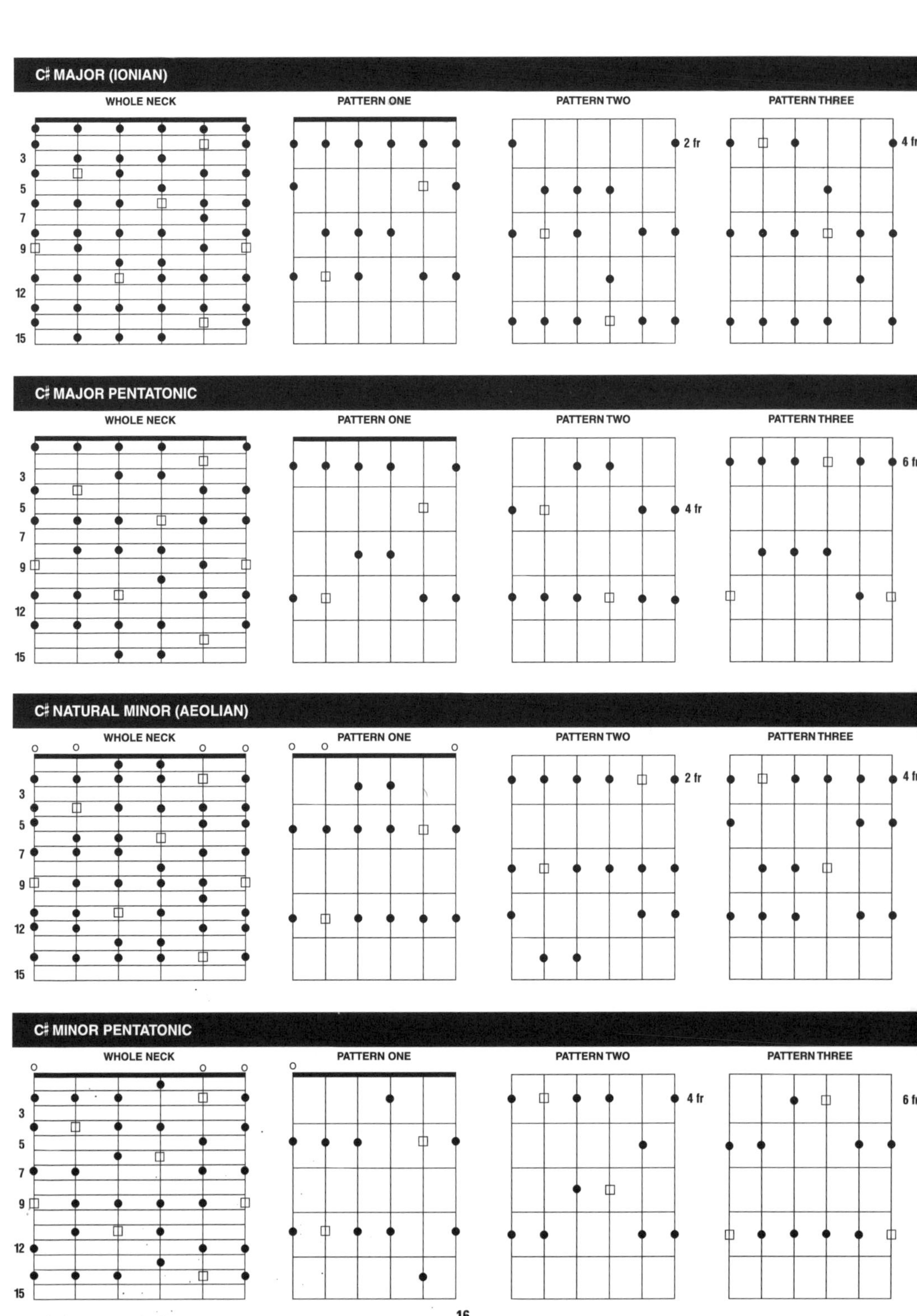

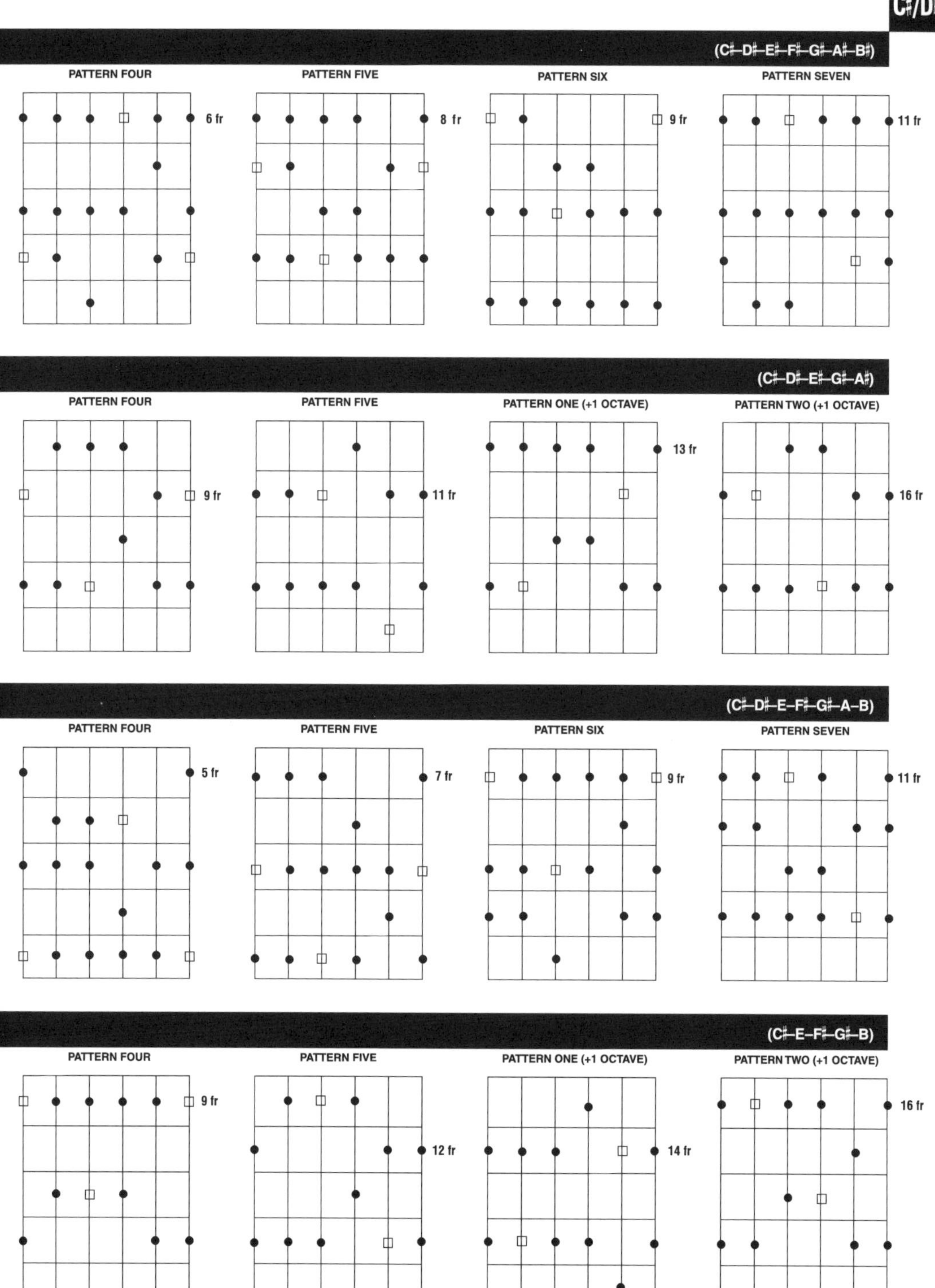
(C♯–D♯–E♯–F♯–G♯–A♯–B♯)
PATTERN FOUR
PATTERN FIVE
PATTERN SIX
PATTERN SEVEN
6 fr
8 fr
9 fr
11 fr
(C♯–D♯–E♯–G♯–A♯)
PATTERN FOUR
PATTERN FIVE
PATTERN ONE (+1 OCTAVE)
PATTERN TWO (+1 OCTAVE)
9 fr
11 fr
13 fr
16 fr
(C♯–D♯–E–F♯–G♯–A–B)
PATTERN FOUR
PATTERN FIVE
PATTERN SIX
PATTERN SEVEN
5 fr
7 fr
9 fr
11 fr
(C♯–E–F♯–G♯–B)
PATTERN FOUR
PATTERN FIVE
PATTERN ONE (+1 OCTAVE)
PATTERN TWO (+1 OCTAVE)
9 fr
12 fr
14 fr
16 fr

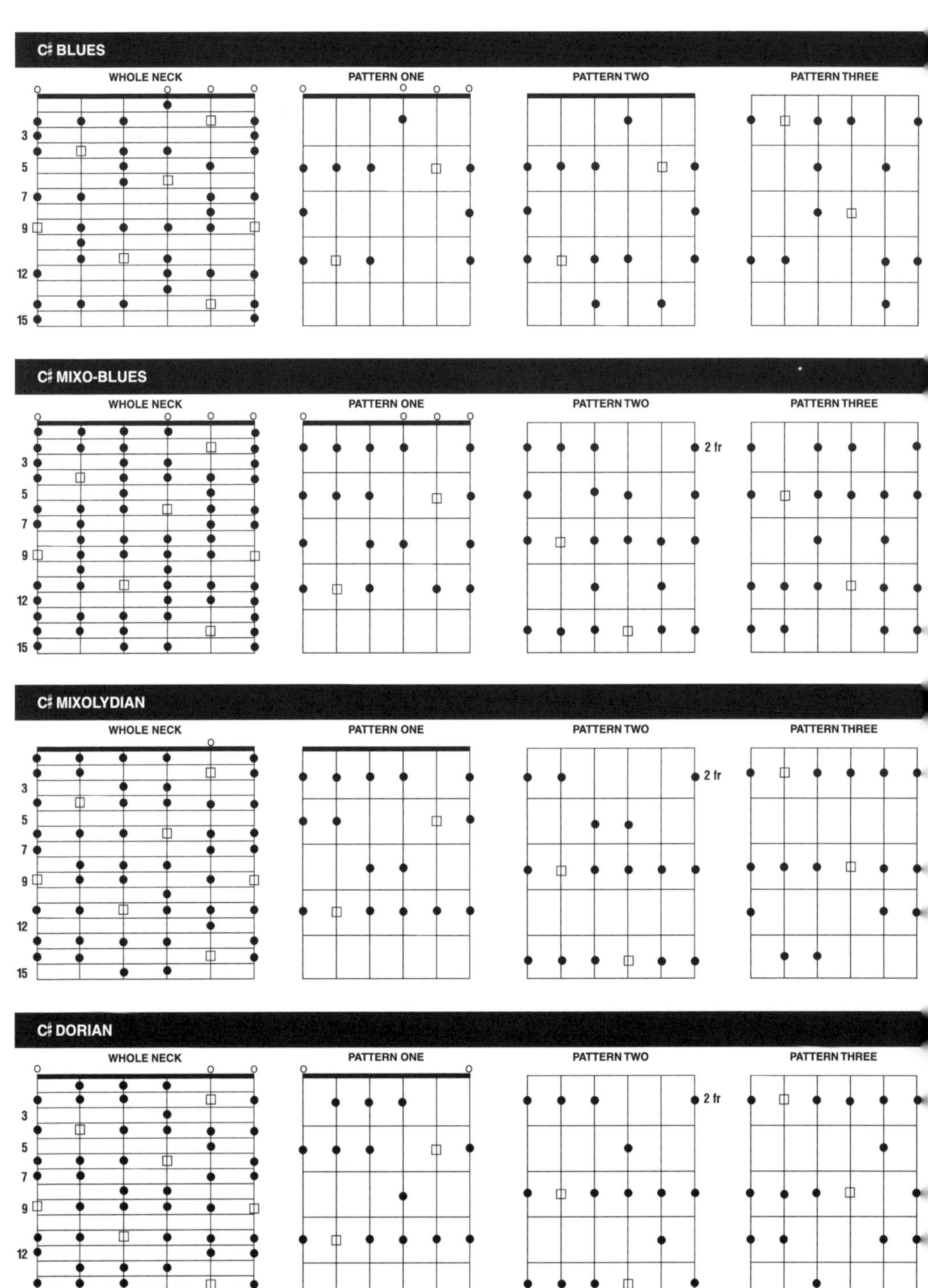

C# BLUES
WHOLE NECK
PATTERN ONE
PATTERN TWO
PATTERN THREE

C# MIXO-BLUES
WHOLE NECK
PATTERN ONE
PATTERN TWO
2 fr
PATTERN THREE

C# MIXOLYDIAN
WHOLE NECK
PATTERN ONE
PATTERN TWO
2 fr
PATTERN THREE

C# DORIAN
WHOLE NECK
PATTERN ONE
PATTERN TWO
2 fr
PATTERN THREE

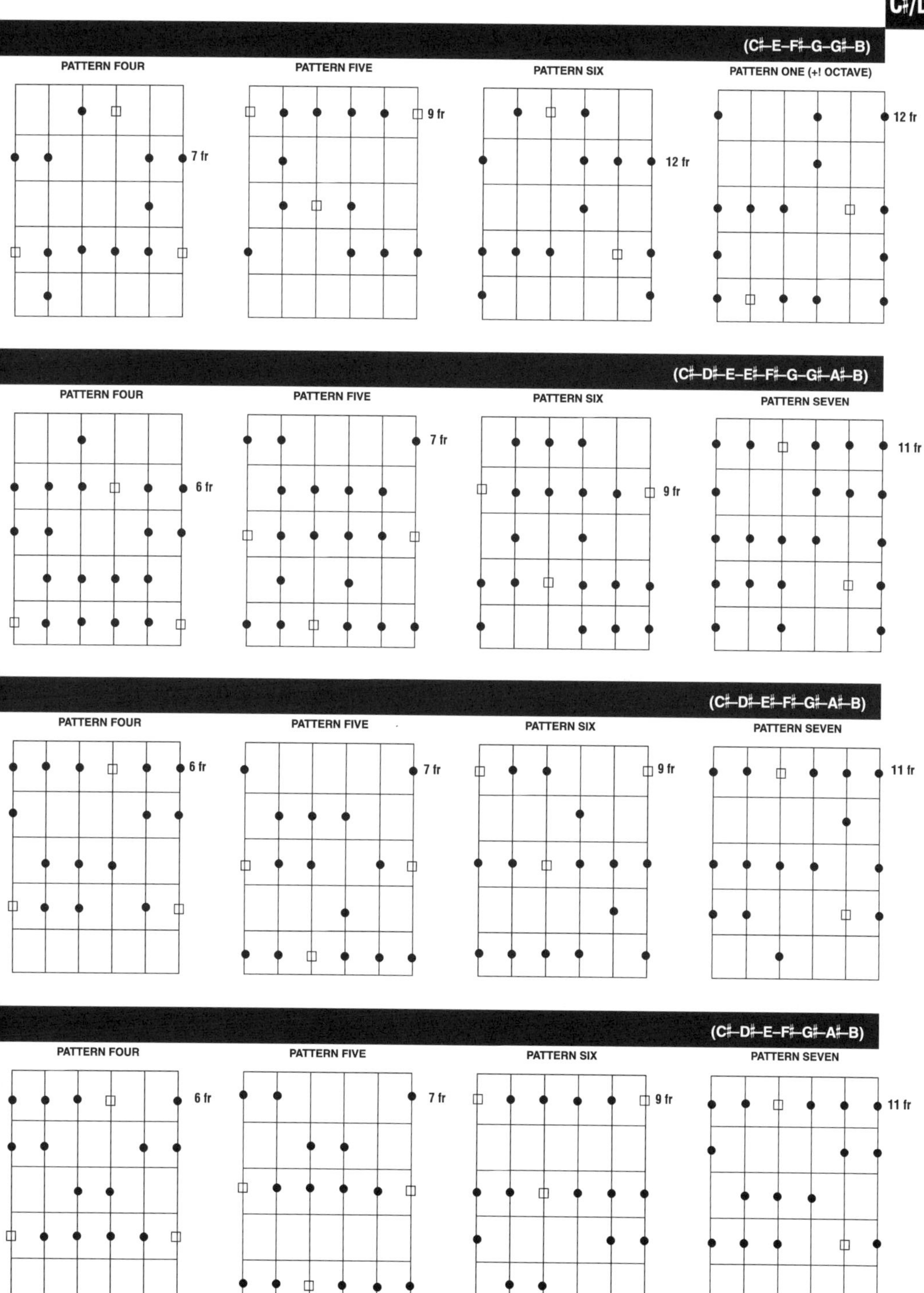
C#/Db
(C#–E–F#–G–G#–B)
PATTERN FOUR
PATTERN FIVE
PATTERN SIX
PATTERN ONE (+! OCTAVE)
7 fr
9 fr
12 fr
12 fr
(C#–D#–E–E#–F#–G–G#–A#–B)
PATTERN FOUR
PATTERN FIVE
PATTERN SIX
PATTERN SEVEN
6 fr
7 fr
9 fr
11 fr
(C#–D#–E#–F#–G#–A#–B)
PATTERN FOUR
PATTERN FIVE
PATTERN SIX
PATTERN SEVEN
6 fr
7 fr
9 fr
11 fr
(C#–D#–E–F#–G#–A#–B)
PATTERN FOUR
PATTERN FIVE
PATTERN SIX
PATTERN SEVEN
6 fr
7 fr
9 fr
11 fr

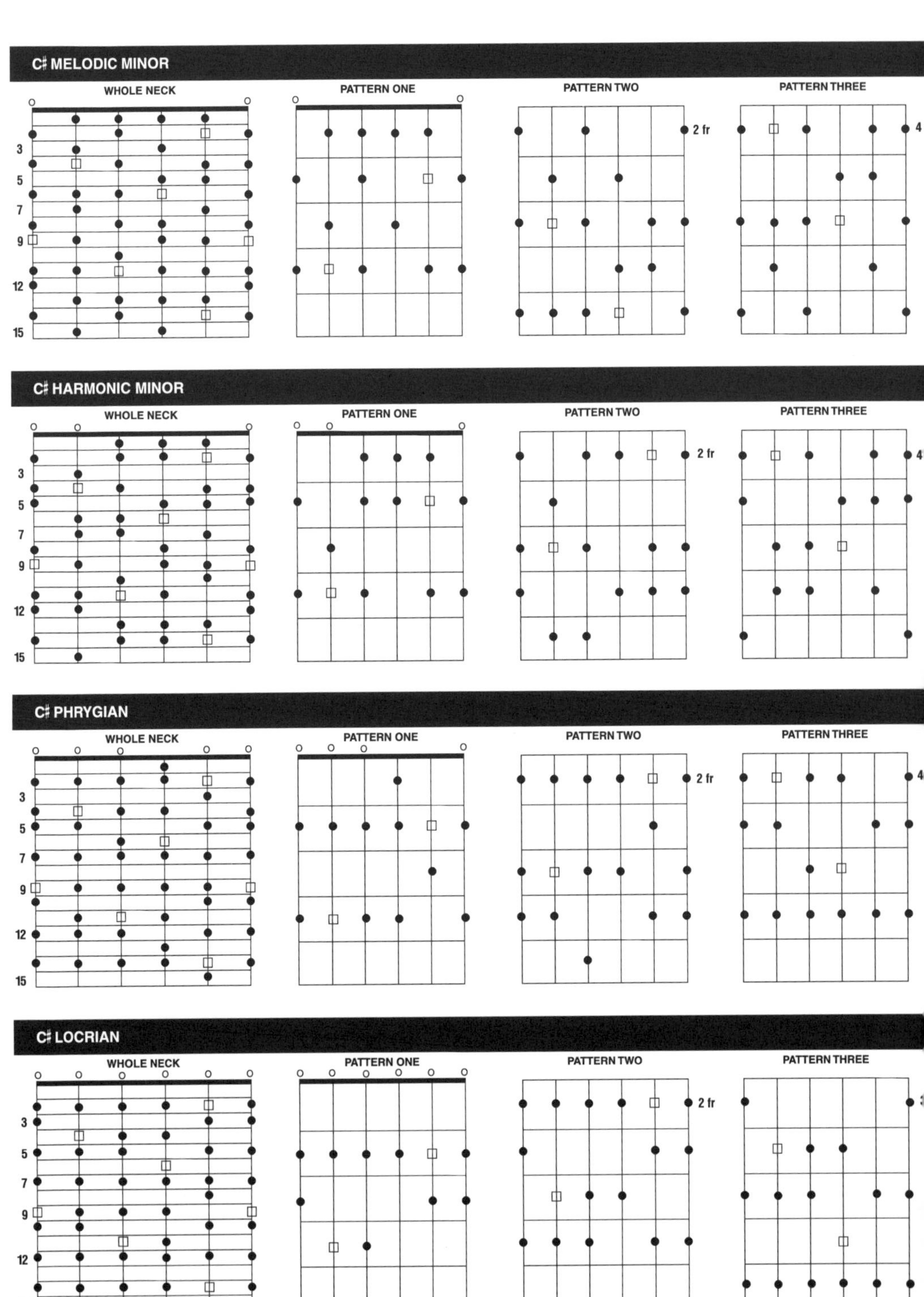


C# MELODIC MINOR
WHOLE NECK
PATTERN ONE
PATTERN TWO
PATTERN THREE
2 fr
4

C# HARMONIC MINOR
WHOLE NECK
PATTERN ONE
PATTERN TWO
PATTERN THREE
2 fr
4

C# PHRYGIAN
WHOLE NECK
PATTERN ONE
PATTERN TWO
PATTERN THREE
2 fr
4

C# LOCRIAN
WHOLE NECK
PATTERN ONE
PATTERN TWO
PATTERN THREE
2 fr

(C#–D#–E–F#–G#–A#–B#)

| PATTERN FOUR | PATTERN FIVE | PATTERN SIX | PATTERN SEVEN |
|---|---|---|---|

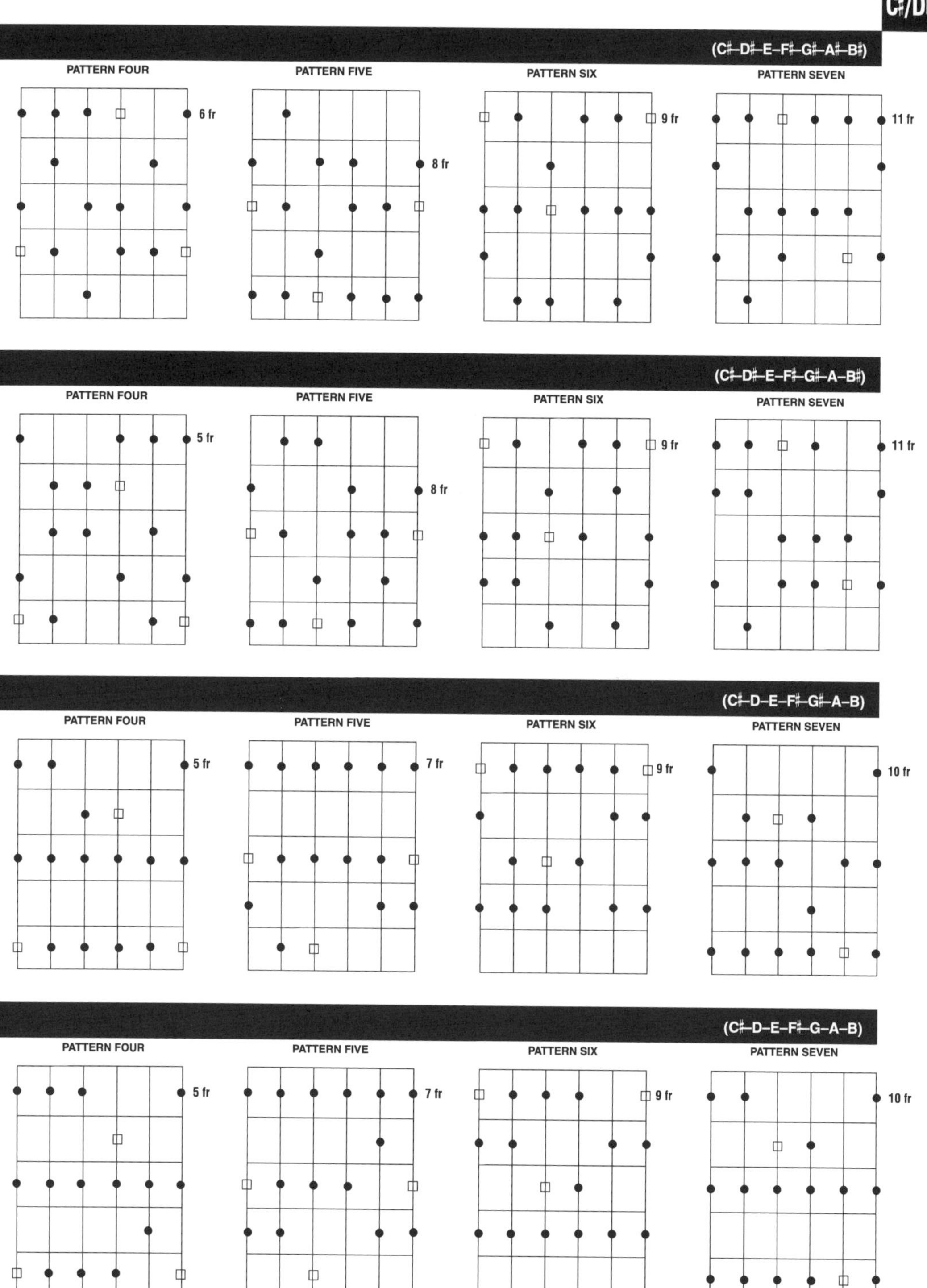

(C#–D#–E–F#–G#–A–B#)

| PATTERN FOUR | PATTERN FIVE | PATTERN SIX | PATTERN SEVEN |
|---|---|---|---|

(C#–D–E–F#–G#–A–B)

| PATTERN FOUR | PATTERN FIVE | PATTERN SIX | PATTERN SEVEN |
|---|---|---|---|

(C#–D–E–F#–G–A–B)

| PATTERN FOUR | PATTERN FIVE | PATTERN SIX | PATTERN SEVEN |
|---|---|---|---|

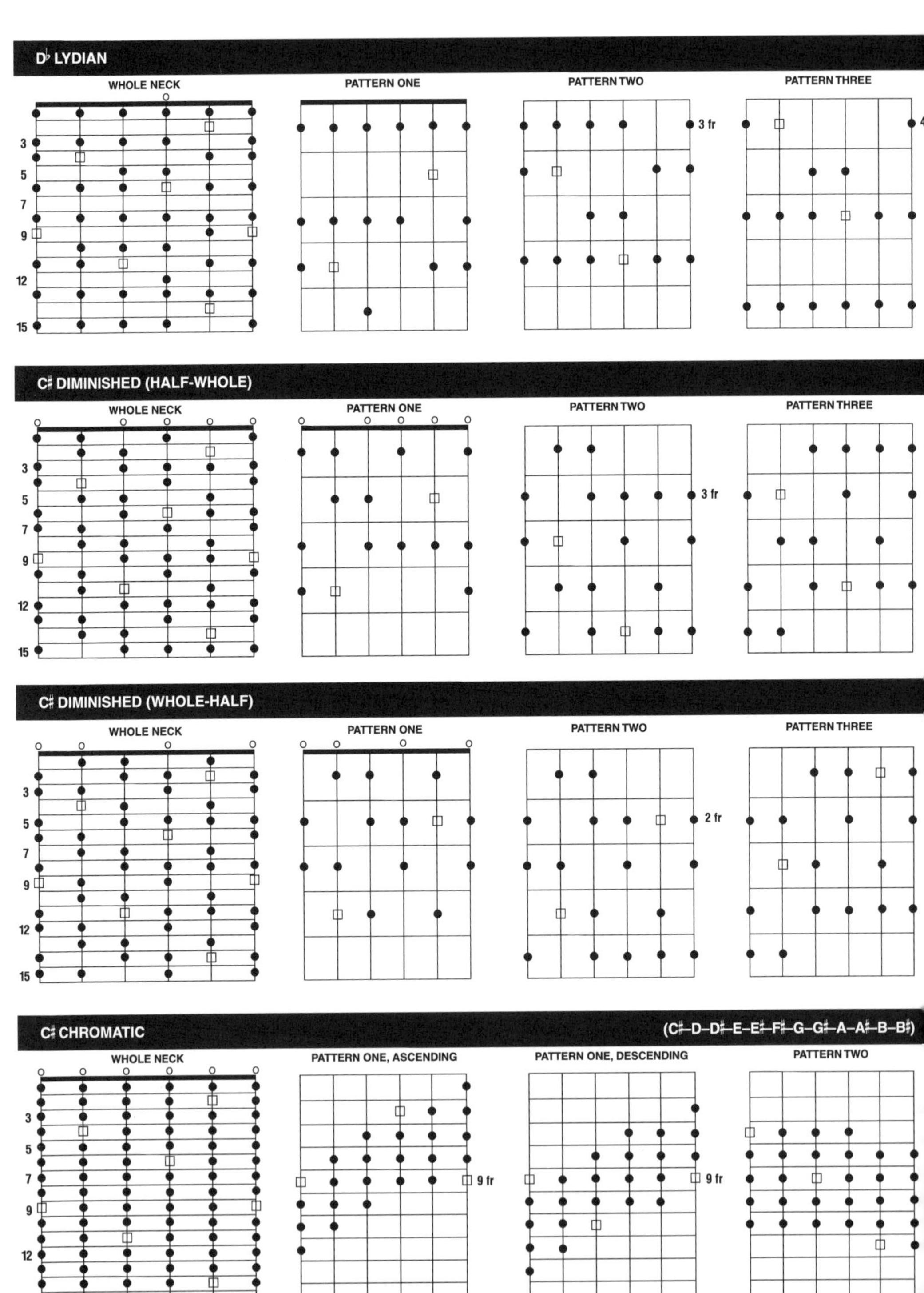

D♭ LYDIAN
WHOLE NECK
PATTERN ONE
PATTERN TWO
PATTERN THREE
3 fr
4
3
5
7
9
12
15
C♯ DIMINISHED (HALF-WHOLE)
WHOLE NECK
PATTERN ONE
PATTERN TWO
PATTERN THREE
3 fr
3
5
7
9
12
15
C♯ DIMINISHED (WHOLE-HALF)
WHOLE NECK
PATTERN ONE
PATTERN TWO
PATTERN THREE
2 fr
3
5
7
9
12
15
C♯ CHROMATIC
(C♯–D–D♯–E–E♯–F♯–G–G♯–A–A♯–B–B♯)
WHOLE NECK
PATTERN ONE, ASCENDING
PATTERN ONE, DESCENDING
PATTERN TWO
9 fr
9 fr
3
5
7
9
12
15

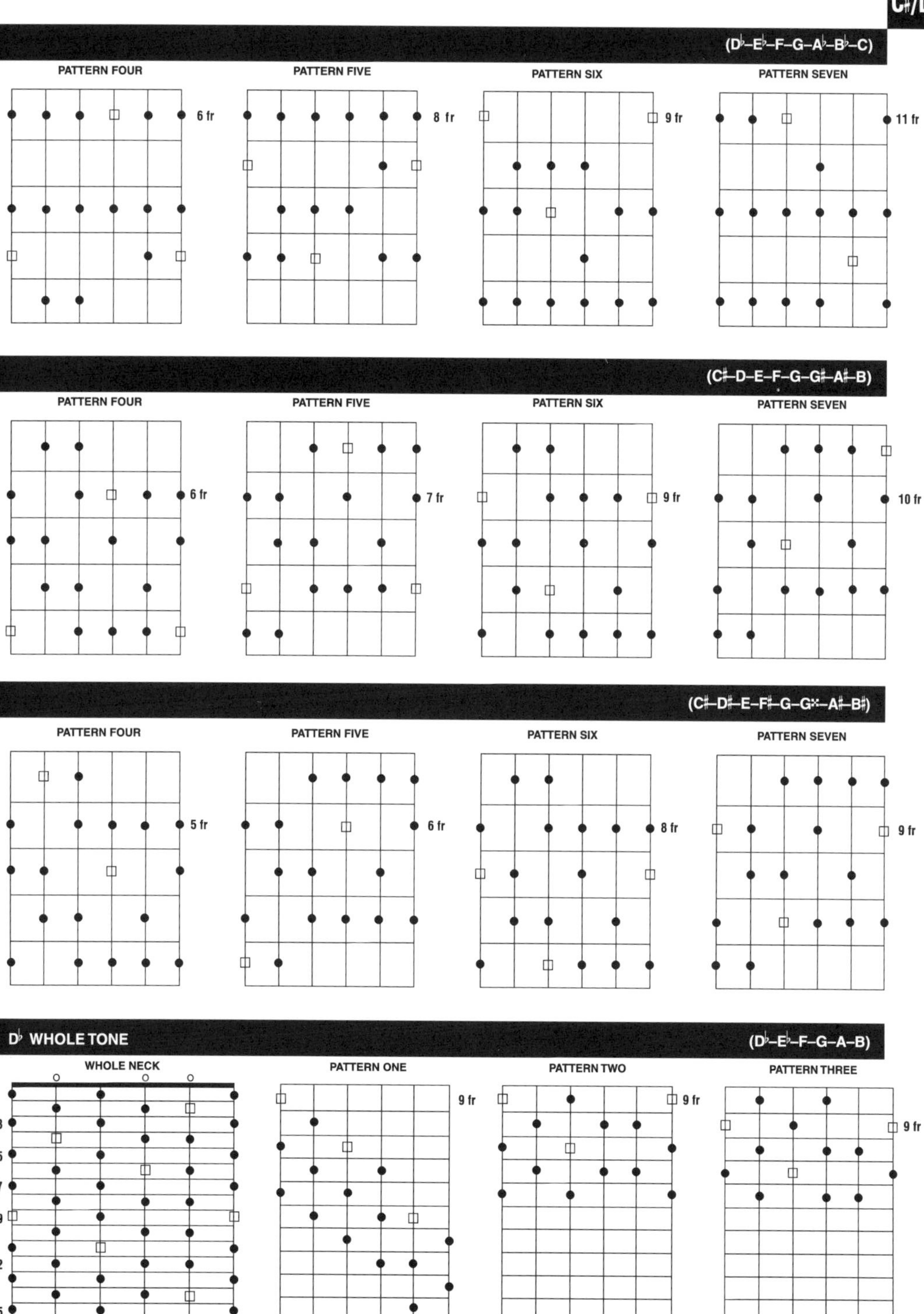


(Db–Eb–F–G–Ab–Bb–C)
PATTERN FOUR
PATTERN FIVE
PATTERN SIX
PATTERN SEVEN
6 fr
8 fr
9 fr
11 fr
(C#–D–E–F–G–G#–A#–B)
PATTERN FOUR
PATTERN FIVE
PATTERN SIX
PATTERN SEVEN
6 fr
7 fr
9 fr
10 fr
(C#–D#–E–F#–G–G𝄪–A#–B#)
PATTERN FOUR
PATTERN FIVE
PATTERN SIX
PATTERN SEVEN
5 fr
6 fr
8 fr
9 fr
Db WHOLE TONE
(Db–Eb–F–G–A–B)
WHOLE NECK
PATTERN ONE
PATTERN TWO
PATTERN THREE
9 fr
9 fr
9 fr
3
5
7
9
2
5

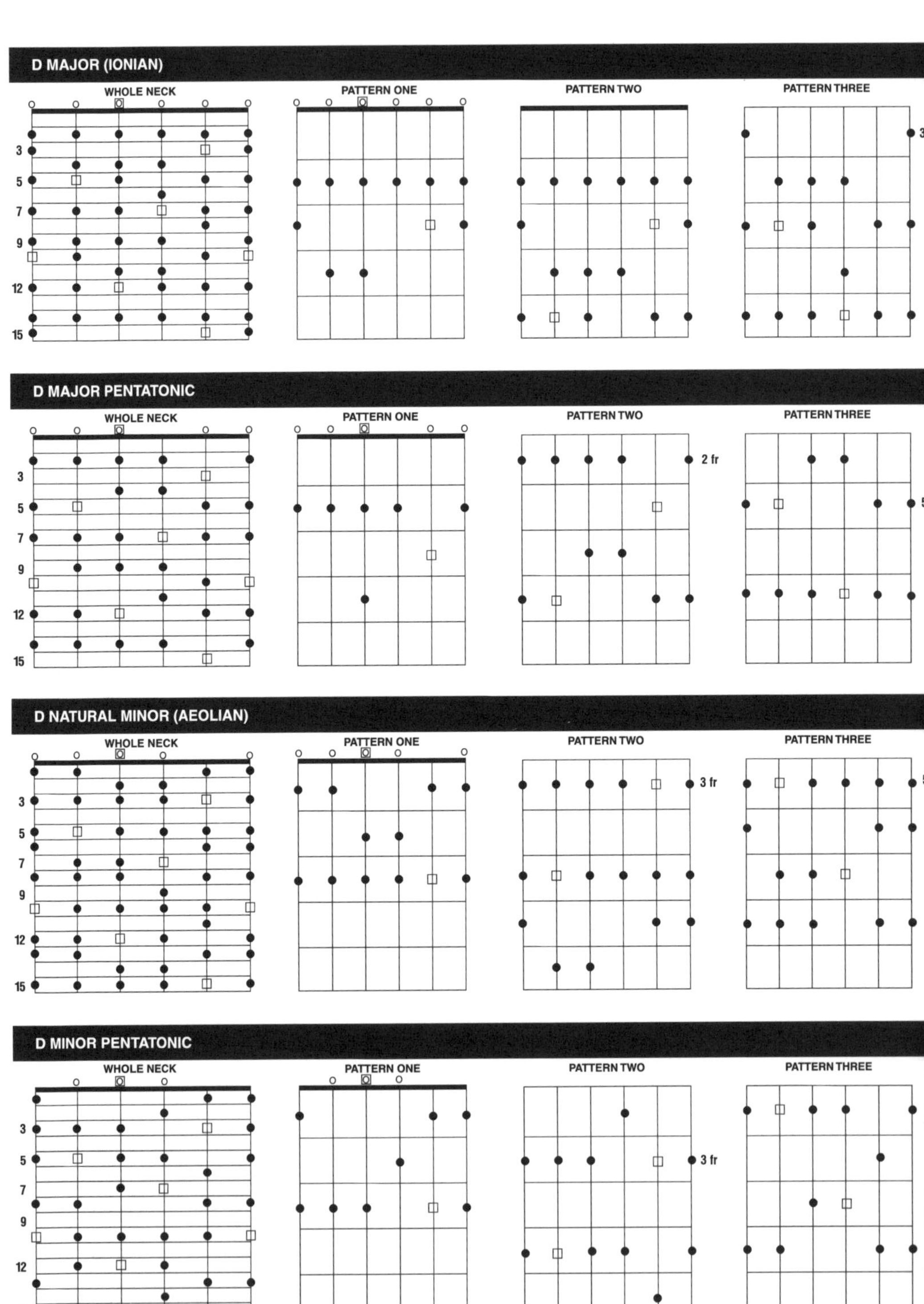
D MAJOR (IONIAN)
WHOLE NECK
PATTERN ONE
PATTERN TWO
PATTERN THREE

D MAJOR PENTATONIC
WHOLE NECK
PATTERN ONE
PATTERN TWO
PATTERN THREE
2 fr

D NATURAL MINOR (AEOLIAN)
WHOLE NECK
PATTERN ONE
PATTERN TWO
PATTERN THREE
3 fr

D MINOR PENTATONIC
WHOLE NECK
PATTERN ONE
PATTERN TWO
PATTERN THREE
3 fr

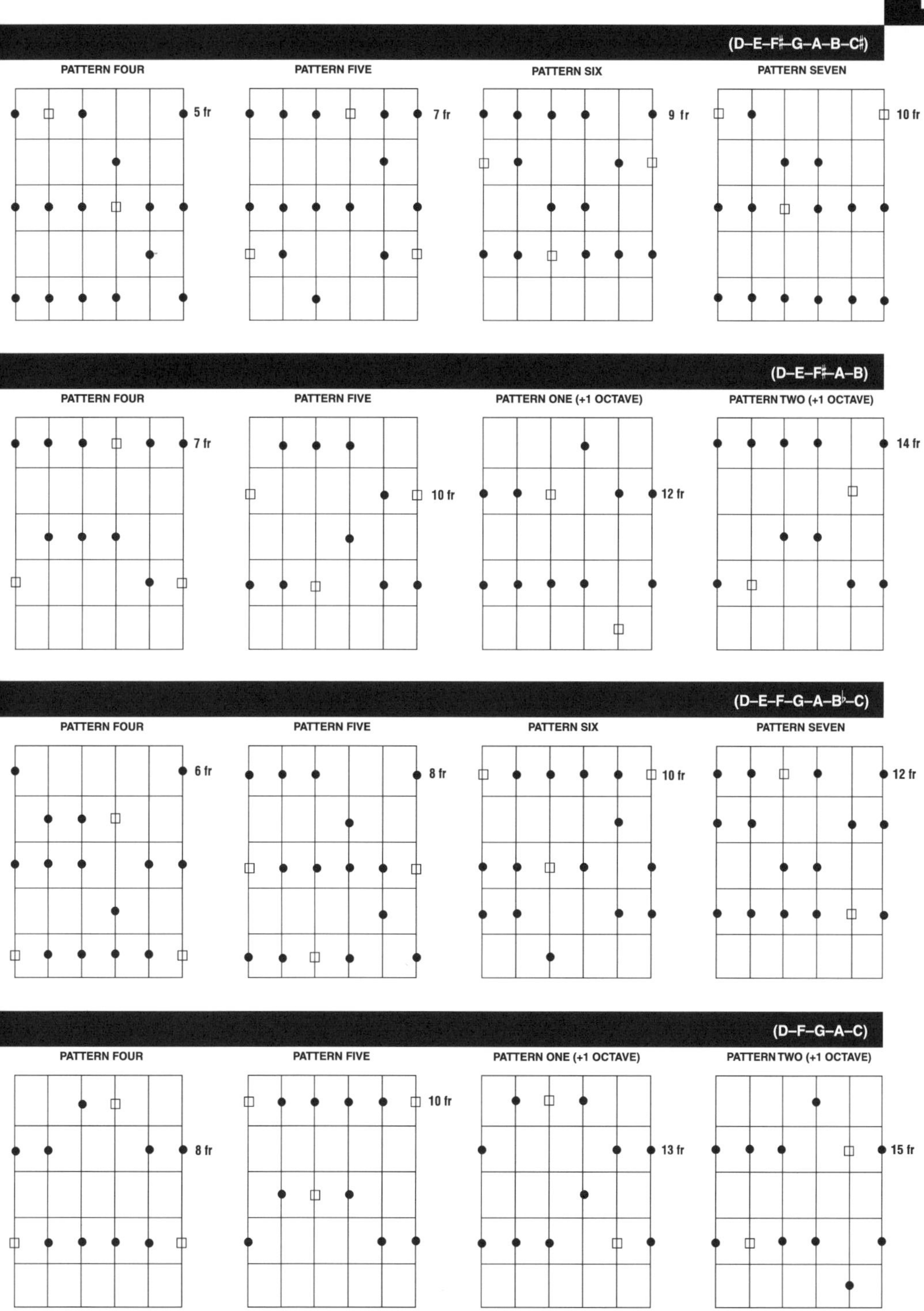
(D–E–F#–G–A–B–C#)
PATTERN FOUR
PATTERN FIVE
PATTERN SIX
PATTERN SEVEN
5 fr
7 fr
9 fr
10 fr

(D–E–F#–A–B)
PATTERN FOUR
PATTERN FIVE
PATTERN ONE (+1 OCTAVE)
PATTERN TWO (+1 OCTAVE)
7 fr
10 fr
12 fr
14 fr

(D–E–F–G–A–Bb–C)
PATTERN FOUR
PATTERN FIVE
PATTERN SIX
PATTERN SEVEN
6 fr
8 fr
10 fr
12 fr

(D–F–G–A–C)
PATTERN FOUR
PATTERN FIVE
PATTERN ONE (+1 OCTAVE)
PATTERN TWO (+1 OCTAVE)
10 fr
8 fr
13 fr
15 fr

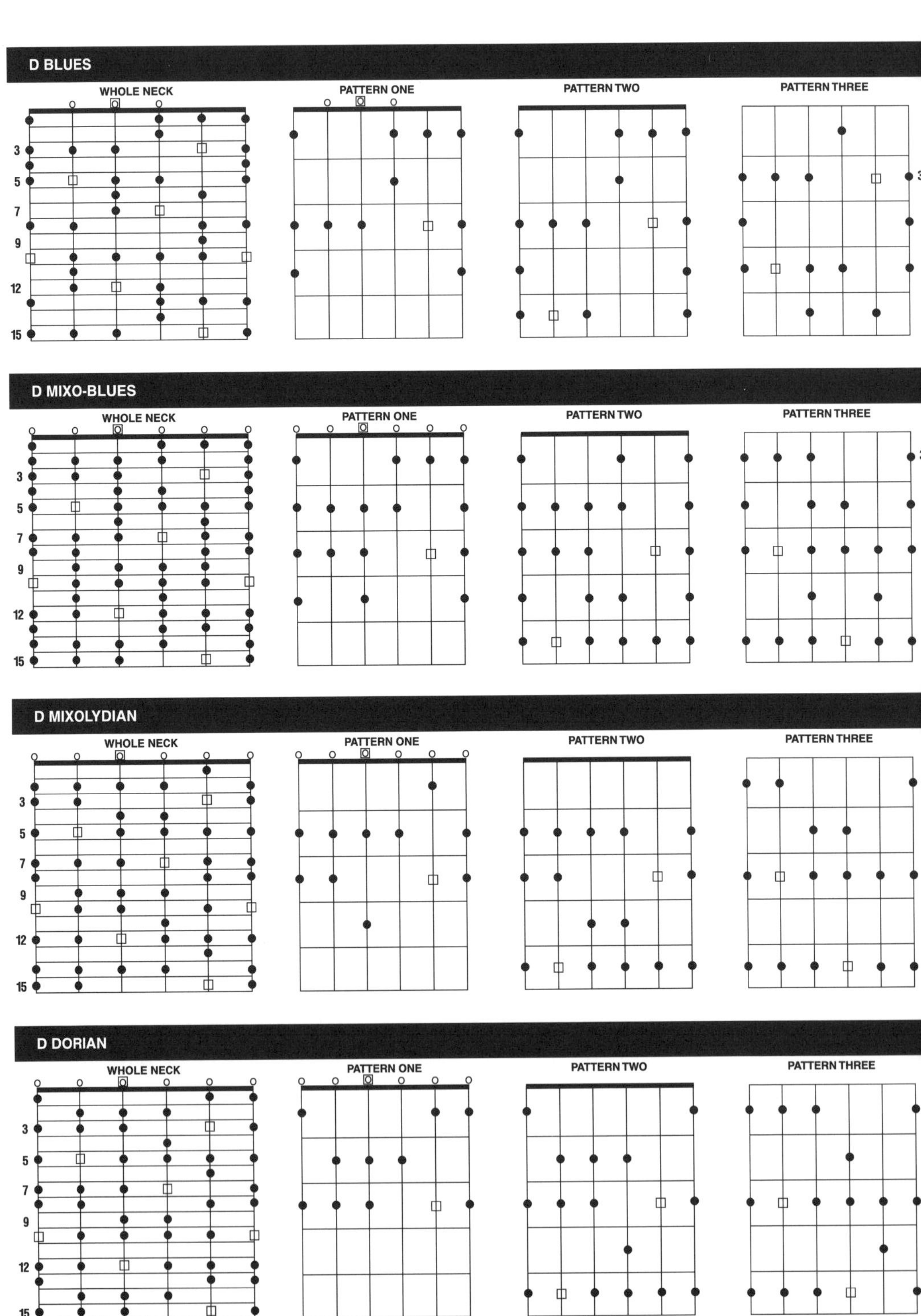

D BLUES
WHOLE NECK
PATTERN ONE
PATTERN TWO
PATTERN THREE
D MIXO-BLUES
WHOLE NECK
PATTERN ONE
PATTERN TWO
PATTERN THREE
D MIXOLYDIAN
WHOLE NECK
PATTERN ONE
PATTERN TWO
PATTERN THREE
D DORIAN
WHOLE NECK
PATTERN ONE
PATTERN TWO
PATTERN THREE

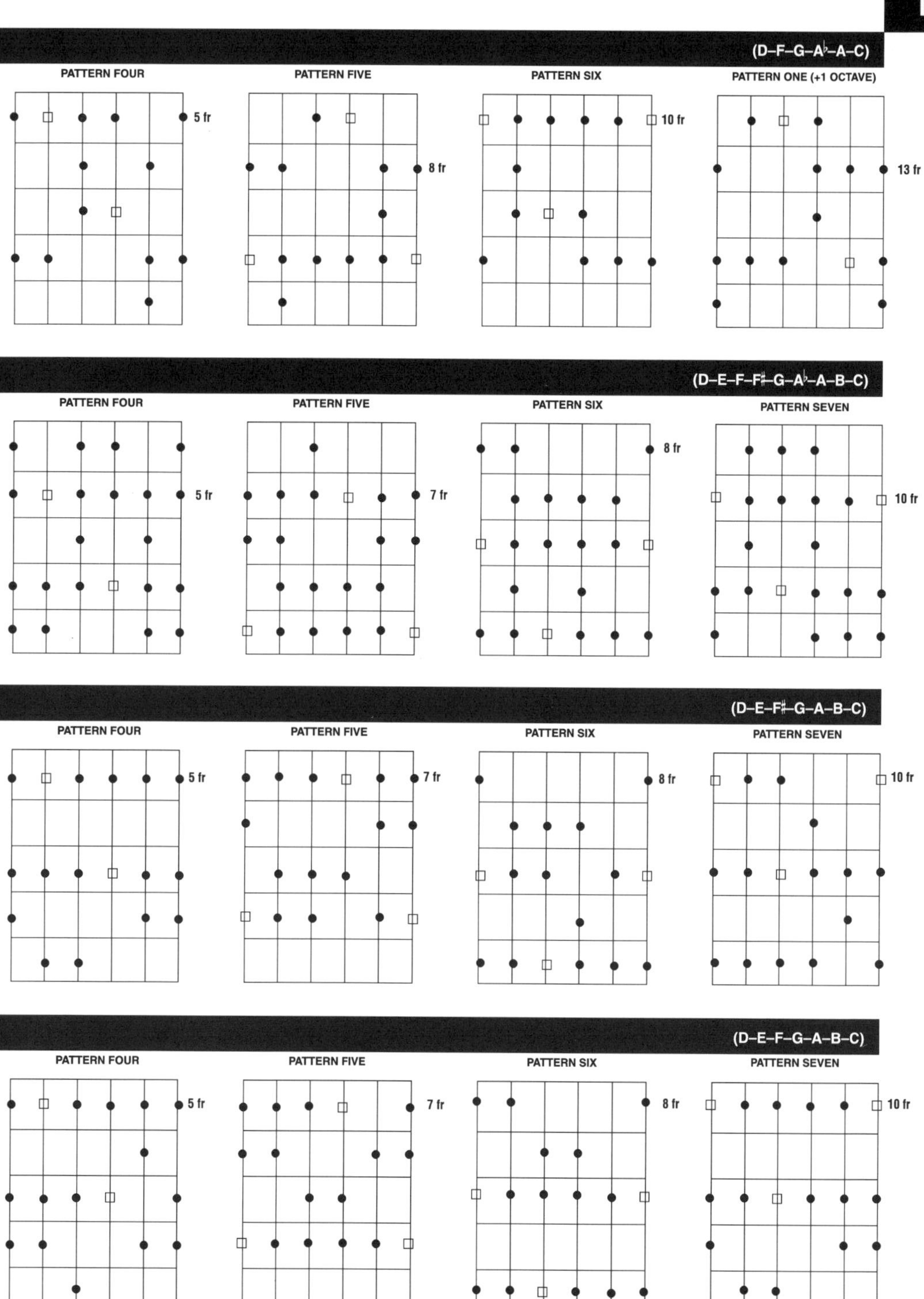

(D–F–G–A♭–A–C)
PATTERN FOUR
PATTERN FIVE
PATTERN SIX
PATTERN ONE (+1 OCTAVE)
5 fr
8 fr
10 fr
13 fr

(D–E–F–F♯–G–A♭–A–B–C)
PATTERN FOUR
PATTERN FIVE
PATTERN SIX
PATTERN SEVEN
5 fr
7 fr
8 fr
10 fr

(D–E–F♯–G–A–B–C)
PATTERN FOUR
PATTERN FIVE
PATTERN SIX
PATTERN SEVEN
5 fr
7 fr
8 fr
10 fr

(D–E–F–G–A–B–C)
PATTERN FOUR
PATTERN FIVE
PATTERN SIX
PATTERN SEVEN
5 fr
7 fr
8 fr
10 fr

# D MELODIC MINOR

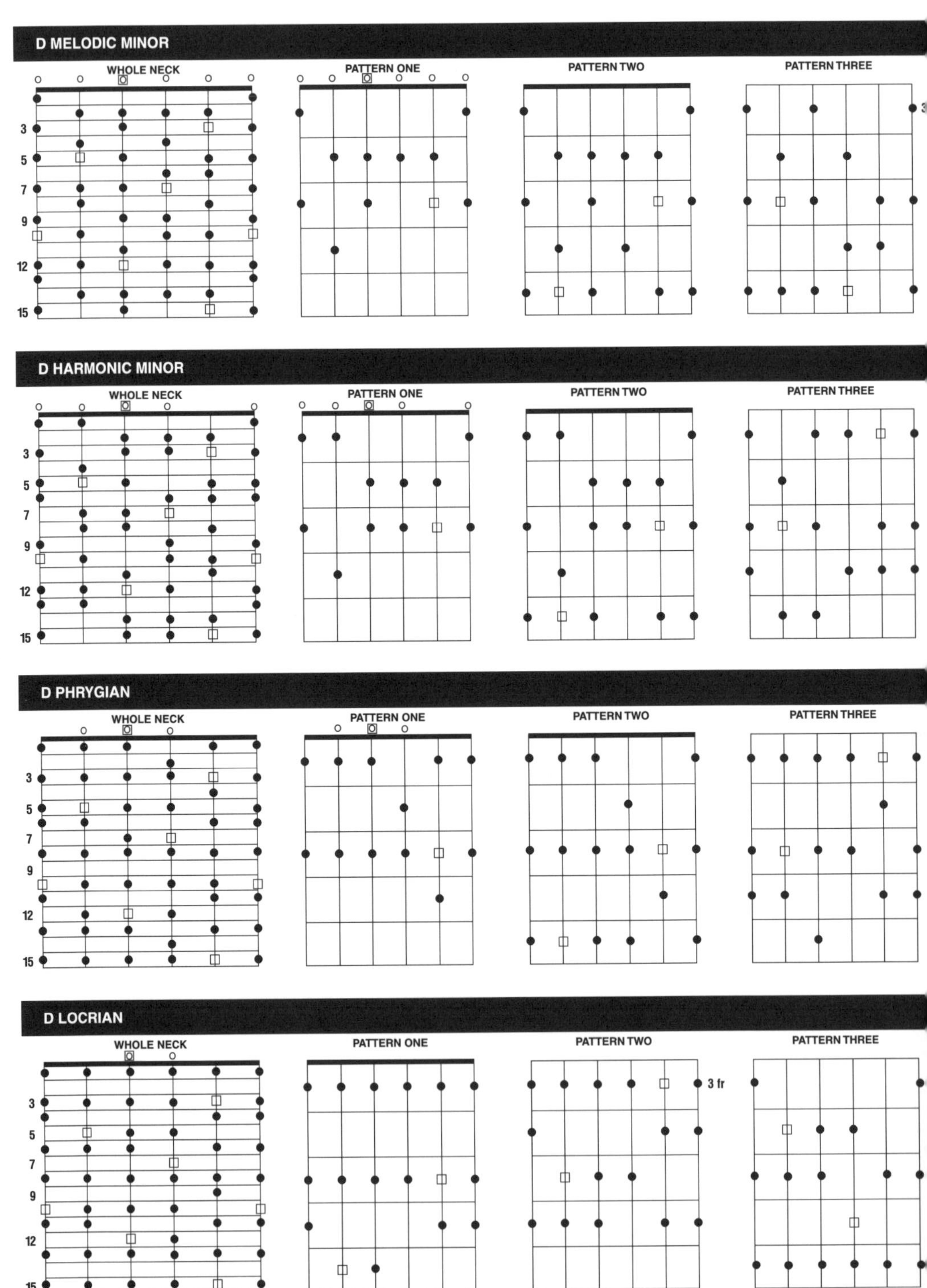

## D HARMONIC MINOR

## D PHRYGIAN

## D LOCRIAN

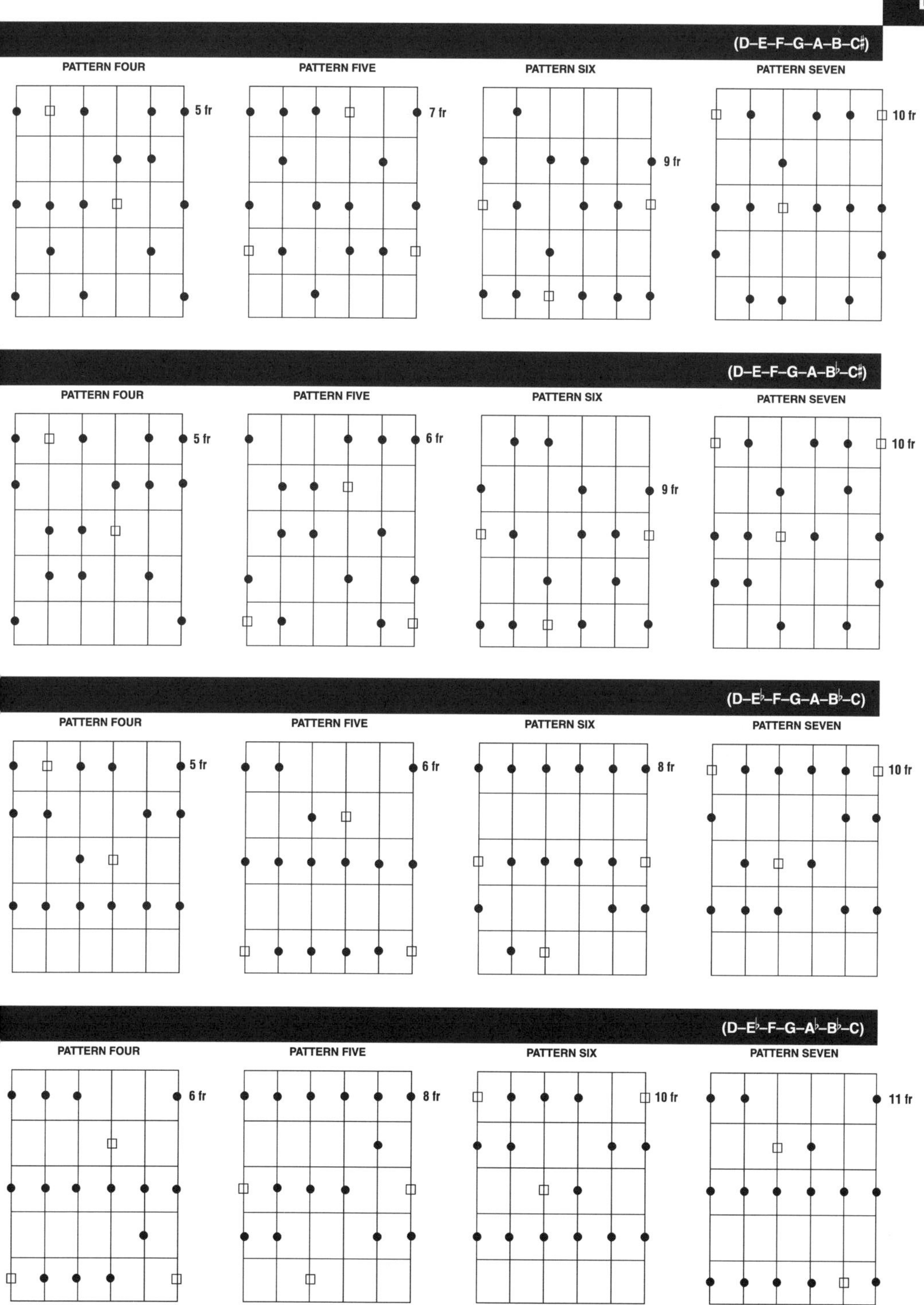
(D–E–F–G–A–B–C♯)
PATTERN FOUR
PATTERN FIVE
PATTERN SIX
PATTERN SEVEN
5 fr
7 fr
9 fr
10 fr
(D–E–F–G–A–B♭–C♯)
PATTERN FOUR
PATTERN FIVE
PATTERN SIX
PATTERN SEVEN
5 fr
6 fr
9 fr
10 fr
(D–E♭–F–G–A–B♭–C)
PATTERN FOUR
PATTERN FIVE
PATTERN SIX
PATTERN SEVEN
5 fr
6 fr
8 fr
10 fr
(D–E♭–F–G–A♭–B♭–C)
PATTERN FOUR
PATTERN FIVE
PATTERN SIX
PATTERN SEVEN
6 fr
8 fr
10 fr
11 fr

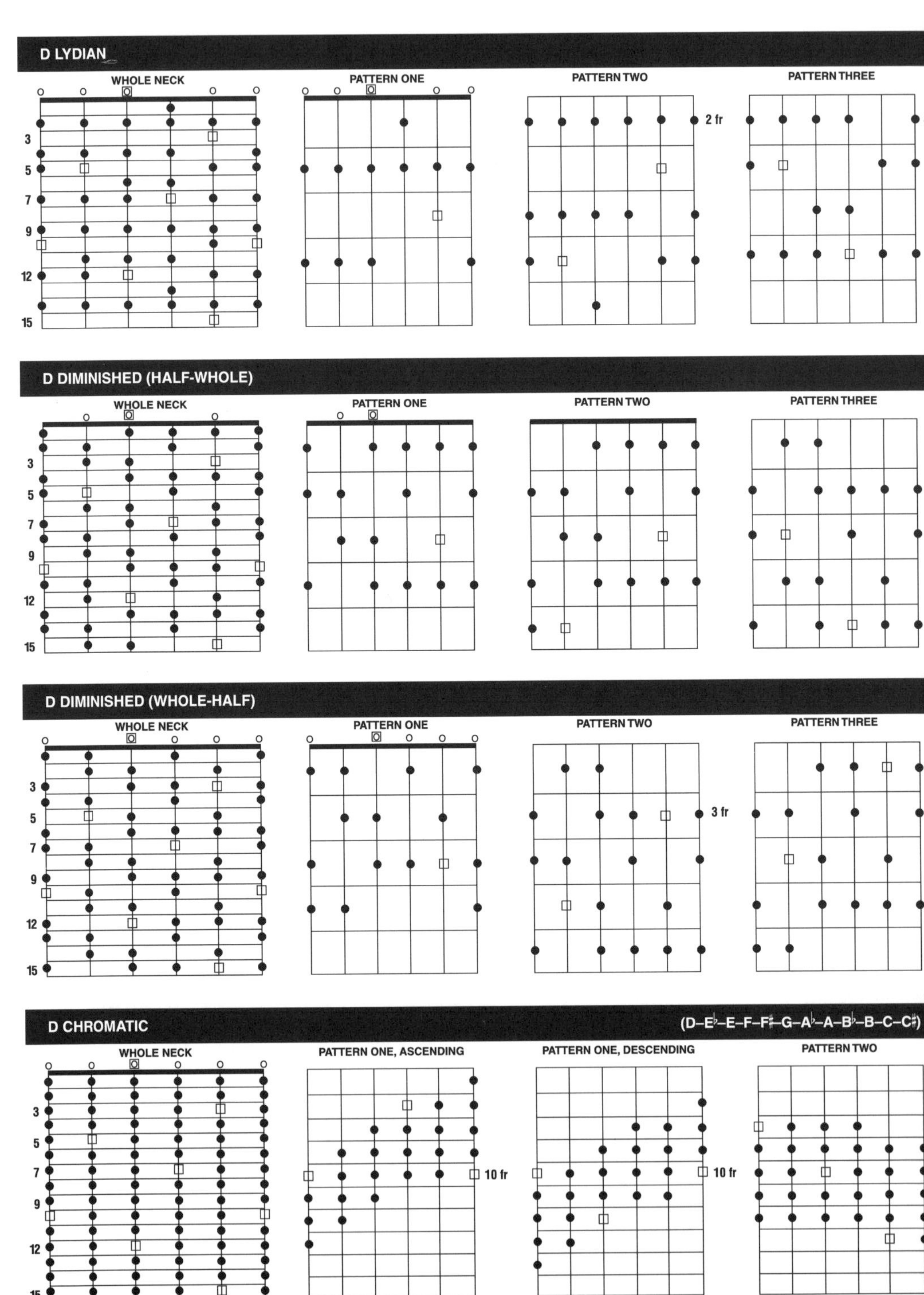


D LYDIAN
WHOLE NECK
PATTERN ONE
PATTERN TWO
2 fr
PATTERN THREE

D DIMINISHED (HALF-WHOLE)
WHOLE NECK
PATTERN ONE
PATTERN TWO
PATTERN THREE

D DIMINISHED (WHOLE-HALF)
WHOLE NECK
PATTERN ONE
PATTERN TWO
3 fr
PATTERN THREE

D CHROMATIC
(D–E♭–E–F–F♯–G–A♭–A–B♭–B–C–C♯)
WHOLE NECK
PATTERN ONE, ASCENDING
10 fr
PATTERN ONE, DESCENDING
10 fr
PATTERN TWO

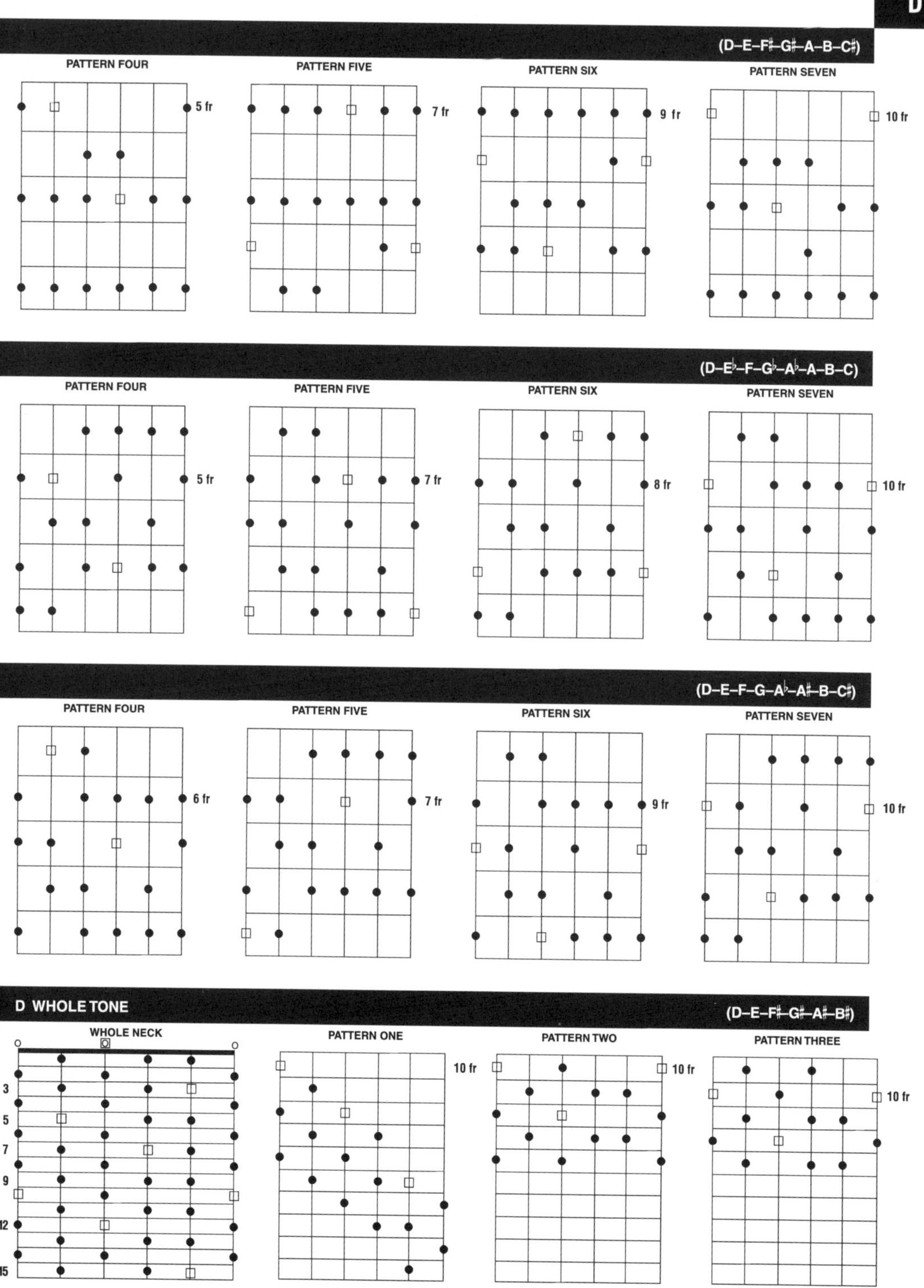

(D–E–F#–G#–A–B–C#)
PATTERN FOUR
PATTERN FIVE
PATTERN SIX
PATTERN SEVEN
5 fr
7 fr
9 fr
10 fr
(D–Eb–F–Gb–A–B–C)
PATTERN FOUR
PATTERN FIVE
PATTERN SIX
PATTERN SEVEN
5 fr
7 fr
8 fr
10 fr
(D–E–F–G–Ab–A#–B–C#)
PATTERN FOUR
PATTERN FIVE
PATTERN SIX
PATTERN SEVEN
6 fr
7 fr
9 fr
10 fr
D WHOLE TONE
(D–E–F#–G#–A#–B#)
WHOLE NECK
PATTERN ONE
PATTERN TWO
PATTERN THREE
3
5
7
9
12
15
10 fr
10 fr
10 fr

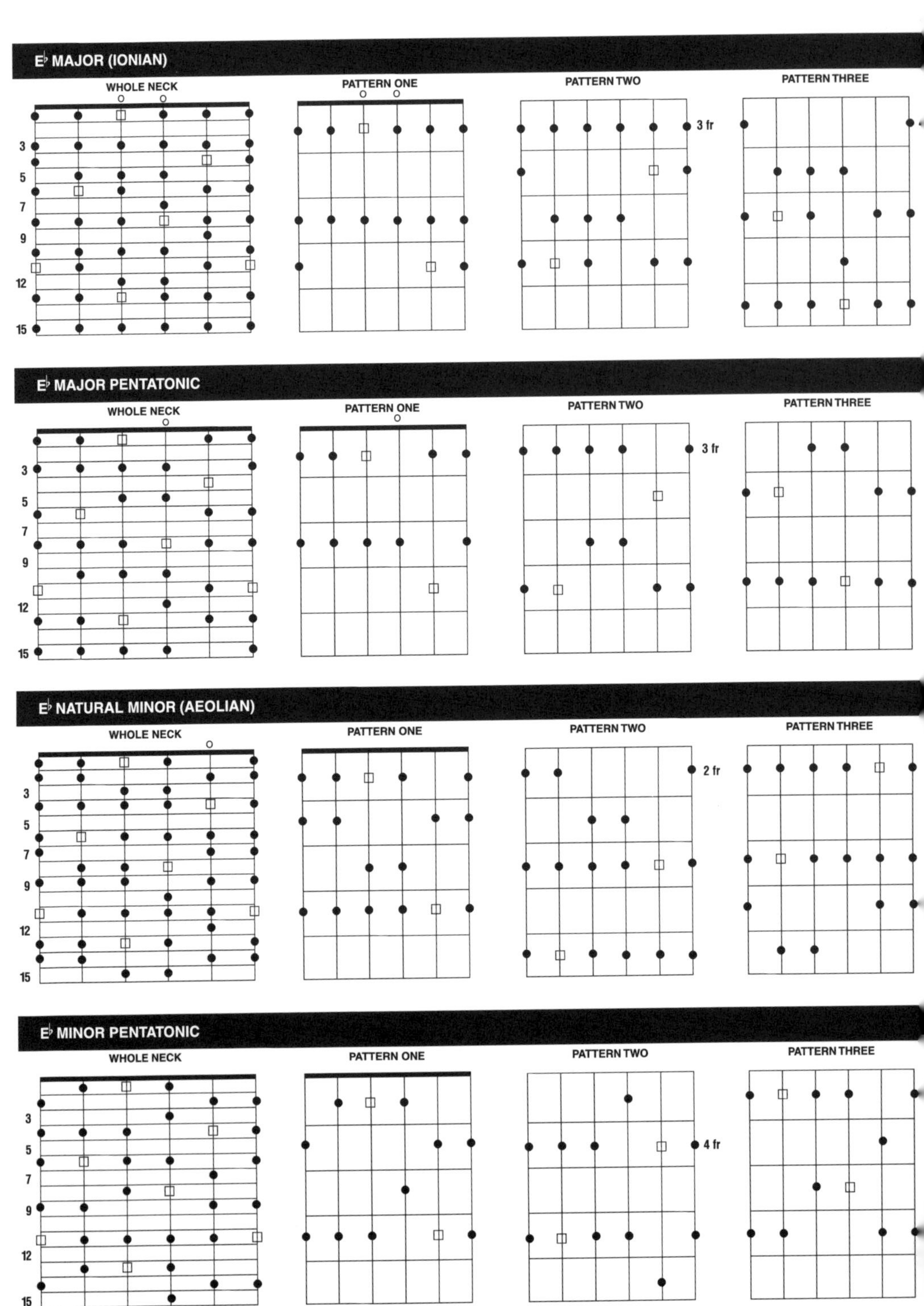

E♭ MAJOR (IONIAN)
WHOLE NECK
PATTERN ONE
PATTERN TWO
PATTERN THREE
3 fr

E♭ MAJOR PENTATONIC
WHOLE NECK
PATTERN ONE
PATTERN TWO
PATTERN THREE
3 fr

E♭ NATURAL MINOR (AEOLIAN)
WHOLE NECK
PATTERN ONE
PATTERN TWO
PATTERN THREE
2 fr

E♭ MINOR PENTATONIC
WHOLE NECK
PATTERN ONE
PATTERN TWO
PATTERN THREE
4 fr

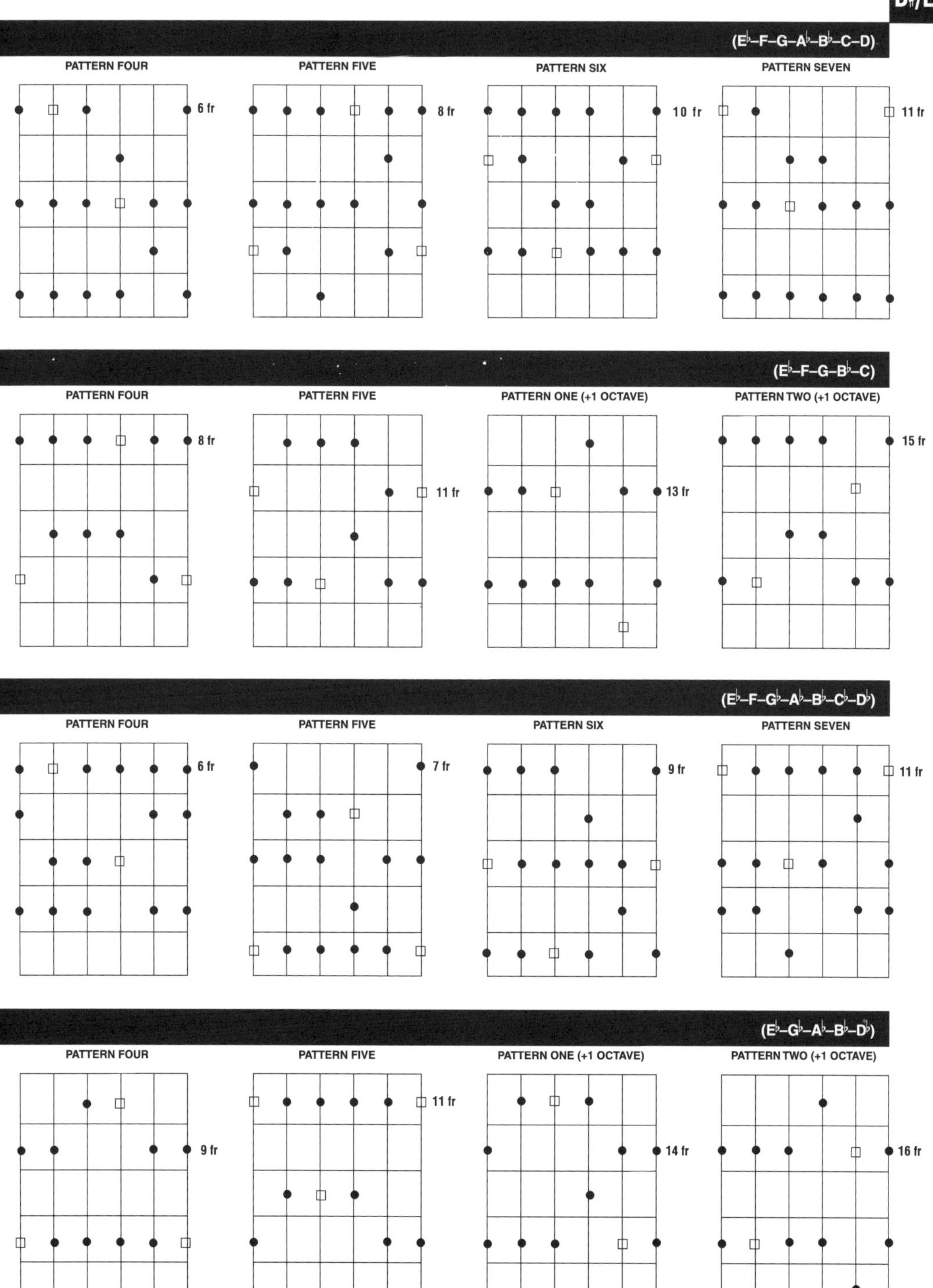
(E♭–F–G–A♭–B♭–C–D)
PATTERN FOUR
PATTERN FIVE
PATTERN SIX
PATTERN SEVEN
6 fr
8 fr
10 fr
11 fr

(E♭–F–G–B♭–C)
PATTERN FOUR
PATTERN FIVE
PATTERN ONE (+1 OCTAVE)
PATTERN TWO (+1 OCTAVE)
8 fr
11 fr
13 fr
15 fr

(E♭–F–G♭–A♭–B♭–C♭–D♭)
PATTERN FOUR
PATTERN FIVE
PATTERN SIX
PATTERN SEVEN
6 fr
7 fr
9 fr
11 fr

(E♭–G♭–A♭–B♭–D♭)
PATTERN FOUR
PATTERN FIVE
PATTERN ONE (+1 OCTAVE)
PATTERN TWO (+1 OCTAVE)
9 fr
11 fr
14 fr
16 fr

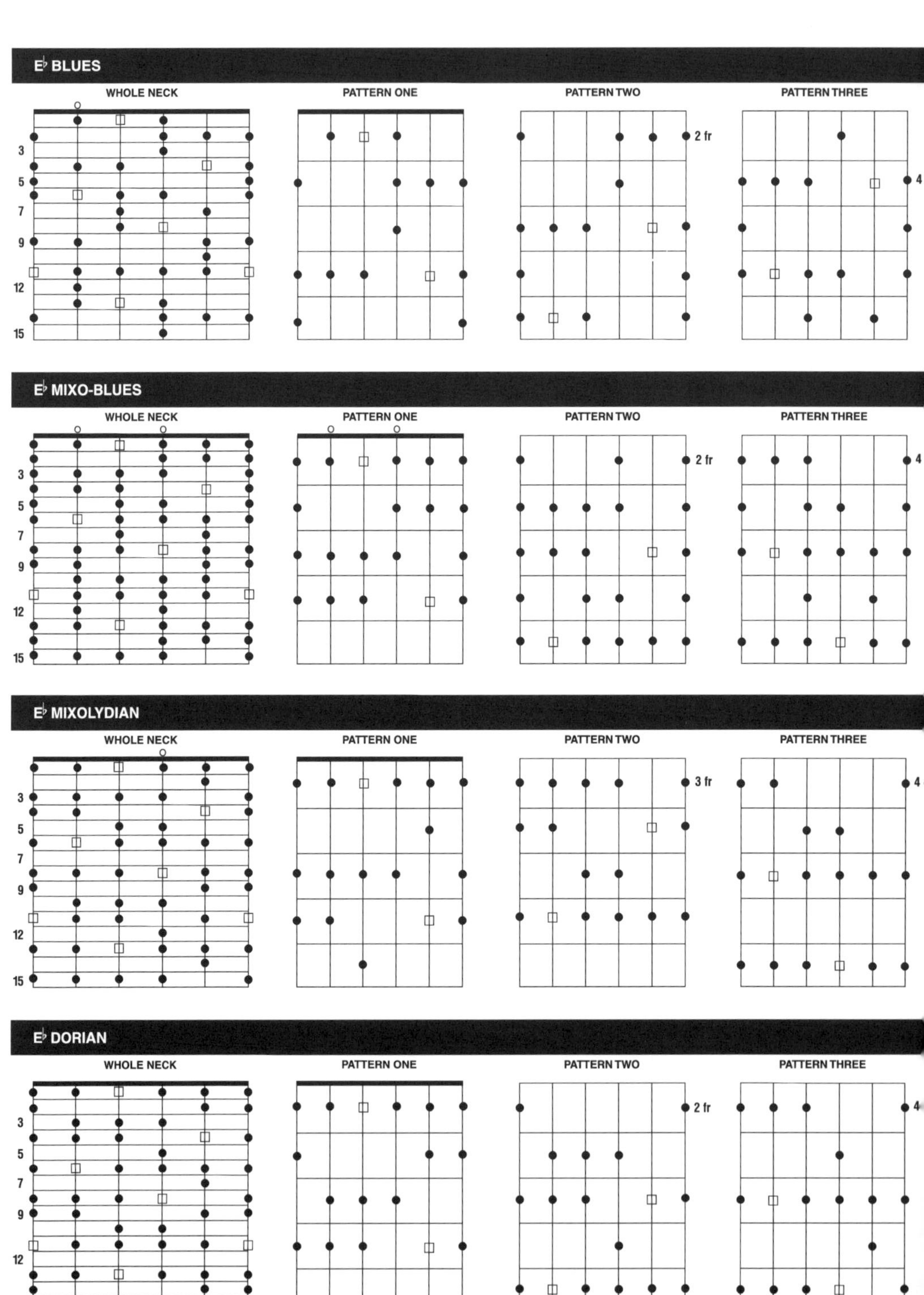

E♭ BLUES
WHOLE NECK
PATTERN ONE
PATTERN TWO
PATTERN THREE
2 fr
4

E♭ MIXO-BLUES
WHOLE NECK
PATTERN ONE
PATTERN TWO
PATTERN THREE
2 fr
4

E♭ MIXOLYDIAN
WHOLE NECK
PATTERN ONE
PATTERN TWO
PATTERN THREE
3 fr
4

E♭ DORIAN
WHOLE NECK
PATTERN ONE
PATTERN TWO
PATTERN THREE
2 fr
4

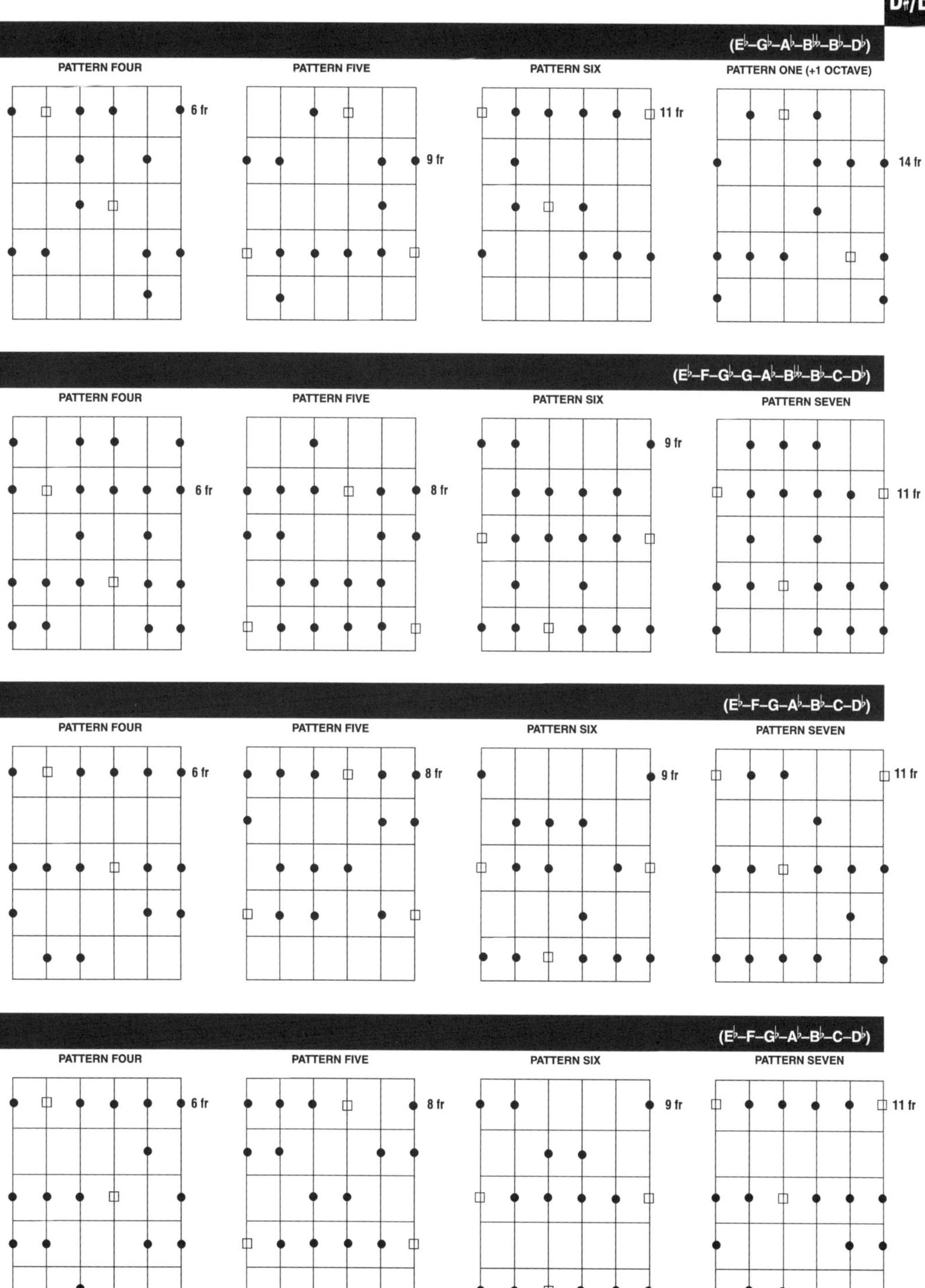
(E♭–G♭–A♭–B♭♭–B♭–D♭)

PATTERN FOUR
PATTERN FIVE
PATTERN SIX
PATTERN ONE (+1 OCTAVE)
6 fr
9 fr
11 fr
14 fr

(E♭–F–G♭–G–A♭–B♭♭–B♭–C–D♭)

PATTERN FOUR
PATTERN FIVE
PATTERN SIX
PATTERN SEVEN
6 fr
8 fr
9 fr
11 fr

(E♭–F–G–A♭–B♭–C–D♭)

PATTERN FOUR
PATTERN FIVE
PATTERN SIX
PATTERN SEVEN
6 fr
8 fr
9 fr
11 fr

(E♭–F–G♭–A♭–B♭–C–D♭)

PATTERN FOUR
PATTERN FIVE
PATTERN SIX
PATTERN SEVEN
6 fr
8 fr
9 fr
11 fr

# E♭ MELODIC MINOR

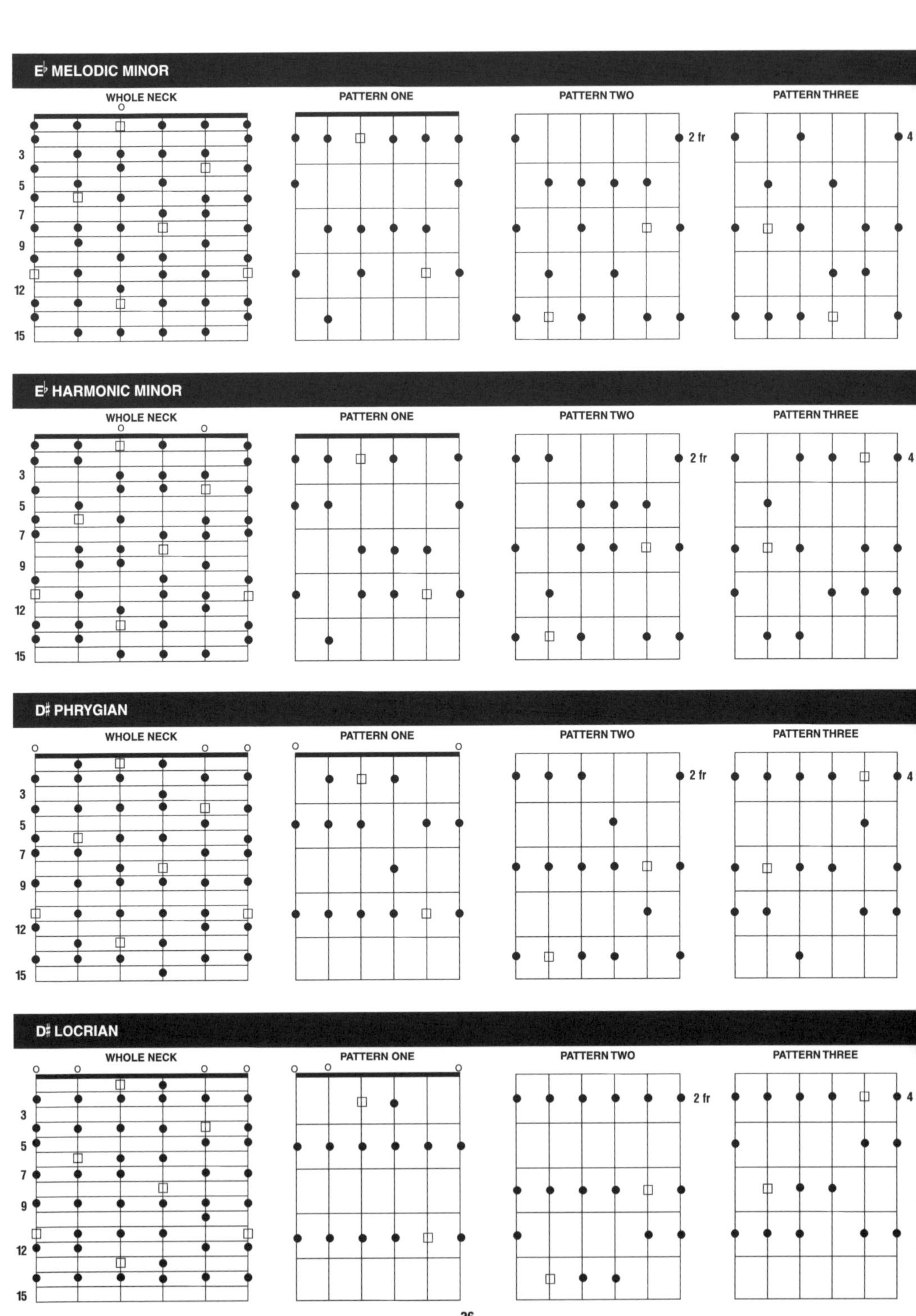

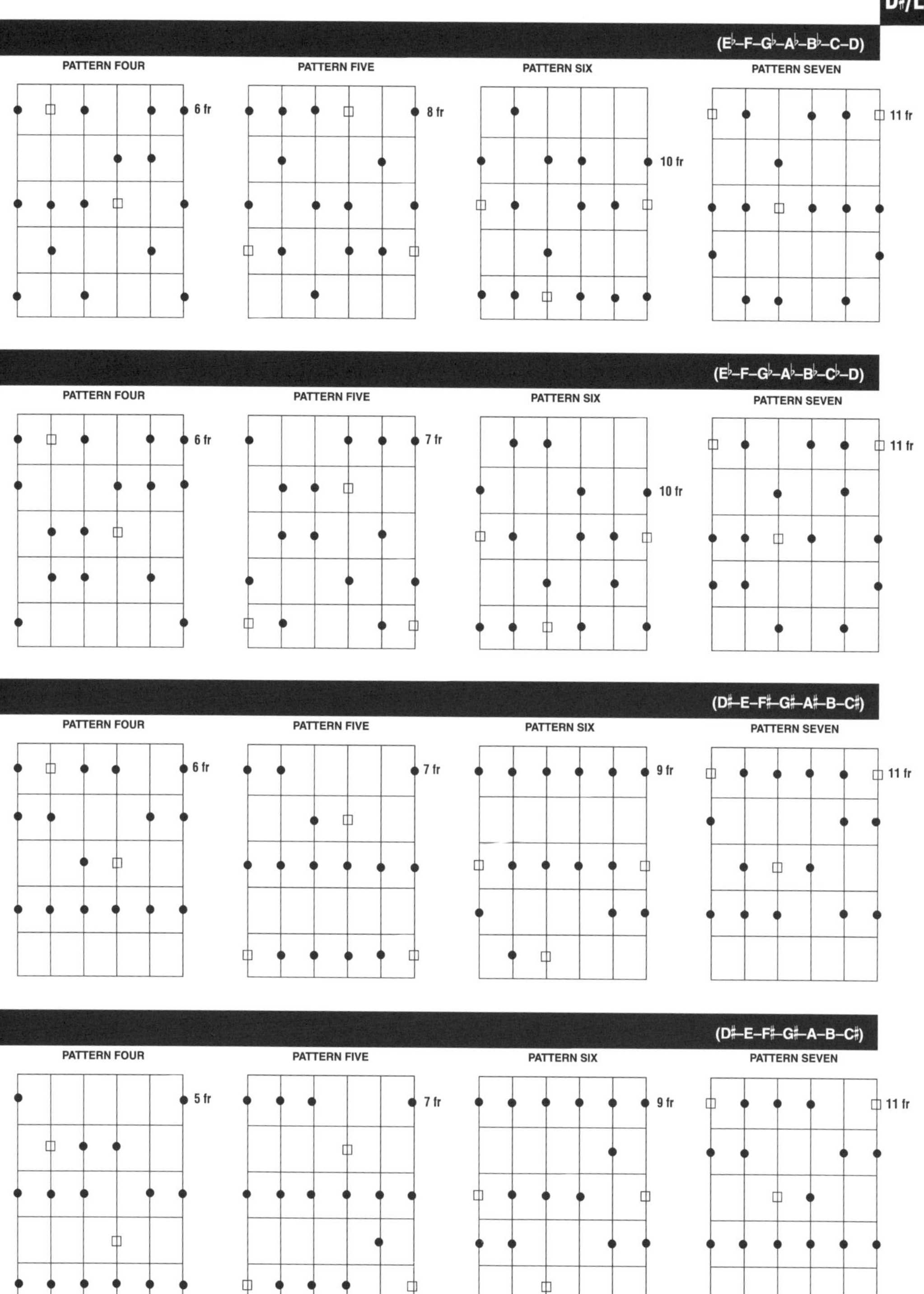
(E♭–F–G♭–A♭–B♭–C–D)
PATTERN FOUR
PATTERN FIVE
PATTERN SIX
PATTERN SEVEN
6 fr
8 fr
10 fr
11 fr

(E♭–F–G♭–A♭–B♭–C♭–D)
PATTERN FOUR
PATTERN FIVE
PATTERN SIX
PATTERN SEVEN
6 fr
7 fr
10 fr
11 fr

(D♯–E–F♯–G♯–A♯–B–C♯)
PATTERN FOUR
PATTERN FIVE
PATTERN SIX
PATTERN SEVEN
6 fr
7 fr
9 fr
11 fr

(D♯–E–F♯–G♯–A–B–C♯)
PATTERN FOUR
PATTERN FIVE
PATTERN SIX
PATTERN SEVEN
5 fr
7 fr
9 fr
11 fr

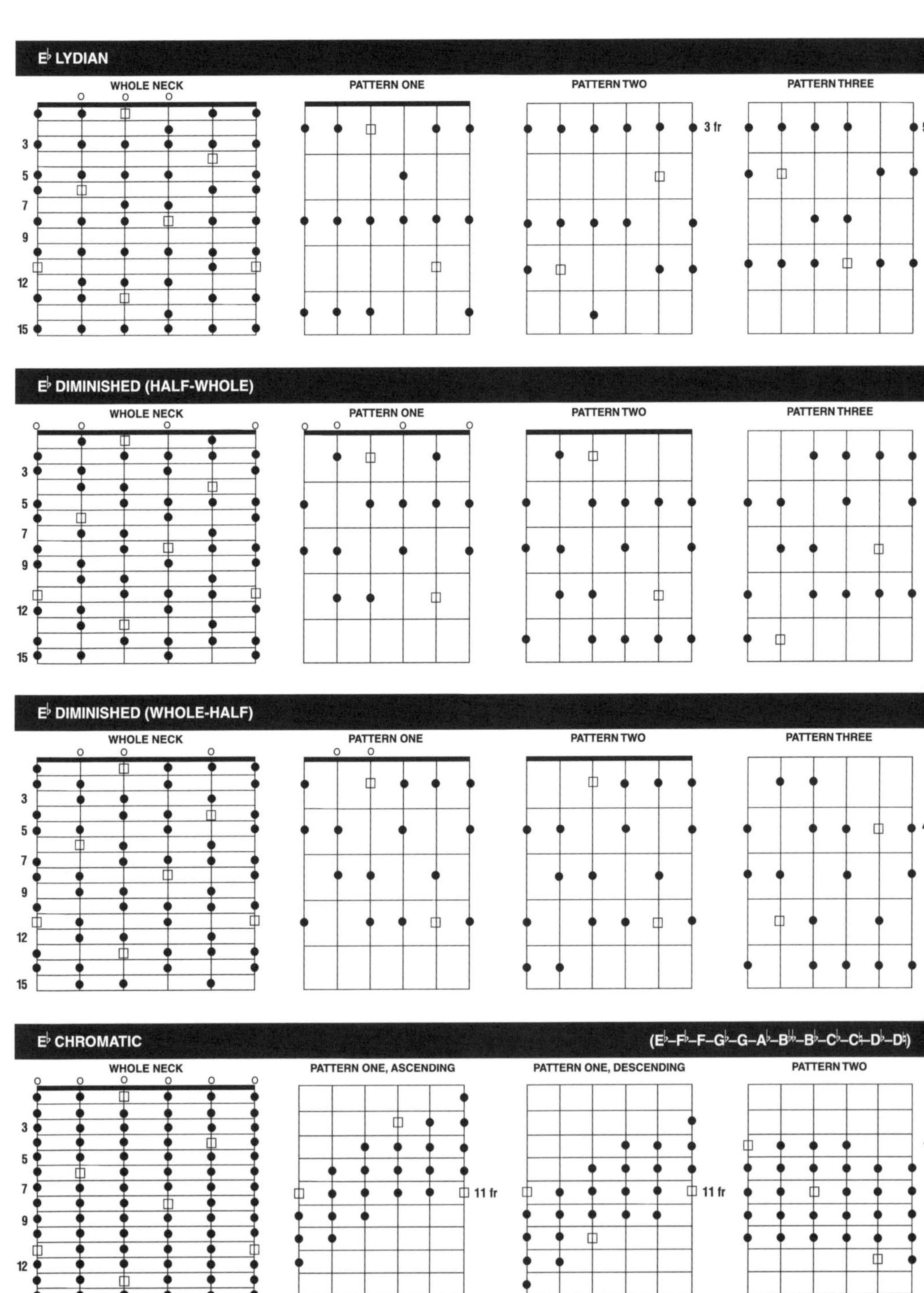

E♭ LYDIAN
WHOLE NECK
PATTERN ONE
PATTERN TWO
3 fr
PATTERN THREE
5

E♭ DIMINISHED (HALF-WHOLE)
WHOLE NECK
PATTERN ONE
PATTERN TWO
PATTERN THREE

E♭ DIMINISHED (WHOLE-HALF)
WHOLE NECK
PATTERN ONE
PATTERN TWO
PATTERN THREE

E♭ CHROMATIC
(E♭–F♭–F–G♭–G–A♭–B♭♭–B♭–C♭–C♮–D♭–D♮)
WHOLE NECK
PATTERN ONE, ASCENDING
PATTERN ONE, DESCENDING
PATTERN TWO
11 fr

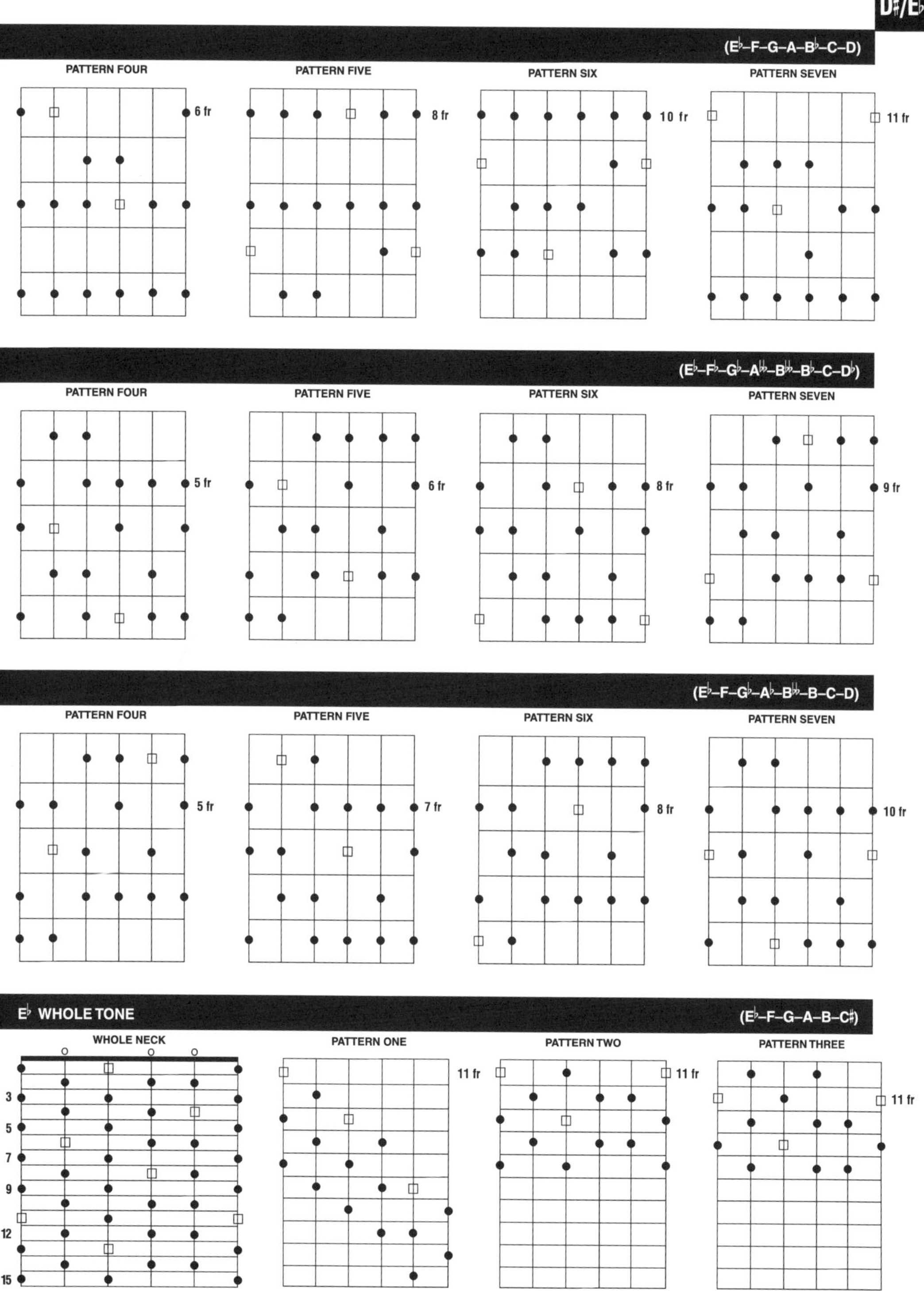
(E♭–F–G–A–B♭–C–D)
PATTERN FOUR
PATTERN FIVE
PATTERN SIX
PATTERN SEVEN
6 fr
8 fr
10 fr
11 fr
(E♭–F–G♭–A♭♭–B♭♭–B♭–C–D♭)
PATTERN FOUR
PATTERN FIVE
PATTERN SIX
PATTERN SEVEN
5 fr
6 fr
8 fr
9 fr
(E♭–F–G♭–A♭–B♭♭–B–C–D)
PATTERN FOUR
PATTERN FIVE
PATTERN SIX
PATTERN SEVEN
5 fr
7 fr
8 fr
10 fr
E♭ WHOLE TONE
(E♭–F–G–A–B–C♯)
WHOLE NECK
PATTERN ONE
PATTERN TWO
PATTERN THREE
3
5
7
9
12
15
11 fr
11 fr
11 fr

## E MAJOR (IONIAN)

WHOLE NECK | PATTERN ONE | PATTERN TWO | PATTERN THREE

## E MAJOR PENTATONIC

WHOLE NECK | PATTERN ONE | PATTERN TWO | PATTERN THREE

## E NATURAL MINOR (AEOLIAN)

WHOLE NECK | PATTERN ONE | PATTERN TWO | PATTERN THREE

## E MINOR PENTATONIC

WHOLE NECK | PATTERN ONE | PATTERN TWO | PATTERN THREE

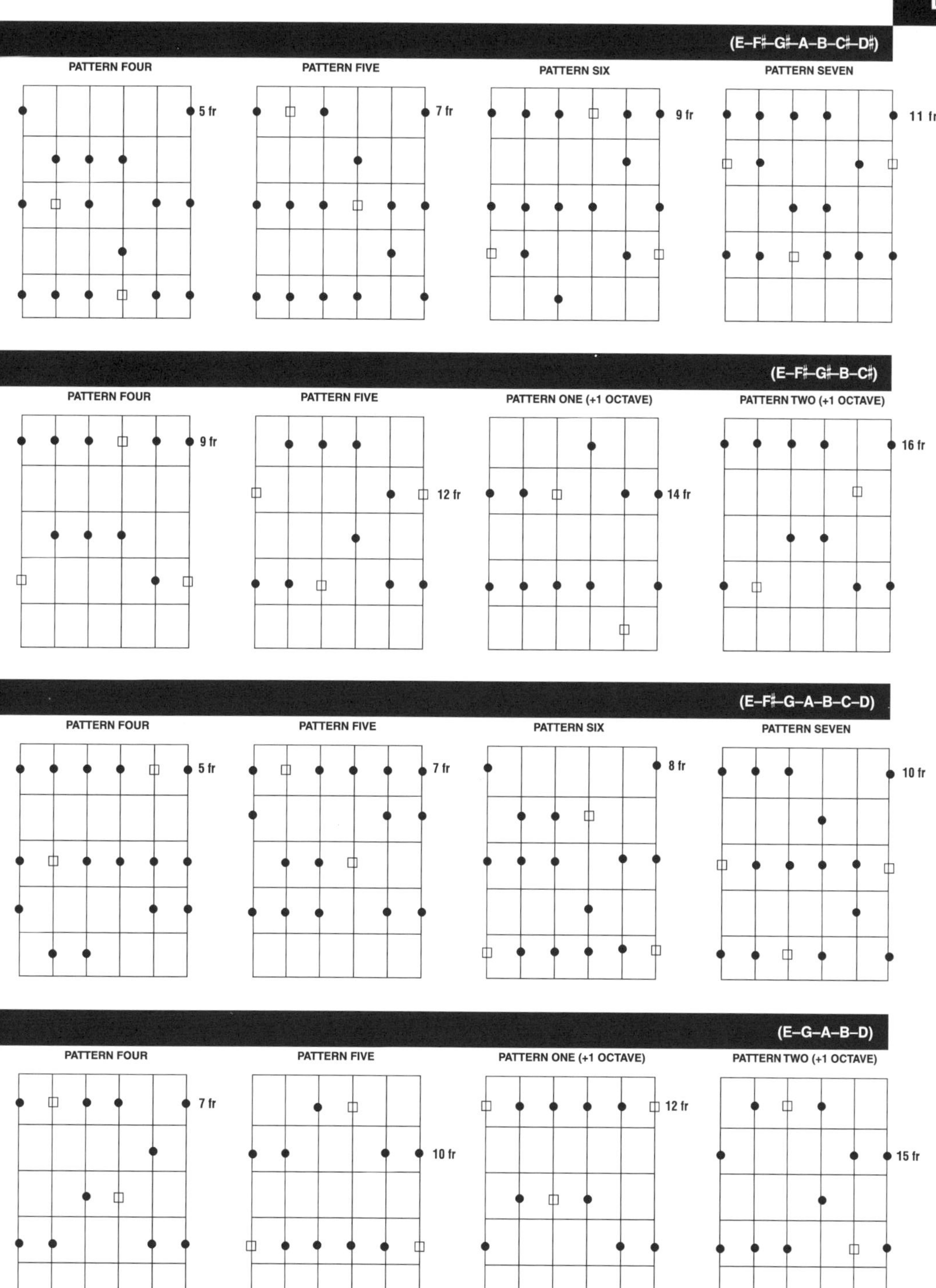
(E–F#–G#–A–B–C#–D#)
PATTERN FOUR
PATTERN FIVE
PATTERN SIX
PATTERN SEVEN
5 fr
7 fr
9 fr
11 fr
(E–F#–G#–B–C#)
PATTERN FOUR
PATTERN FIVE
PATTERN ONE (+1 OCTAVE)
PATTERN TWO (+1 OCTAVE)
9 fr
12 fr
14 fr
16 fr
(E–F#–G–A–B–C–D)
PATTERN FOUR
PATTERN FIVE
PATTERN SIX
PATTERN SEVEN
5 fr
7 fr
8 fr
10 fr
(E–G–A–B–D)
PATTERN FOUR
PATTERN FIVE
PATTERN ONE (+1 OCTAVE)
PATTERN TWO (+1 OCTAVE)
7 fr
10 fr
12 fr
15 fr

# E BLUES

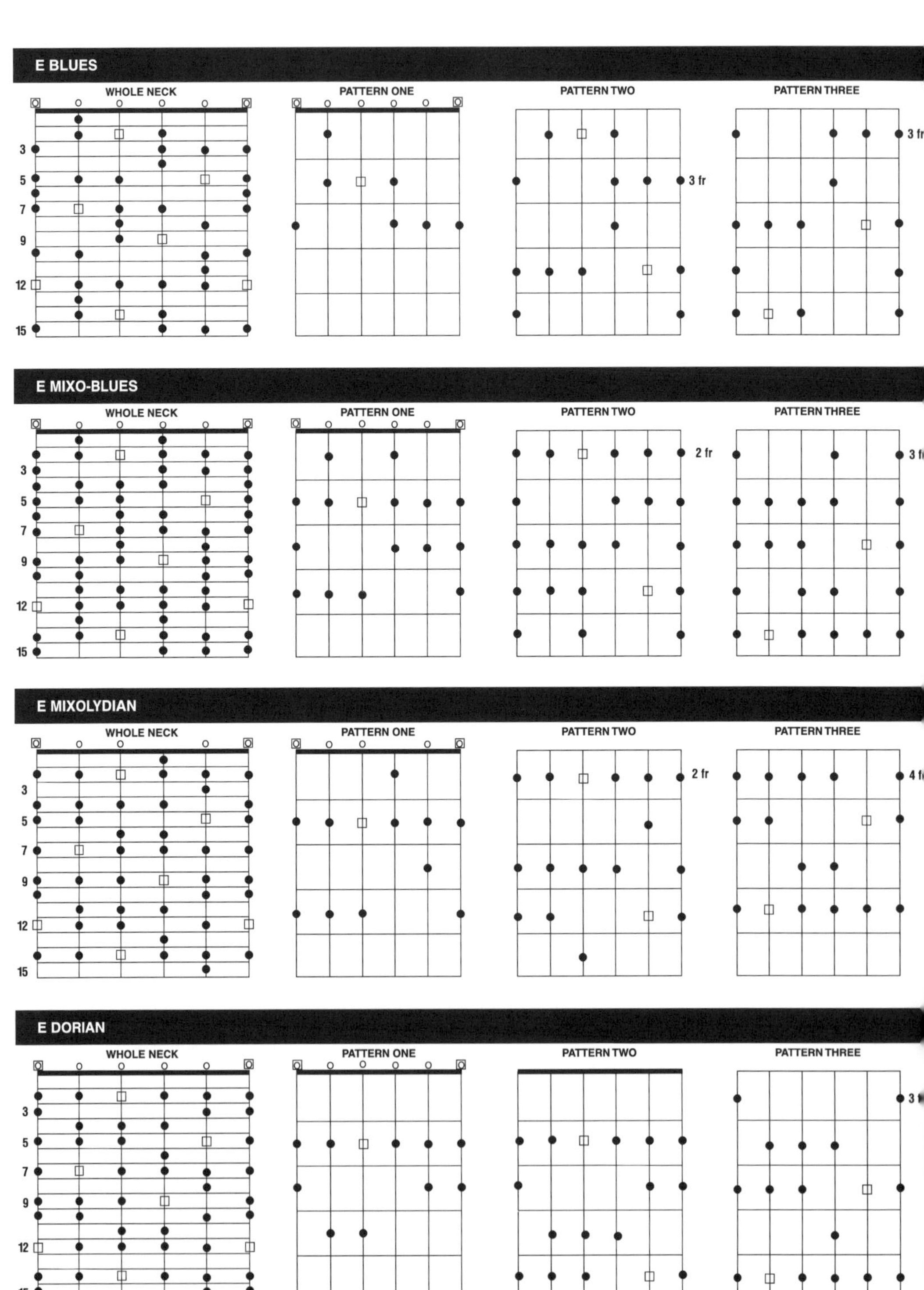

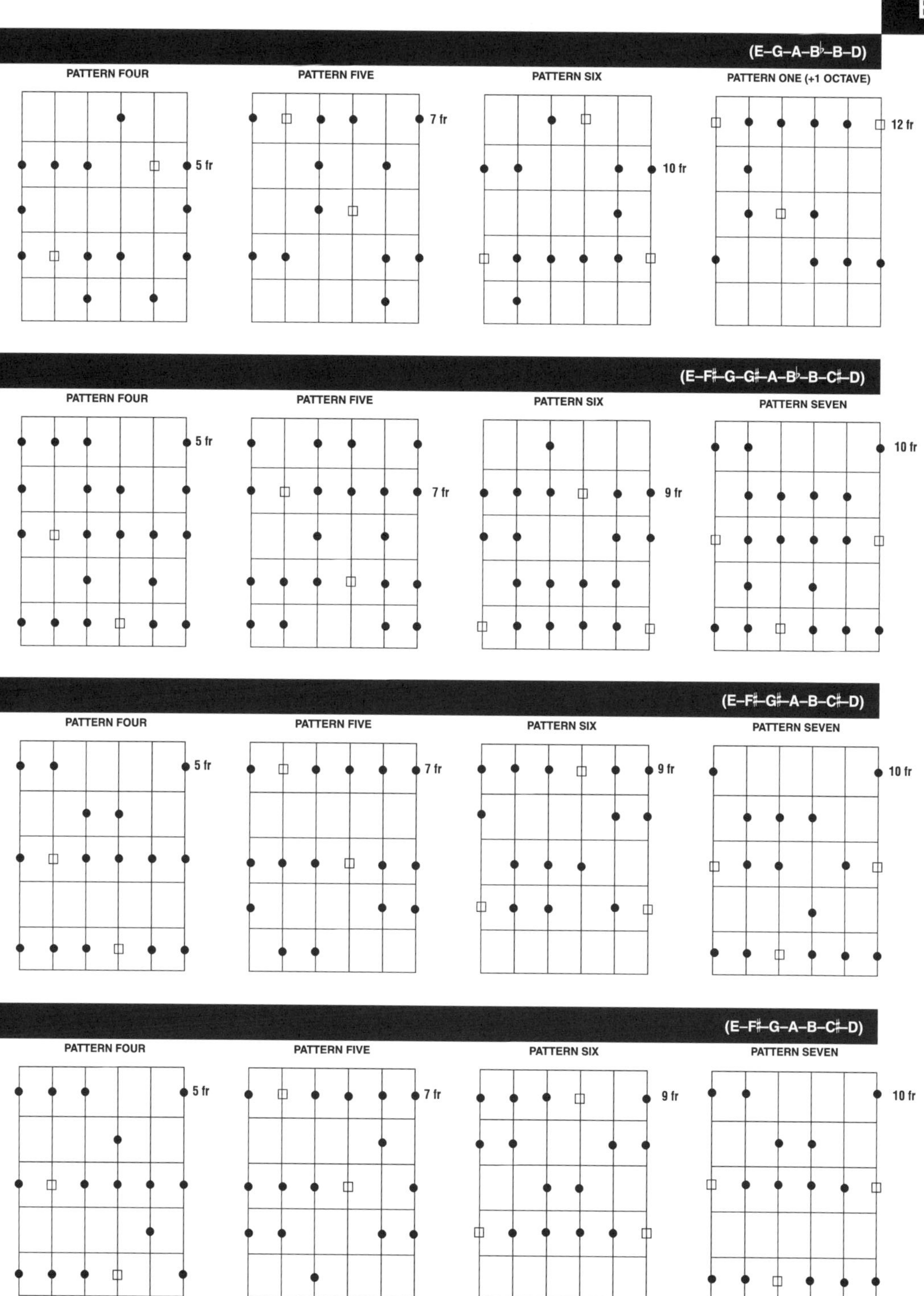
(E–G–A–B♭–B–D)
PATTERN FOUR
PATTERN FIVE
7 fr
5 fr
PATTERN SIX
10 fr
PATTERN ONE (+1 OCTAVE)
12 fr
(E–F♯–G–G♯–A–B♭–B–C♯–D)
PATTERN FOUR
5 fr
PATTERN FIVE
7 fr
PATTERN SIX
9 fr
PATTERN SEVEN
10 fr
(E–F♯–G♯–A–B–C♯–D)
PATTERN FOUR
5 fr
PATTERN FIVE
7 fr
PATTERN SIX
9 fr
PATTERN SEVEN
10 fr
(E–F♯–G–A–B–C♯–D)
PATTERN FOUR
5 fr
PATTERN FIVE
7 fr
PATTERN SIX
9 fr
PATTERN SEVEN
10 fr

# E MELODIC MINOR

WHOLE NECK | PATTERN ONE | PATTERN TWO | PATTERN THREE

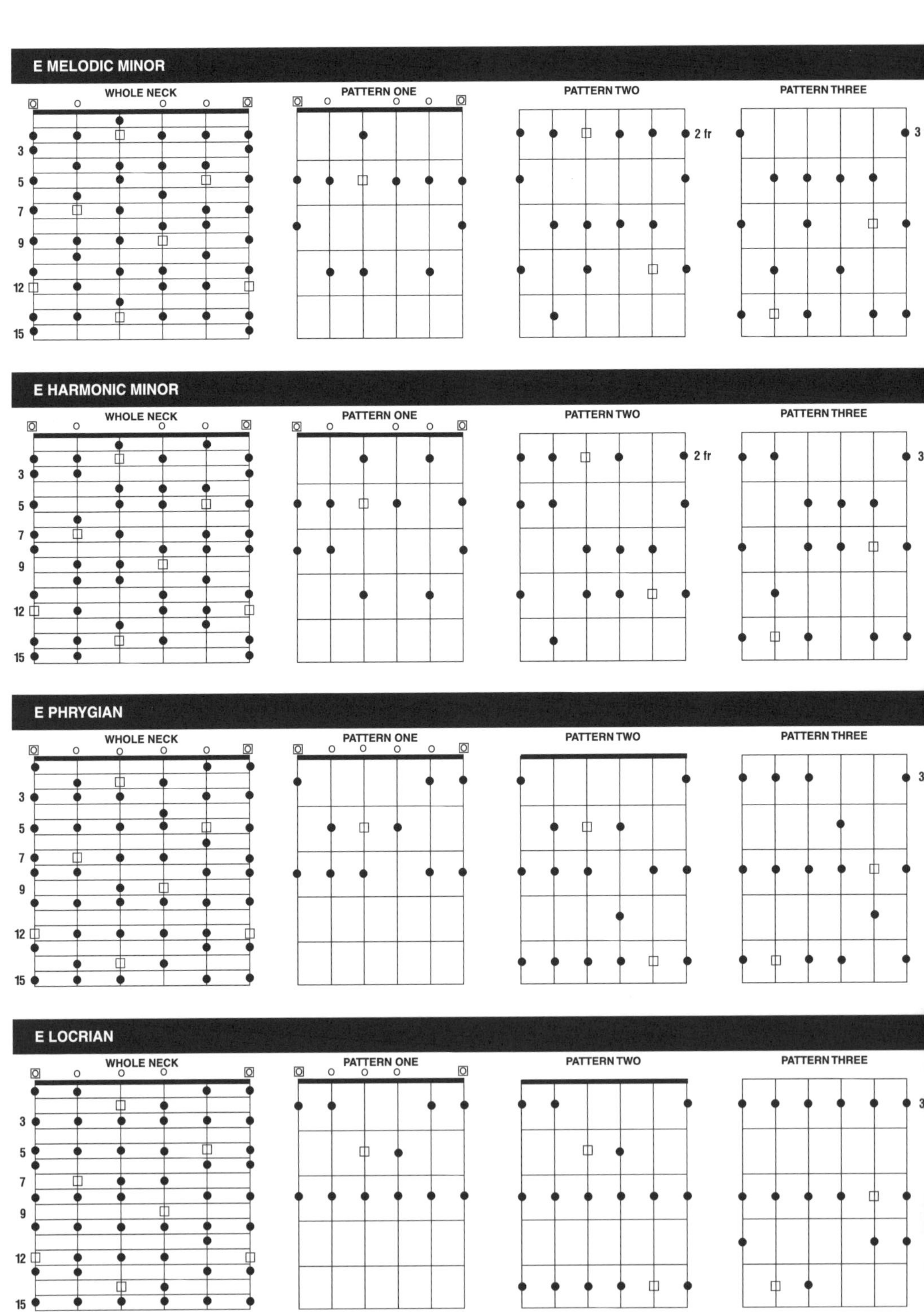

# E HARMONIC MINOR

WHOLE NECK | PATTERN ONE | PATTERN TWO | PATTERN THREE

# E PHRYGIAN

WHOLE NECK | PATTERN ONE | PATTERN TWO | PATTERN THREE

# E LOCRIAN

WHOLE NECK | PATTERN ONE | PATTERN TWO | PATTERN THREE

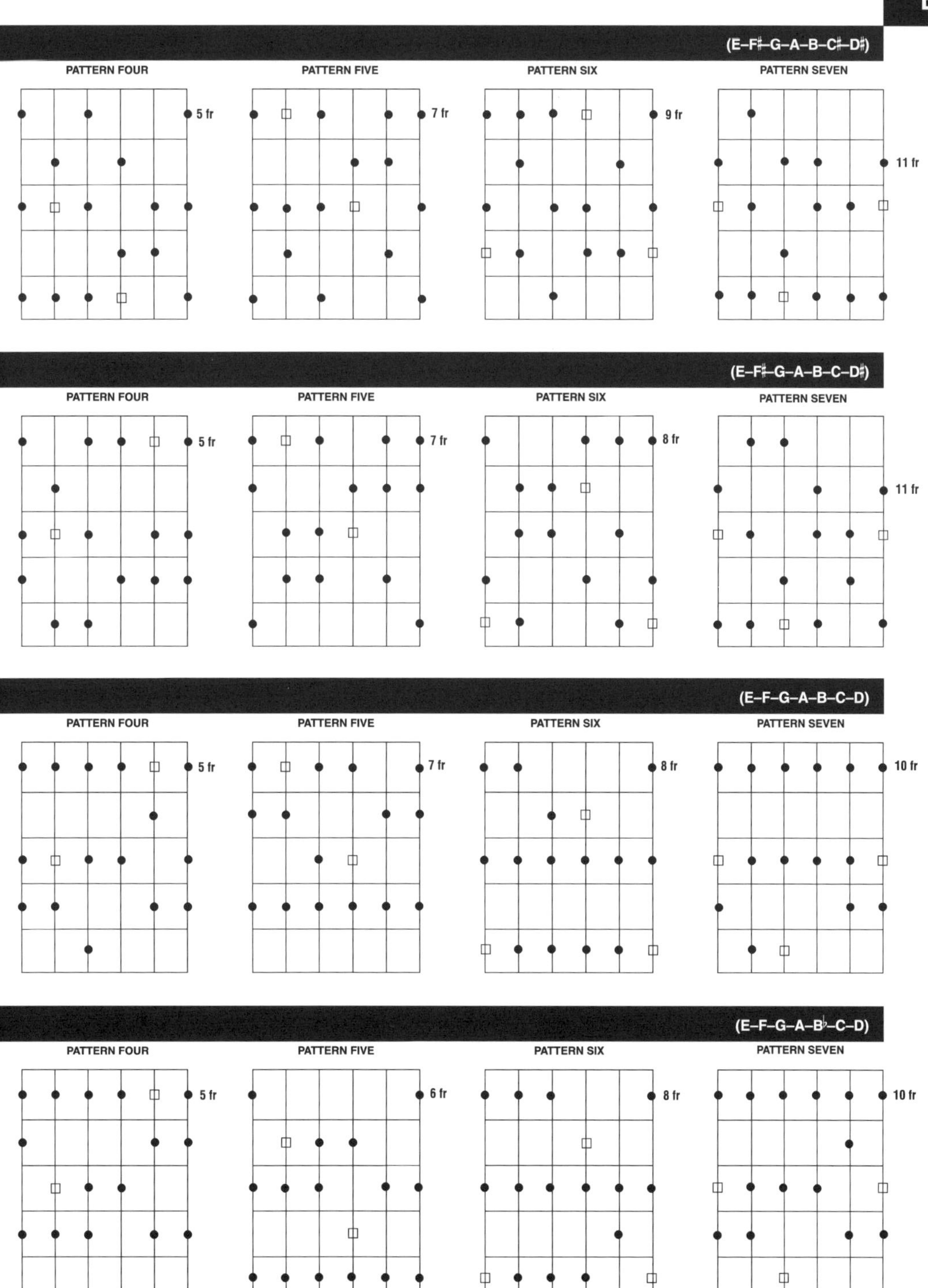
(E–F♯–G–A–B–C♯–D♯)
PATTERN FOUR
PATTERN FIVE
PATTERN SIX
PATTERN SEVEN
5 fr
7 fr
9 fr
11 fr
(E–F♯–G–A–B–C–D♯)
PATTERN FOUR
PATTERN FIVE
PATTERN SIX
PATTERN SEVEN
5 fr
7 fr
8 fr
11 fr
(E–F–G–A–B–C–D)
PATTERN FOUR
PATTERN FIVE
PATTERN SIX
PATTERN SEVEN
5 fr
7 fr
8 fr
10 fr
(E–F–G–A–B♭–C–D)
PATTERN FOUR
PATTERN FIVE
PATTERN SIX
PATTERN SEVEN
5 fr
6 fr
8 fr
10 fr

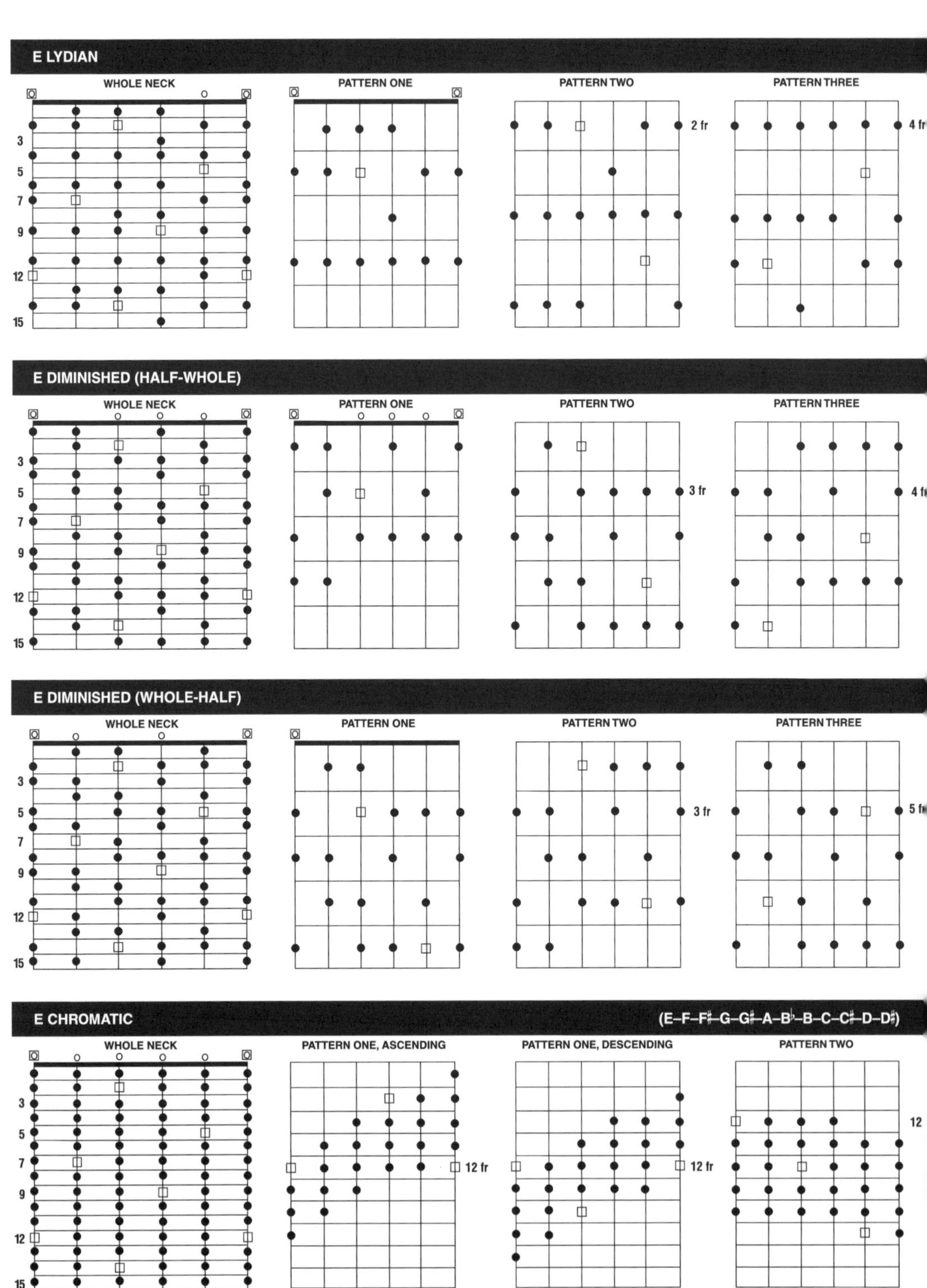


E LYDIAN
WHOLE NECK
PATTERN ONE
PATTERN TWO
2 fr
PATTERN THREE
4 fr

E DIMINISHED (HALF-WHOLE)
WHOLE NECK
PATTERN ONE
PATTERN TWO
3 fr
PATTERN THREE
4 fr

E DIMINISHED (WHOLE-HALF)
WHOLE NECK
PATTERN ONE
PATTERN TWO
3 fr
PATTERN THREE
5 fr

E CHROMATIC
(E–F–F#–G–G#–A–Bb–B–C–C#–D–D#)
WHOLE NECK
PATTERN ONE, ASCENDING
12 fr
PATTERN ONE, DESCENDING
12 fr
PATTERN TWO
12

(E–F#–G#–A#–B–C#–D#)

| PATTERN FOUR | PATTERN FIVE | PATTERN SIX | PATTERN SEVEN |
| --- | --- | --- | --- |

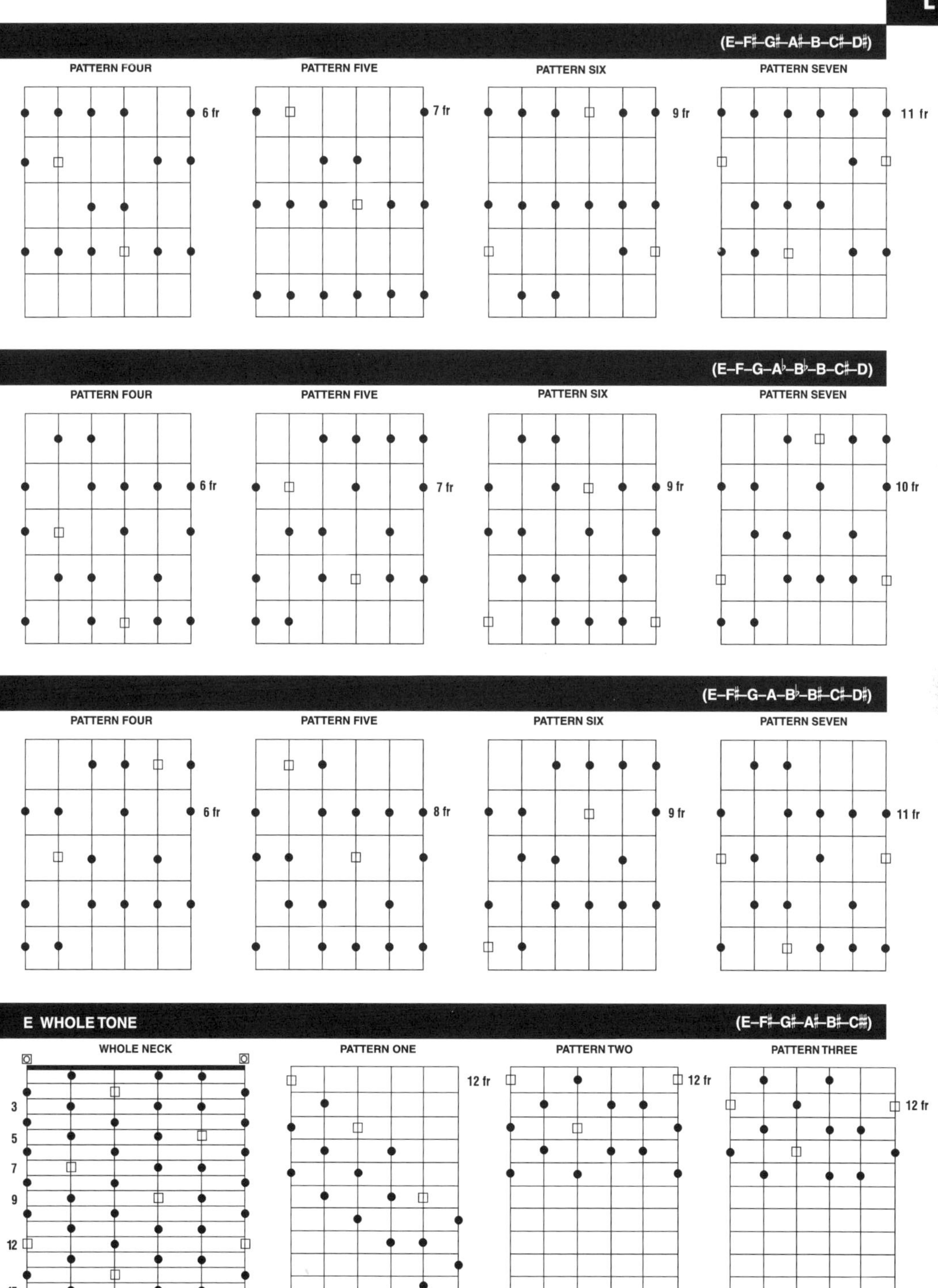

(E–F–G–A♭–B♭–B–C#–D)

| PATTERN FOUR | PATTERN FIVE | PATTERN SIX | PATTERN SEVEN |
| --- | --- | --- | --- |

(E–F#–G–A–B♭–B#–C#–D#)

| PATTERN FOUR | PATTERN FIVE | PATTERN SIX | PATTERN SEVEN |
| --- | --- | --- | --- |

## E WHOLE TONE

(E–F#–G#–A#–B#–C#)

| WHOLE NECK | PATTERN ONE | PATTERN TWO | PATTERN THREE |
| --- | --- | --- | --- |

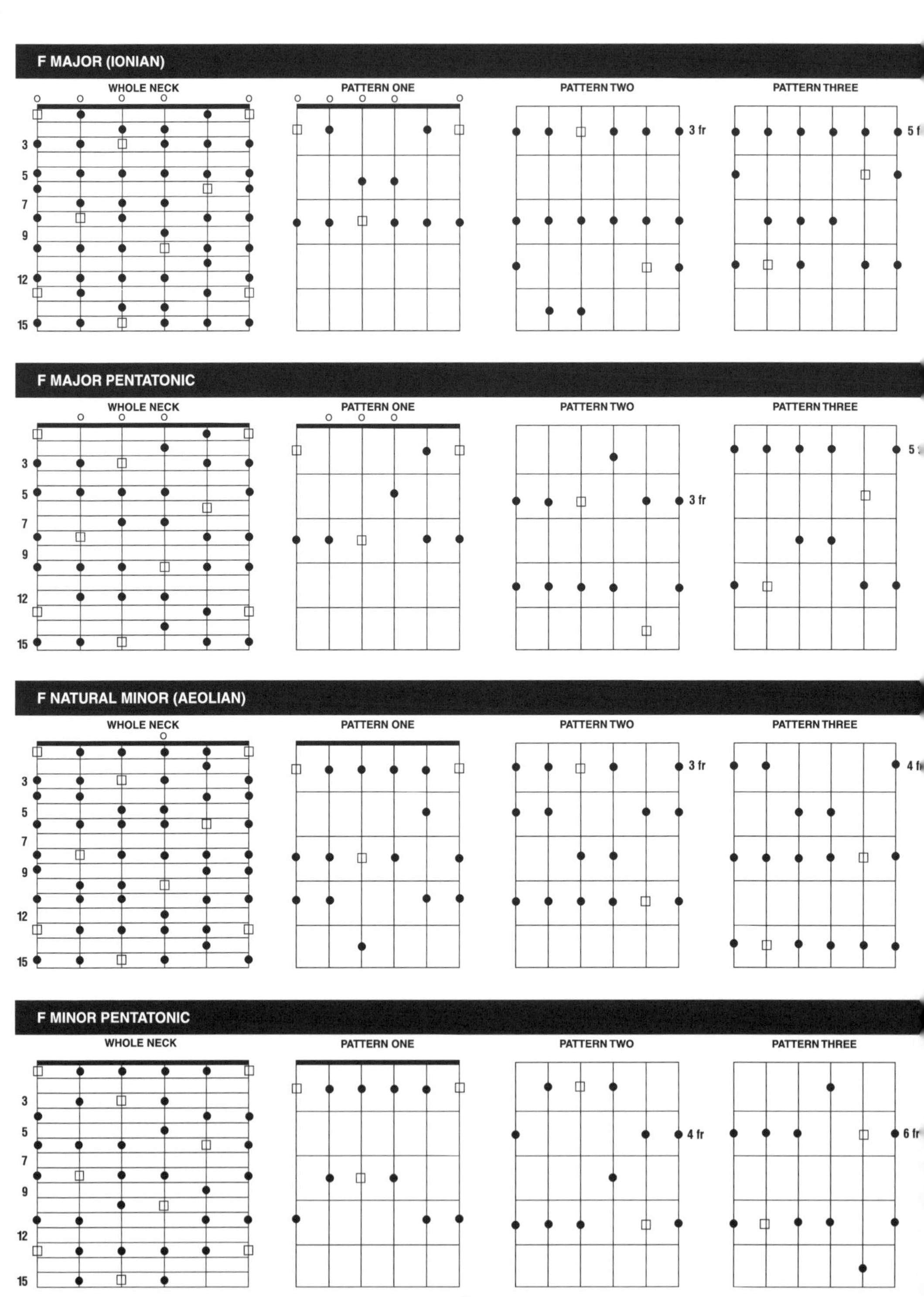

F MAJOR (IONIAN)
WHOLE NECK
PATTERN ONE
PATTERN TWO
PATTERN THREE
3 fr
5 fr
F MAJOR PENTATONIC
WHOLE NECK
PATTERN ONE
PATTERN TWO
PATTERN THREE
3 fr
5 fr
F NATURAL MINOR (AEOLIAN)
WHOLE NECK
PATTERN ONE
PATTERN TWO
PATTERN THREE
3 fr
4 fr
F MINOR PENTATONIC
WHOLE NECK
PATTERN ONE
PATTERN TWO
PATTERN THREE
4 fr
6 fr

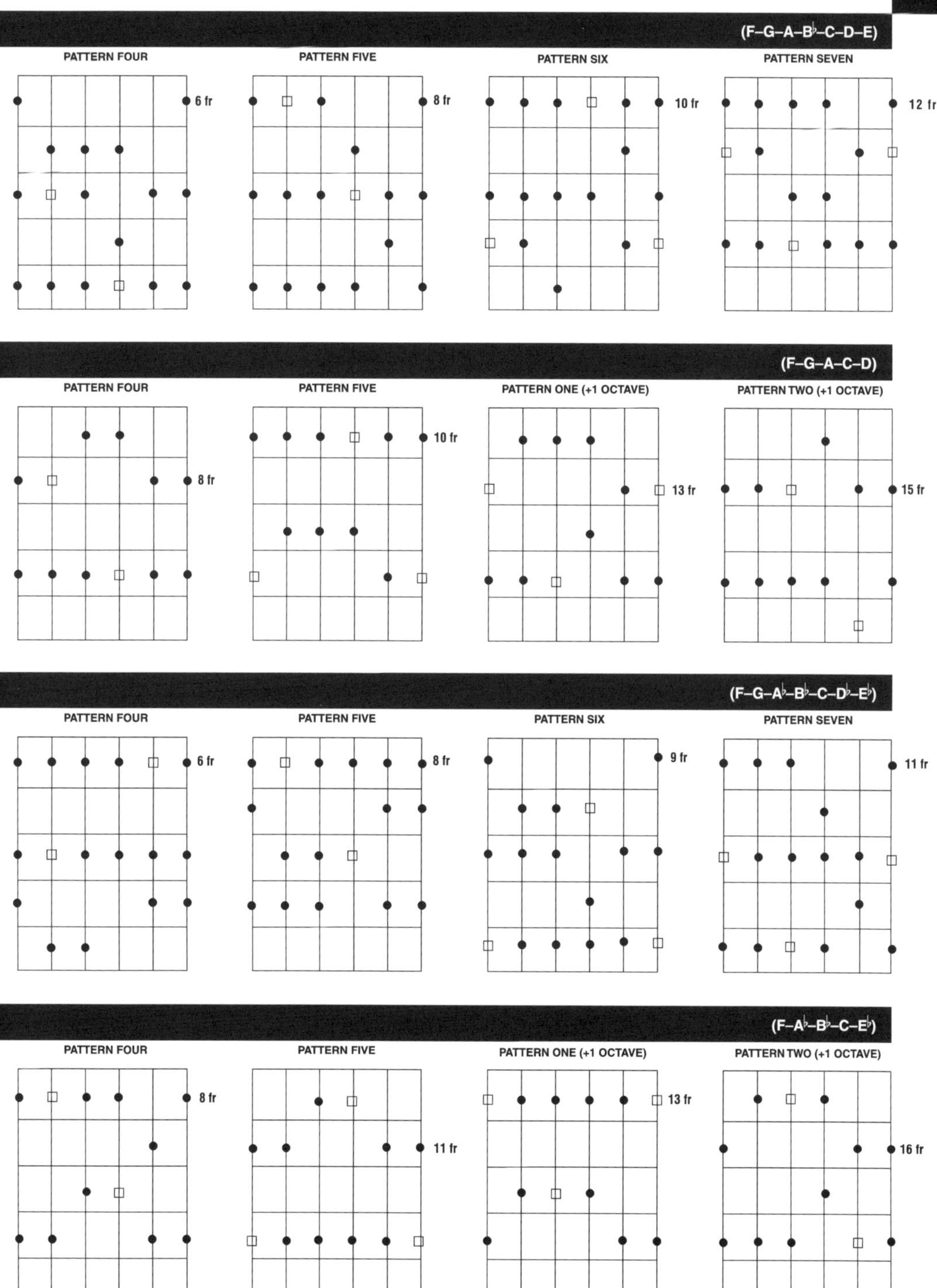


(F–G–A–B♭–C–D–E)
PATTERN FOUR
PATTERN FIVE
PATTERN SIX
PATTERN SEVEN
6 fr
8 fr
10 fr
12 fr

(F–G–A–C–D)
PATTERN FOUR
PATTERN FIVE
PATTERN ONE (+1 OCTAVE)
PATTERN TWO (+1 OCTAVE)
8 fr
10 fr
13 fr
15 fr

(F–G–A♭–B♭–C–D♭–E♭)
PATTERN FOUR
PATTERN FIVE
PATTERN SIX
PATTERN SEVEN
6 fr
8 fr
9 fr
11 fr

(F–A♭–B♭–C–E♭)
PATTERN FOUR
PATTERN FIVE
PATTERN ONE (+1 OCTAVE)
PATTERN TWO (+1 OCTAVE)
8 fr
11 fr
13 fr
16 fr

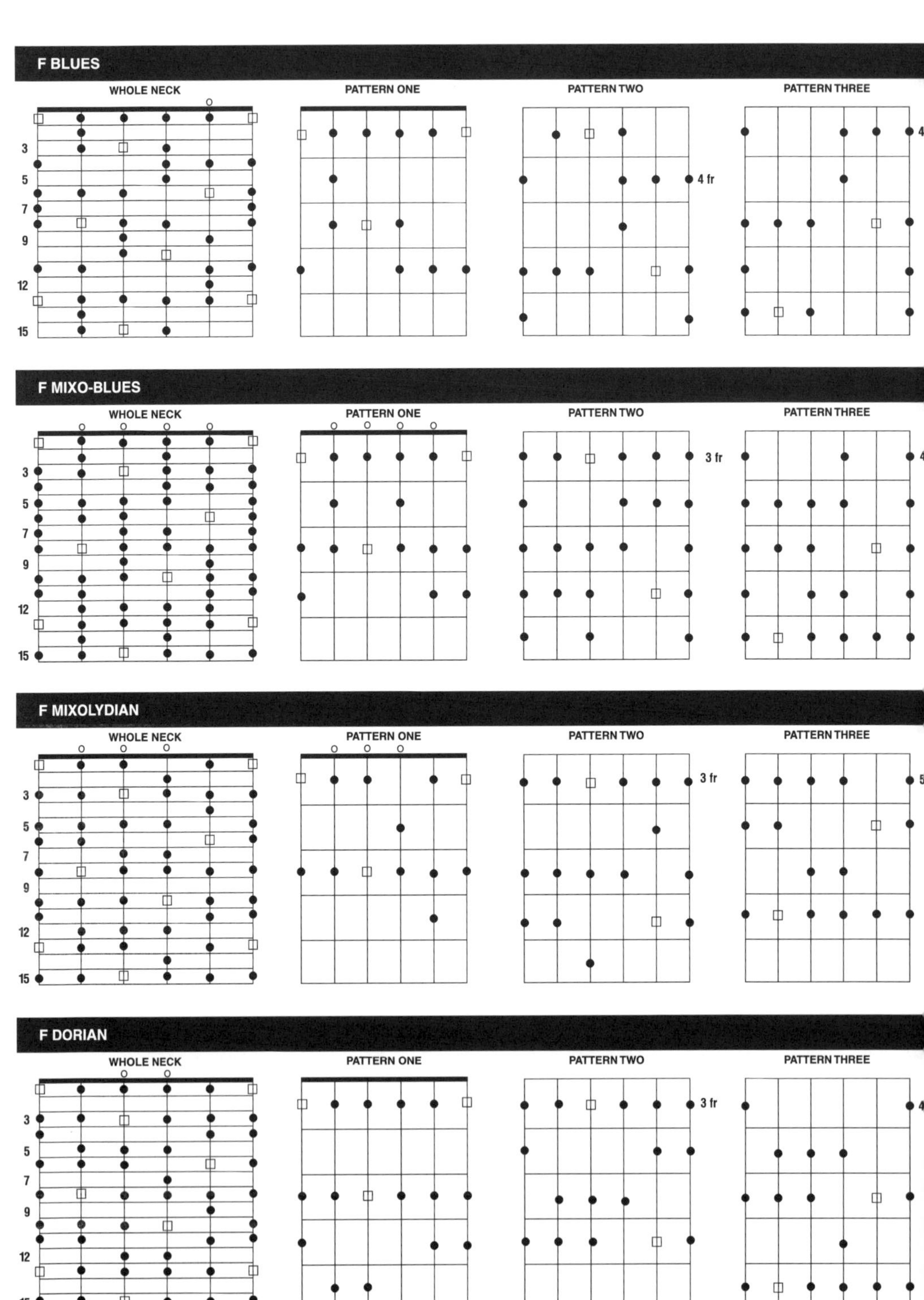

F BLUES
WHOLE NECK
PATTERN ONE
PATTERN TWO
PATTERN THREE
F MIXO-BLUES
WHOLE NECK
PATTERN ONE
PATTERN TWO
PATTERN THREE
F MIXOLYDIAN
WHOLE NECK
PATTERN ONE
PATTERN TWO
PATTERN THREE
F DORIAN
WHOLE NECK
PATTERN ONE
PATTERN TWO
PATTERN THREE

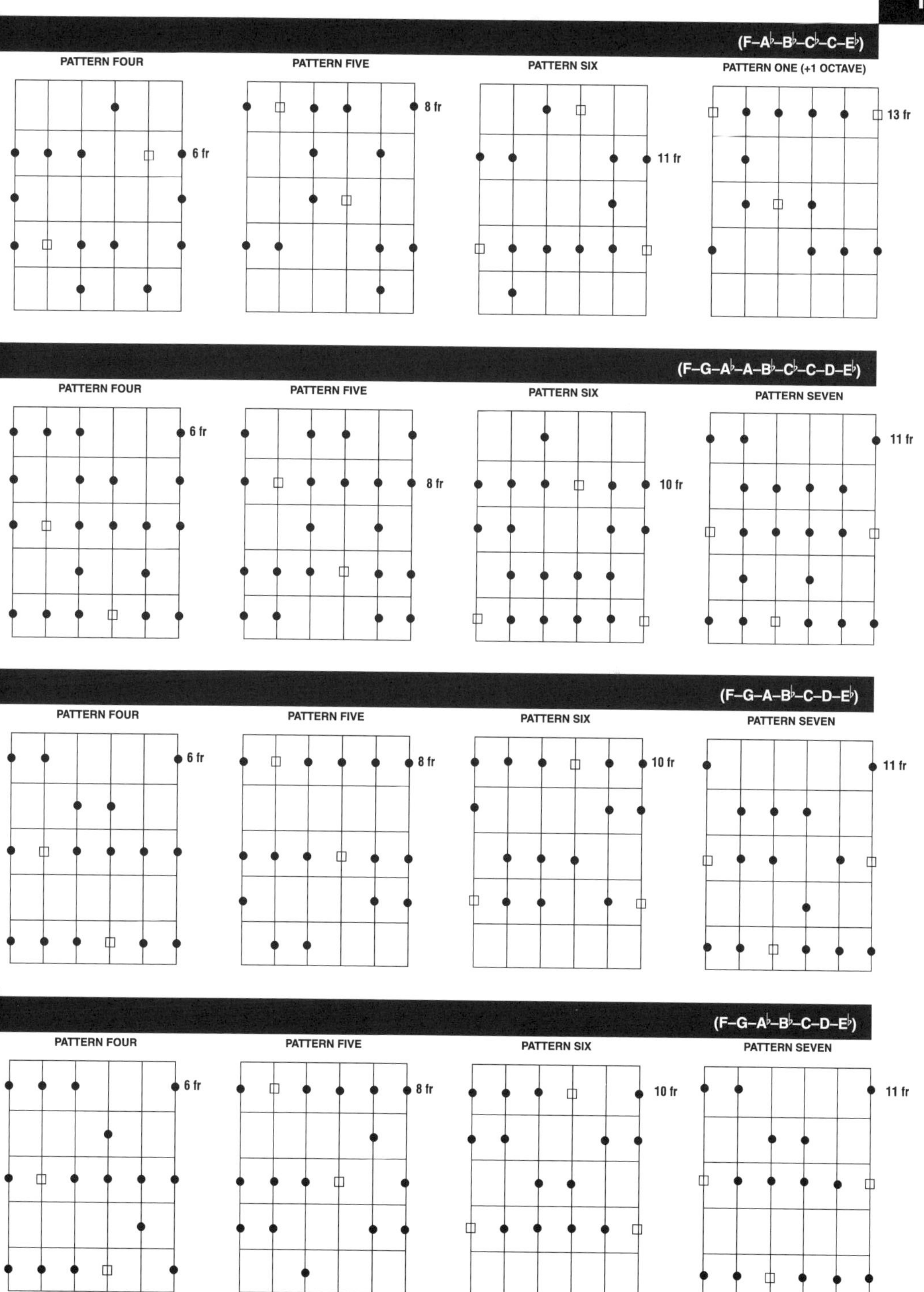


(F–A♭–B–C♭–C–E♭)
PATTERN FOUR
PATTERN FIVE
PATTERN SIX
PATTERN ONE (+1 OCTAVE)
8 fr
6 fr
11 fr
13 fr

(F–G–A♭–A–B♭–C♭–C–D–E♭)
PATTERN FOUR
PATTERN FIVE
PATTERN SIX
PATTERN SEVEN
6 fr
8 fr
10 fr
11 fr

(F–G–A–B♭–C–D–E♭)
PATTERN FOUR
PATTERN FIVE
PATTERN SIX
PATTERN SEVEN
6 fr
8 fr
10 fr
11 fr

(F–G–A♭–B♭–C–D–E♭)
PATTERN FOUR
PATTERN FIVE
PATTERN SIX
PATTERN SEVEN
6 fr
8 fr
10 fr
11 fr

# F MELODIC MINOR

WHOLE NECK | PATTERN ONE | PATTERN TWO | PATTERN THREE

# F HARMONIC MINOR

WHOLE NECK | PATTERN ONE | PATTERN TWO | PATTERN THREE

# F PHRYGIAN

WHOLE NECK | PATTERN ONE | PATTERN TWO | PATTERN THREE

# F LOCRIAN

WHOLE NECK | PATTERN ONE | PATTERN TWO | PATTERN THREE

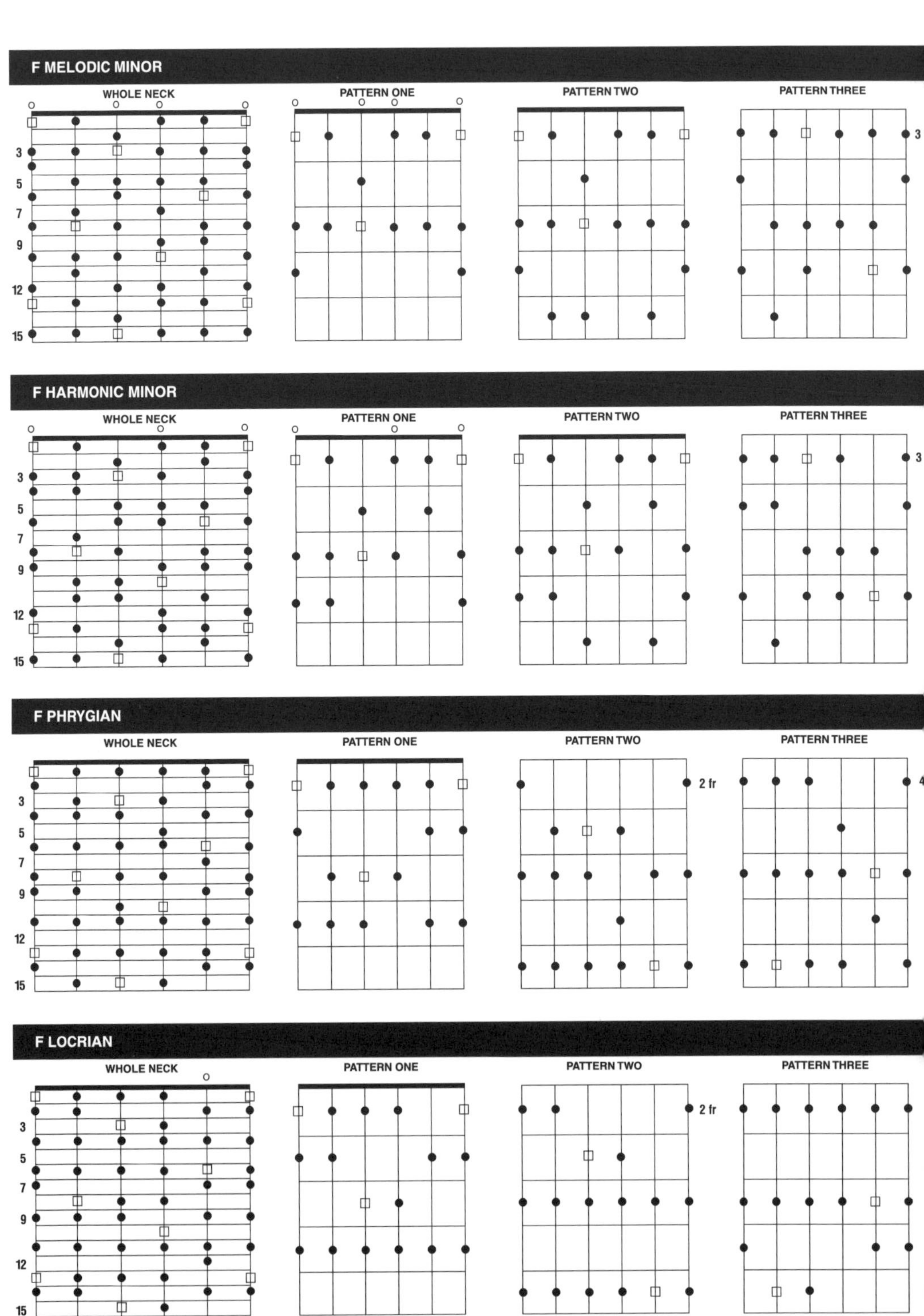

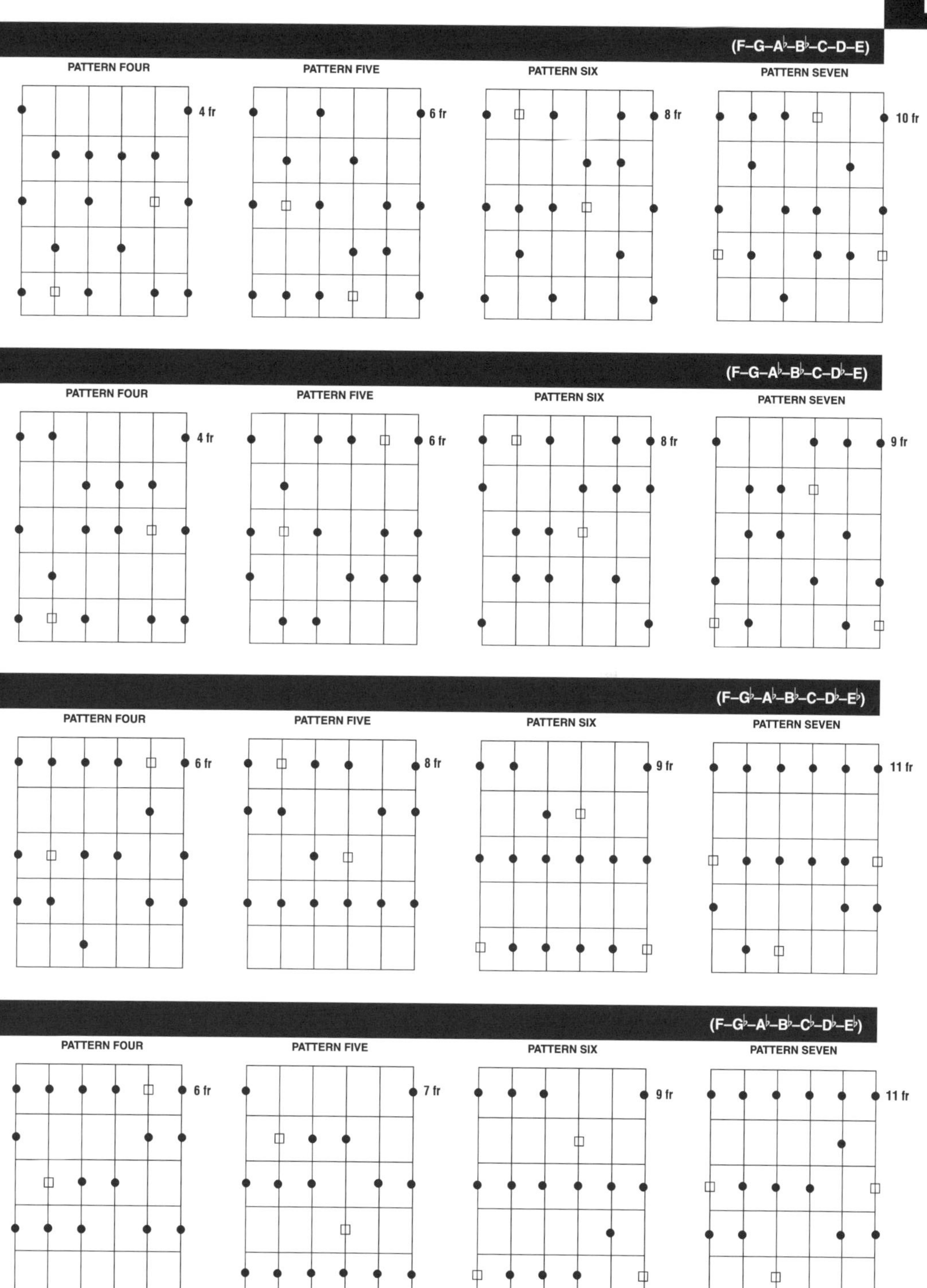


(F–G–A♭–B♭–C–D–E)
PATTERN FOUR
PATTERN FIVE
PATTERN SIX
PATTERN SEVEN
4 fr
6 fr
8 fr
10 fr

(F–G–A♭–B♭–C–D♭–E)
PATTERN FOUR
PATTERN FIVE
PATTERN SIX
PATTERN SEVEN
4 fr
6 fr
8 fr
9 fr

(F–G♭–A♭–B♭–C–D♭–E♭)
PATTERN FOUR
PATTERN FIVE
PATTERN SIX
PATTERN SEVEN
6 fr
8 fr
9 fr
11 fr

(F–G♭–A♭–B♭–C♭–D♭–E♭)
PATTERN FOUR
PATTERN FIVE
PATTERN SIX
PATTERN SEVEN
6 fr
7 fr
9 fr
11 fr

F

# F LYDIAN

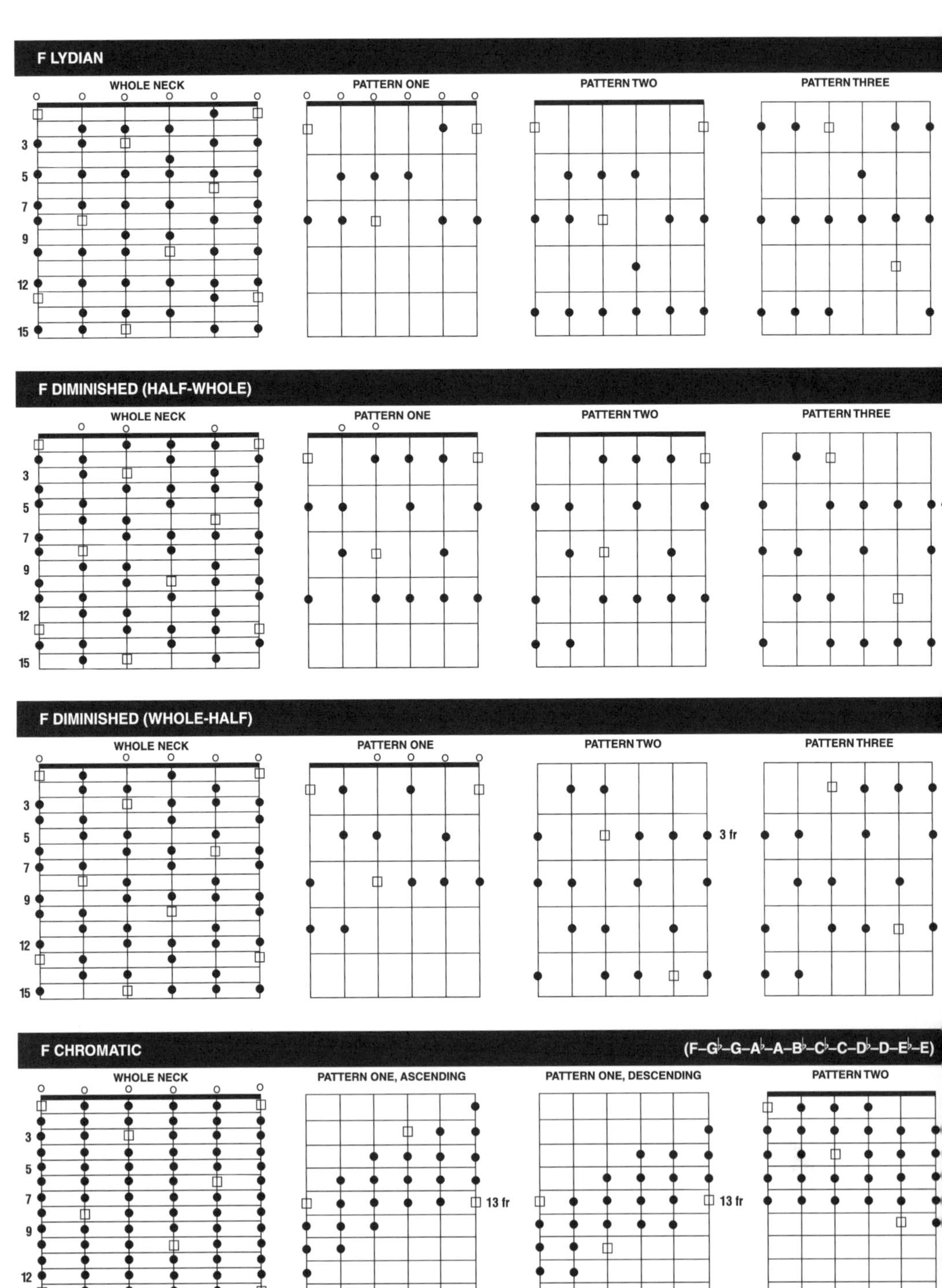

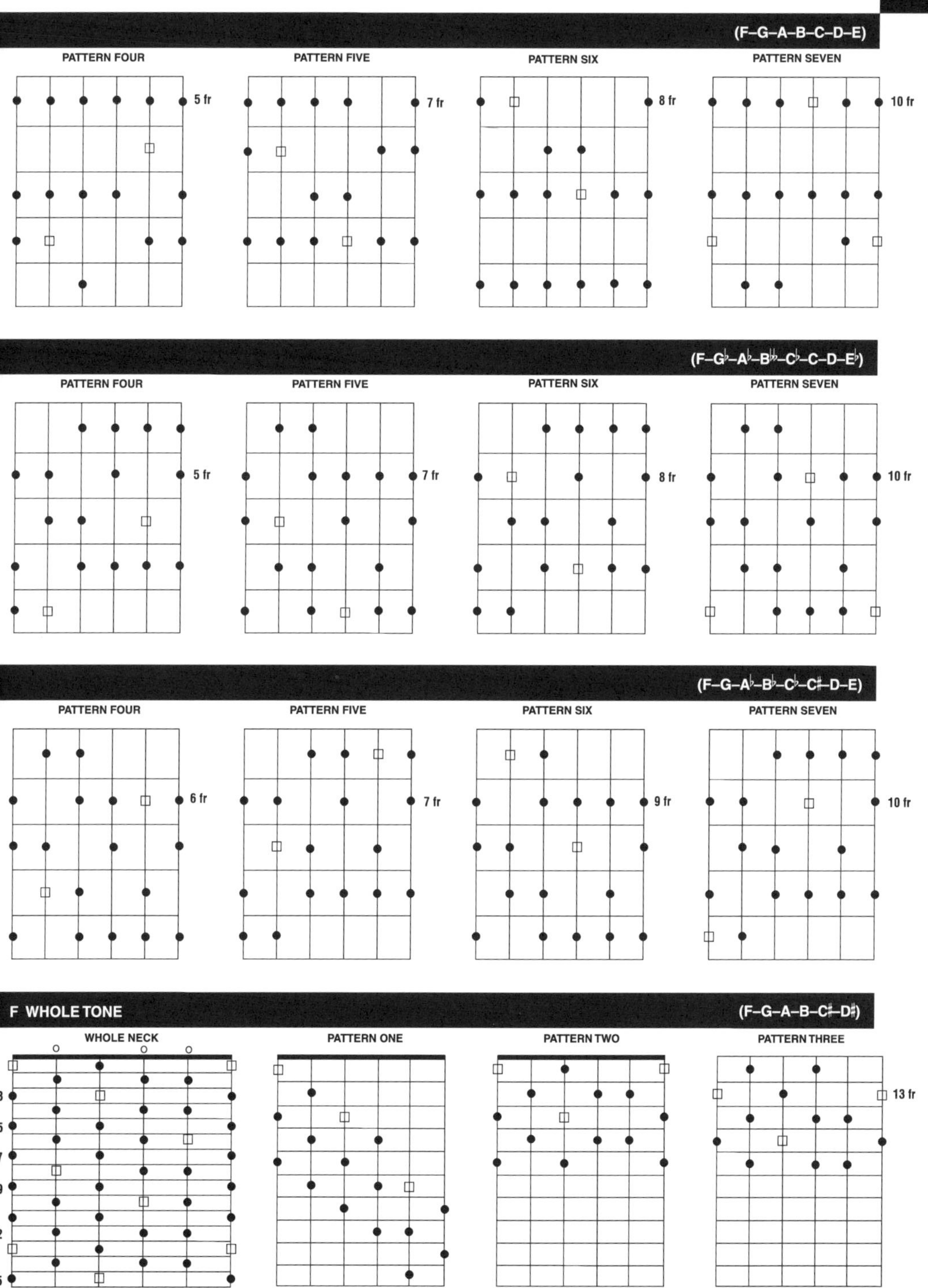

(F–G–A–B–C–D–E)
PATTERN FOUR
PATTERN FIVE
PATTERN SIX
PATTERN SEVEN
5 fr
7 fr
8 fr
10 fr
(F–G♭–A♭–B♭♭–C♭–C–D–E♭)
PATTERN FOUR
PATTERN FIVE
PATTERN SIX
PATTERN SEVEN
5 fr
7 fr
8 fr
10 fr
(F–G–A♭–B♭–C♭–C♯–D–E)
PATTERN FOUR
PATTERN FIVE
PATTERN SIX
PATTERN SEVEN
6 fr
7 fr
9 fr
10 fr
F WHOLE TONE
(F–G–A–B–C♯–D♯)
WHOLE NECK
PATTERN ONE
PATTERN TWO
PATTERN THREE
13 fr

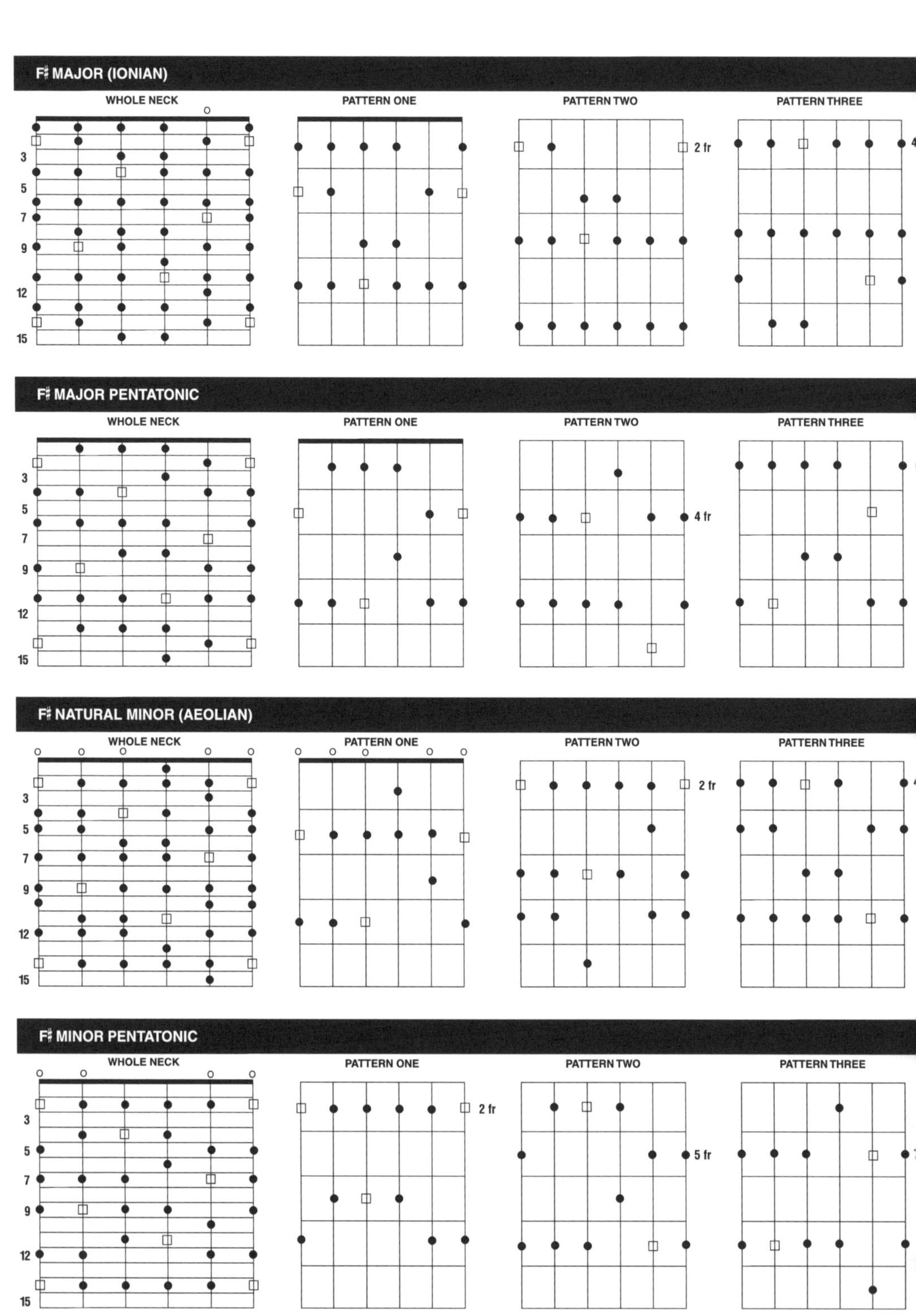


F# MAJOR (IONIAN)
WHOLE NECK
PATTERN ONE
PATTERN TWO
PATTERN THREE
2 fr

F# MAJOR PENTATONIC
WHOLE NECK
PATTERN ONE
PATTERN TWO
PATTERN THREE
4 fr

F# NATURAL MINOR (AEOLIAN)
WHOLE NECK
PATTERN ONE
PATTERN TWO
PATTERN THREE
2 fr

F# MINOR PENTATONIC
WHOLE NECK
PATTERN ONE
PATTERN TWO
PATTERN THREE
2 fr
5 fr

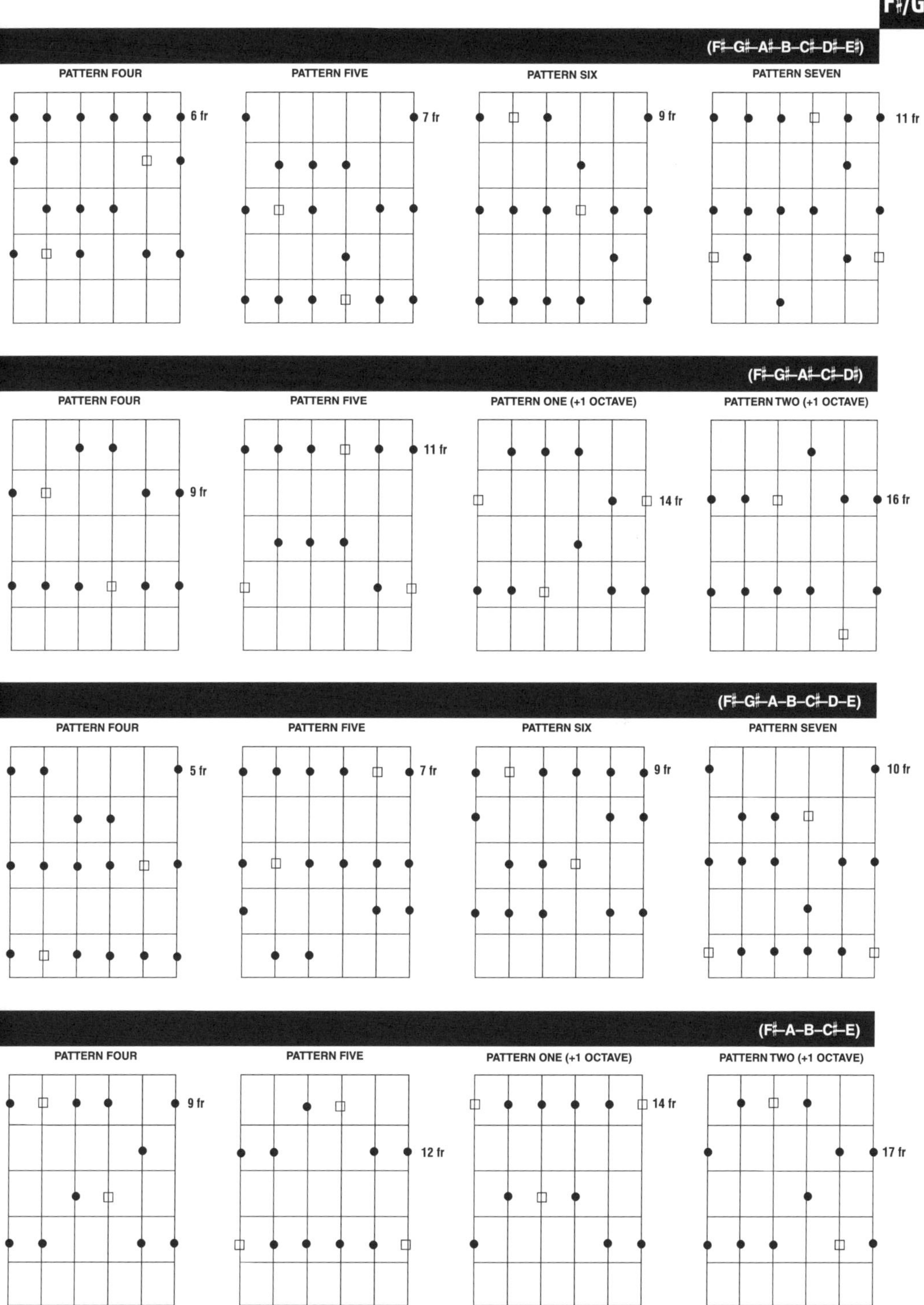

F#/Gb
(F#–G#–A#–B–C#–D#–E#)
PATTERN FOUR
PATTERN FIVE
PATTERN SIX
PATTERN SEVEN
6 fr
7 fr
9 fr
11 fr
(F#–G#–A#–C#–D#)
PATTERN FOUR
PATTERN FIVE
PATTERN ONE (+1 OCTAVE)
PATTERN TWO (+1 OCTAVE)
9 fr
11 fr
14 fr
16 fr
(F#–G#–A–B–C#–D–E)
PATTERN FOUR
PATTERN FIVE
PATTERN SIX
PATTERN SEVEN
5 fr
7 fr
9 fr
10 fr
(F#–A–B–C#–E)
PATTERN FOUR
PATTERN FIVE
PATTERN ONE (+1 OCTAVE)
PATTERN TWO (+1 OCTAVE)
9 fr
12 fr
14 fr
17 fr

F# BLUES
WHOLE NECK
PATTERN ONE
PATTERN TWO
PATTERN THREE

F# MIXO-BLUES
WHOLE NECK
PATTERN ONE
PATTERN TWO
PATTERN THREE

F# MIXOLYDIAN
WHOLE NECK
PATTERN ONE
PATTERN TWO
PATTERN THREE

F# DORIAN
WHOLE NECK
PATTERN ONE
PATTERN TWO
PATTERN THREE

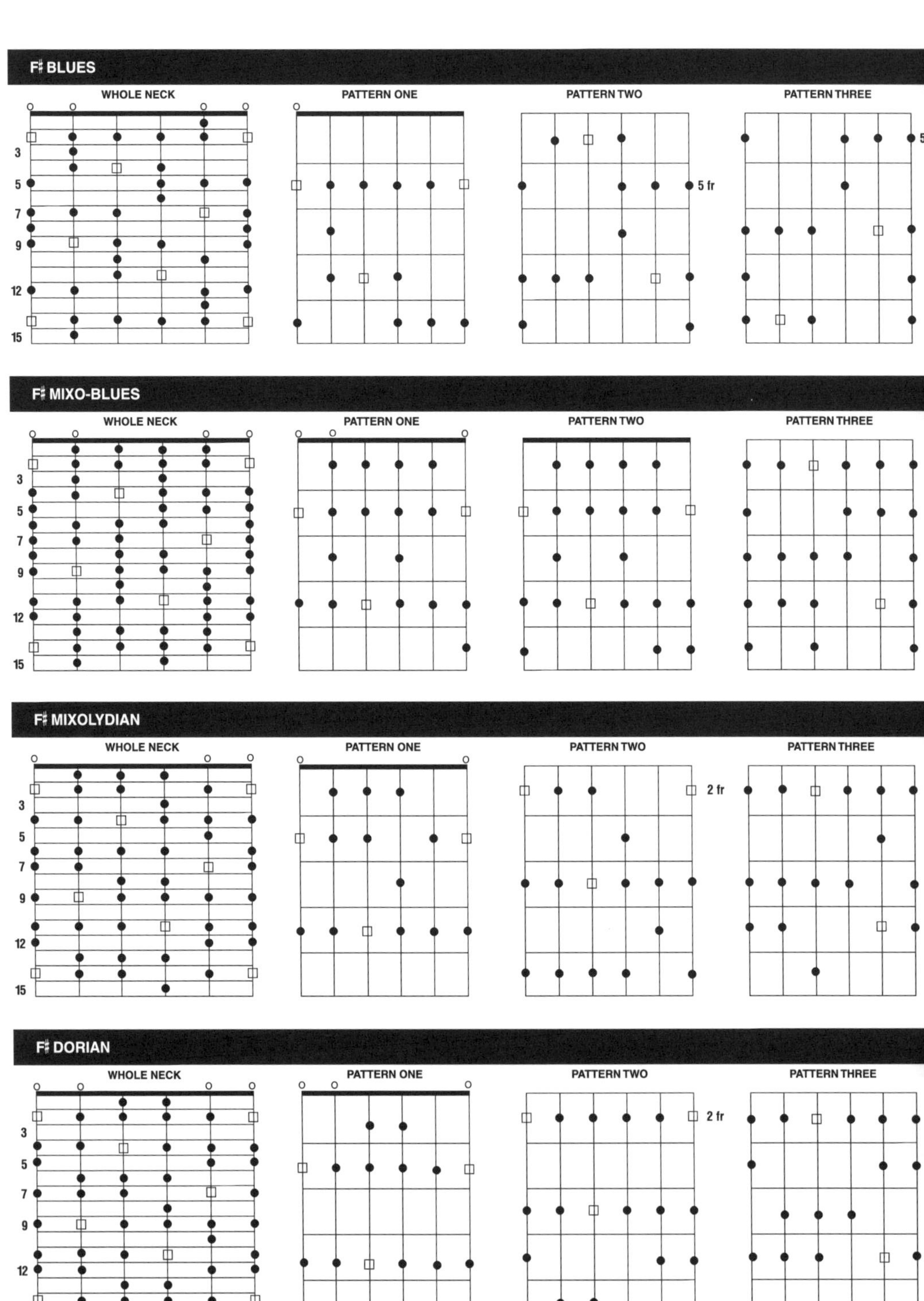

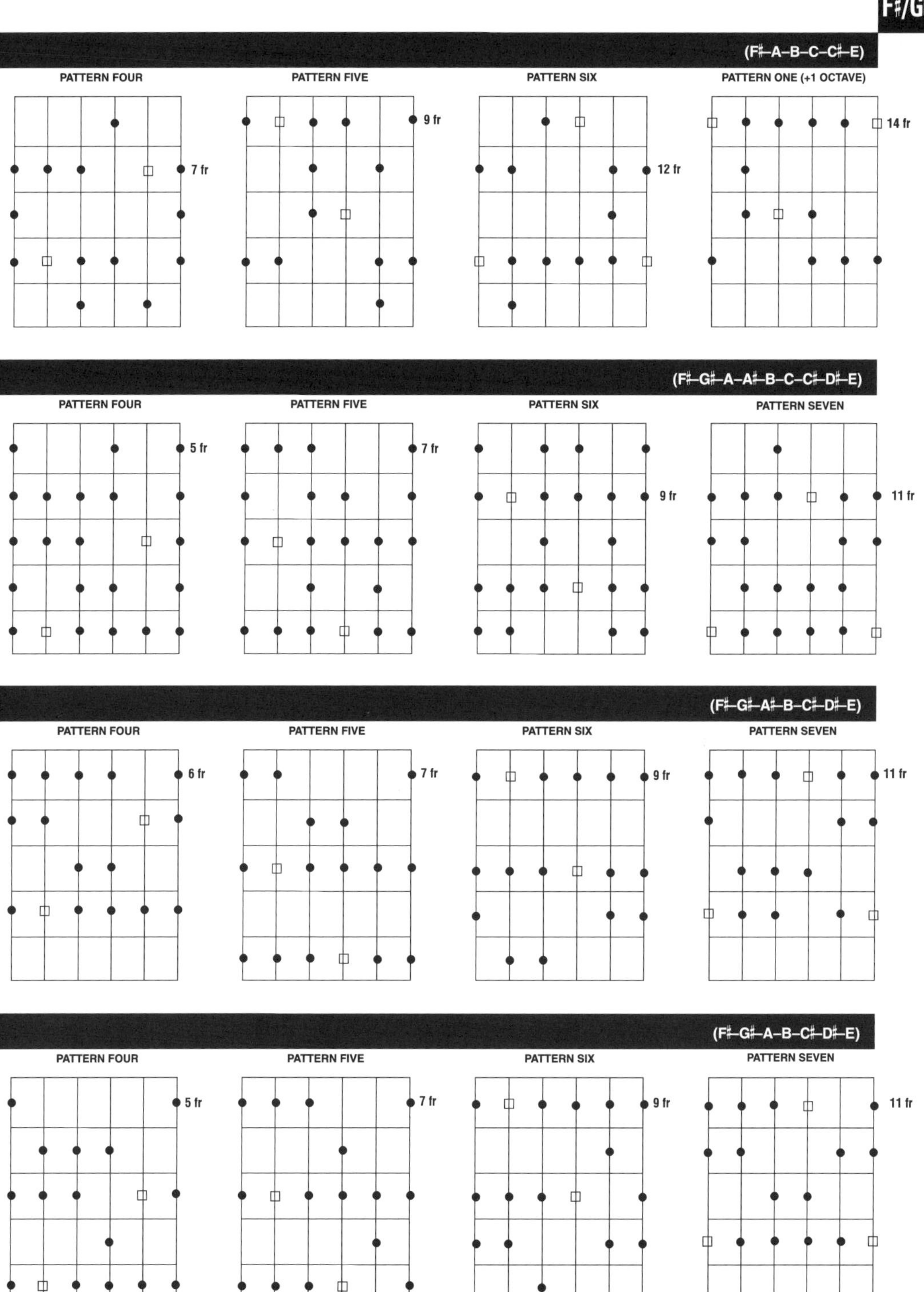
(F#–A–B–C–C#–E)
PATTERN FOUR
PATTERN FIVE
9 fr
7 fr
PATTERN SIX
12 fr
PATTERN ONE (+1 OCTAVE)
14 fr
(F#–G#–A–A#–B–C–C#–D#–E)
PATTERN FOUR
5 fr
PATTERN FIVE
7 fr
PATTERN SIX
9 fr
PATTERN SEVEN
11 fr
(F#–G#–A#–B–C#–D#–E)
PATTERN FOUR
6 fr
PATTERN FIVE
7 fr
PATTERN SIX
9 fr
PATTERN SEVEN
11 fr
(F#–G#–A–B–C#–D#–E)
PATTERN FOUR
5 fr
PATTERN FIVE
7 fr
PATTERN SIX
9 fr
PATTERN SEVEN
11 fr

# F♯ MELODIC MINOR

WHOLE NECK | PATTERN ONE | PATTERN TWO | PATTERN THREE

# F♯ HARMONIC MINOR

WHOLE NECK | PATTERN ONE | PATTERN TWO | PATTERN THREE

# F♯ PHRYGIAN

WHOLE NECK | PATTERN ONE | PATTERN TWO | PATTERN THREE

# F♯ LOCRIAN

WHOLE NECK | PATTERN ONE | PATTERN TWO | PATTERN THREE

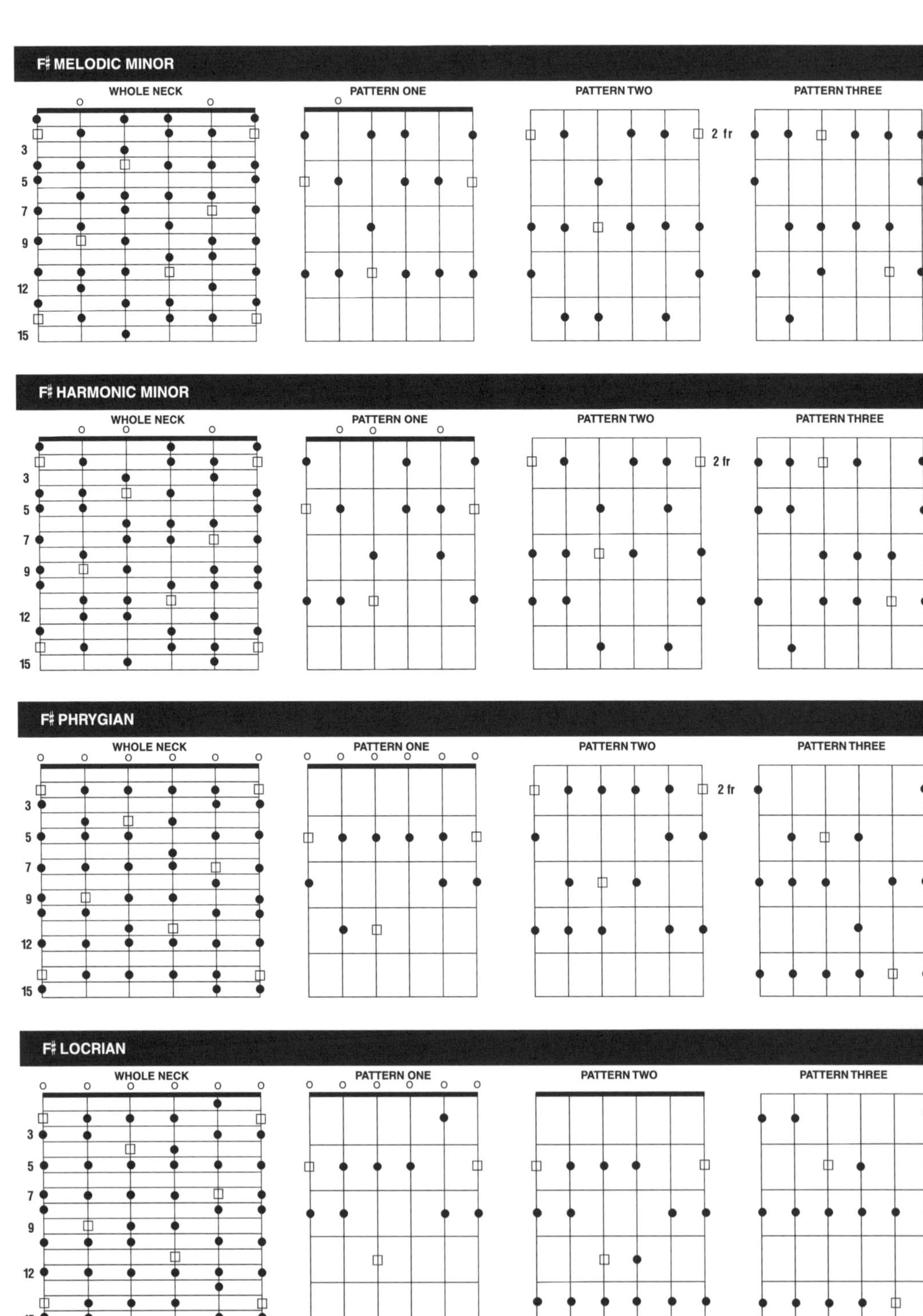

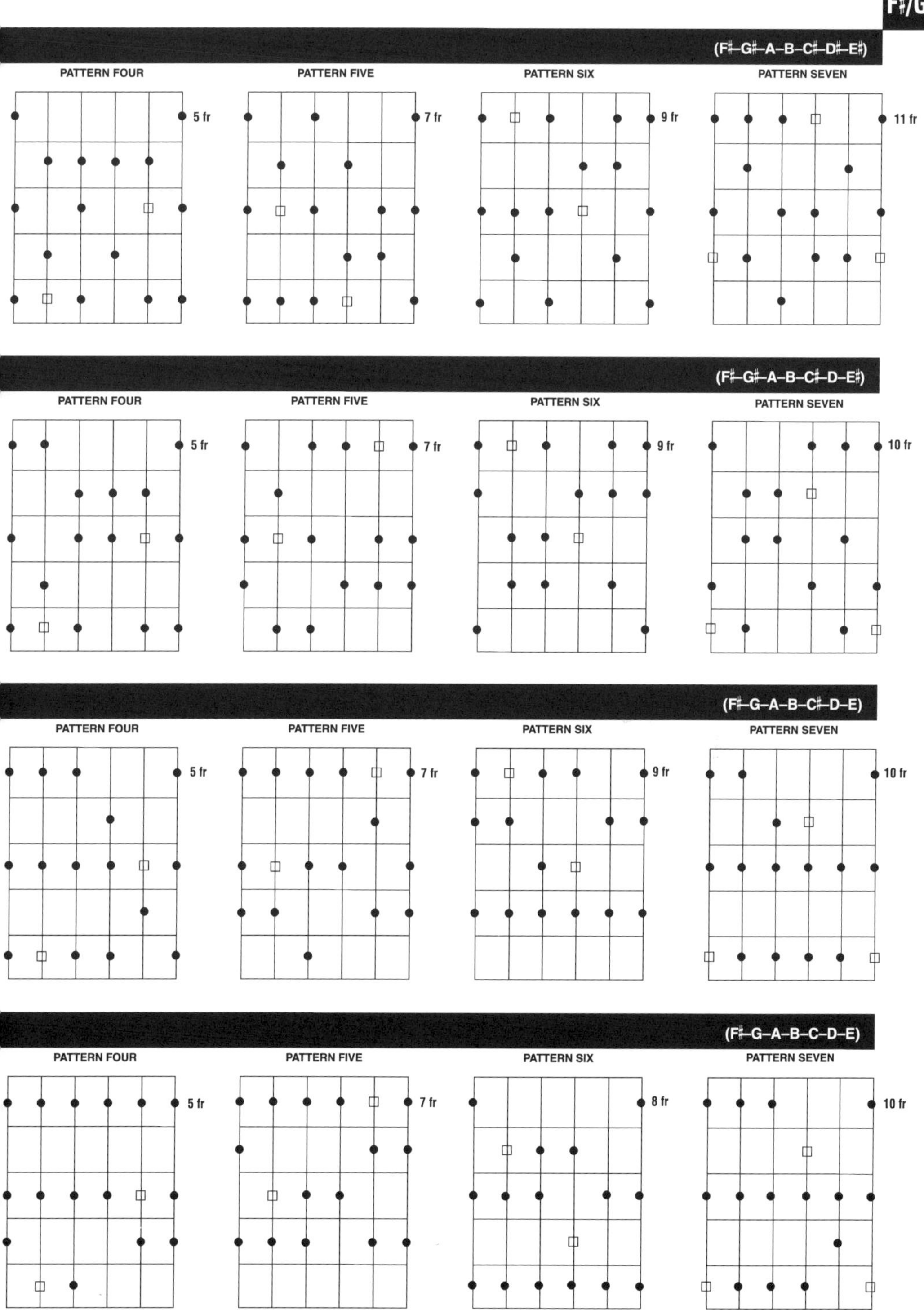
(F#–G#–A–B–C#–D–E#)
PATTERN FOUR
PATTERN FIVE
PATTERN SIX
PATTERN SEVEN
5 fr
7 fr
9 fr
11 fr

(F#–G#–A–B–C#–D–E#)
PATTERN FOUR
PATTERN FIVE
PATTERN SIX
PATTERN SEVEN
5 fr
7 fr
9 fr
10 fr

(F#–G–A–B–C#–D–E)
PATTERN FOUR
PATTERN FIVE
PATTERN SIX
PATTERN SEVEN
5 fr
7 fr
9 fr
10 fr

(F#–G–A–B–C–D–E)
PATTERN FOUR
PATTERN FIVE
PATTERN SIX
PATTERN SEVEN
5 fr
7 fr
8 fr
10 fr

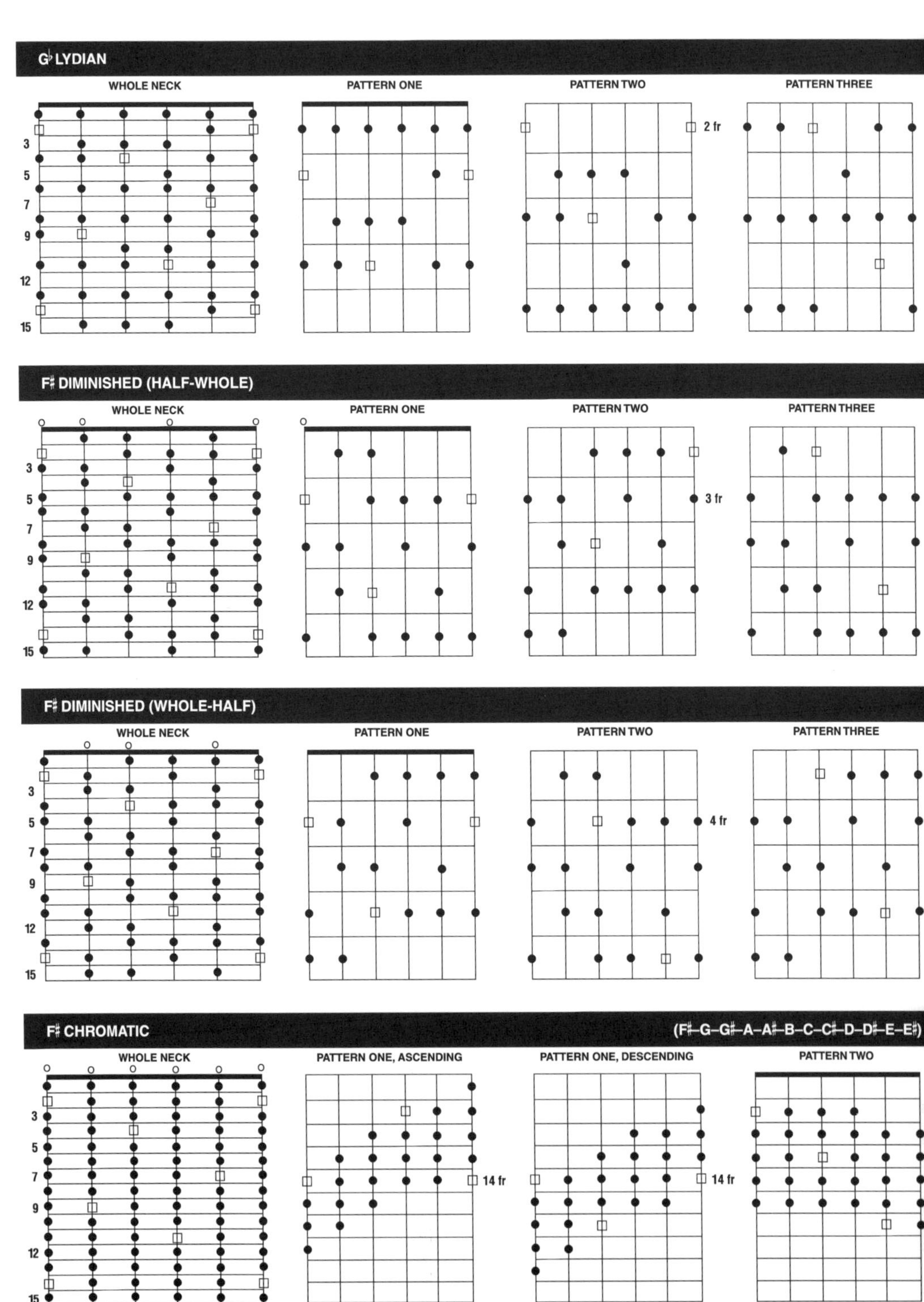

G♭ LYDIAN
WHOLE NECK
PATTERN ONE
PATTERN TWO
PATTERN THREE
2 fr

F♯ DIMINISHED (HALF-WHOLE)
WHOLE NECK
PATTERN ONE
PATTERN TWO
PATTERN THREE
3 fr

F♯ DIMINISHED (WHOLE-HALF)
WHOLE NECK
PATTERN ONE
PATTERN TWO
PATTERN THREE
4 fr

F♯ CHROMATIC
(F♯–G–G♯–A–A♯–B–C–C♯–D–D♯–E–E♯)
WHOLE NECK
PATTERN ONE, ASCENDING
PATTERN ONE, DESCENDING
PATTERN TWO
14 fr
14 fr

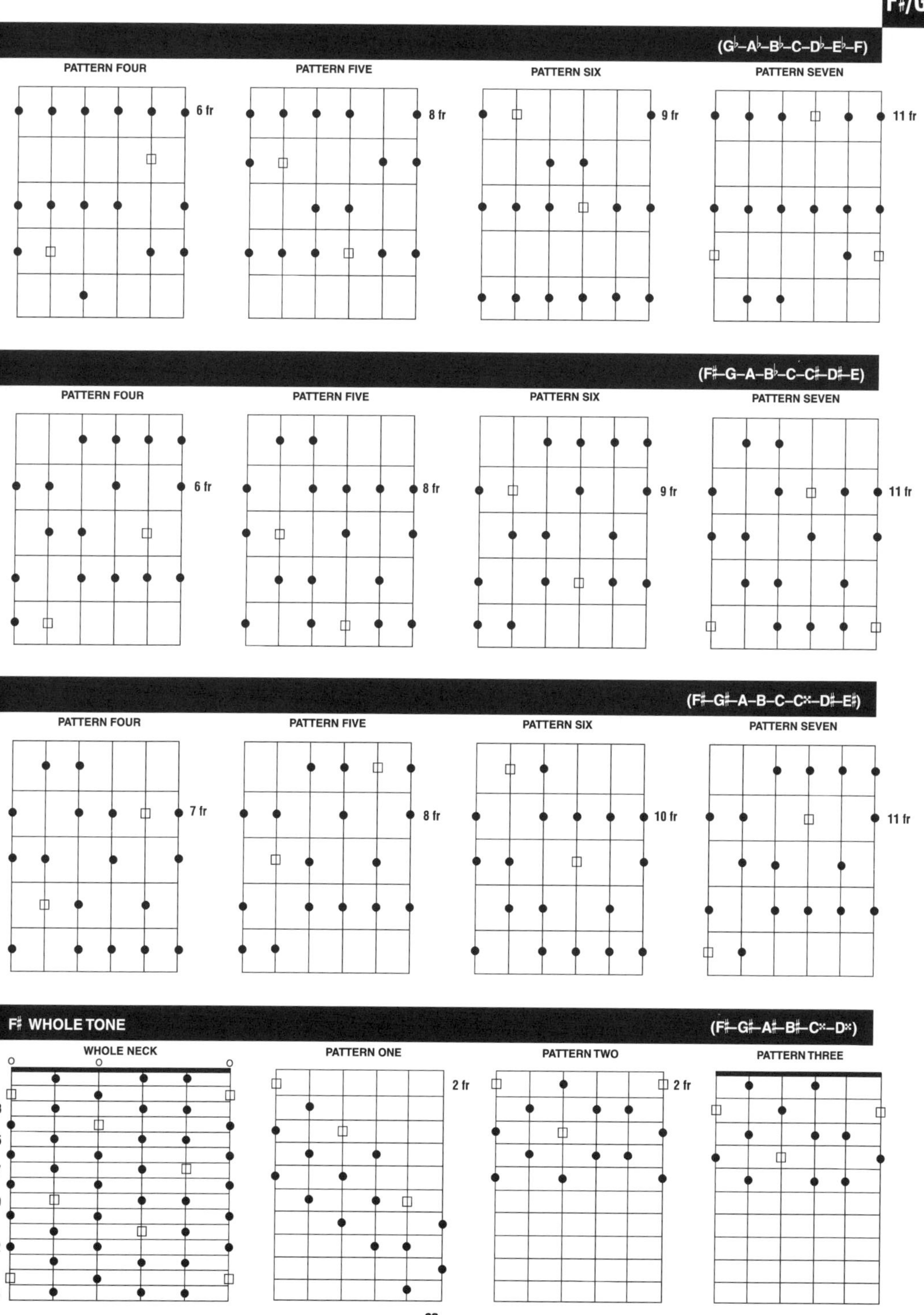
(Gb–Ab–Bb–C–Db–Eb–F)
PATTERN FOUR
PATTERN FIVE
PATTERN SIX
PATTERN SEVEN
6 fr
8 fr
9 fr
11 fr

(F#–G–A–Bb–C–C#–D#–E)
PATTERN FOUR
PATTERN FIVE
PATTERN SIX
PATTERN SEVEN
6 fr
8 fr
9 fr
11 fr

(F#–G#–A–B–C–C𝄪–D#–E#)
PATTERN FOUR
PATTERN FIVE
PATTERN SIX
PATTERN SEVEN
7 fr
8 fr
10 fr
11 fr

F# WHOLE TONE
(F#–G#–A#–B#–C𝄪–D𝄪)
WHOLE NECK
PATTERN ONE
PATTERN TWO
PATTERN THREE
2 fr
2 fr

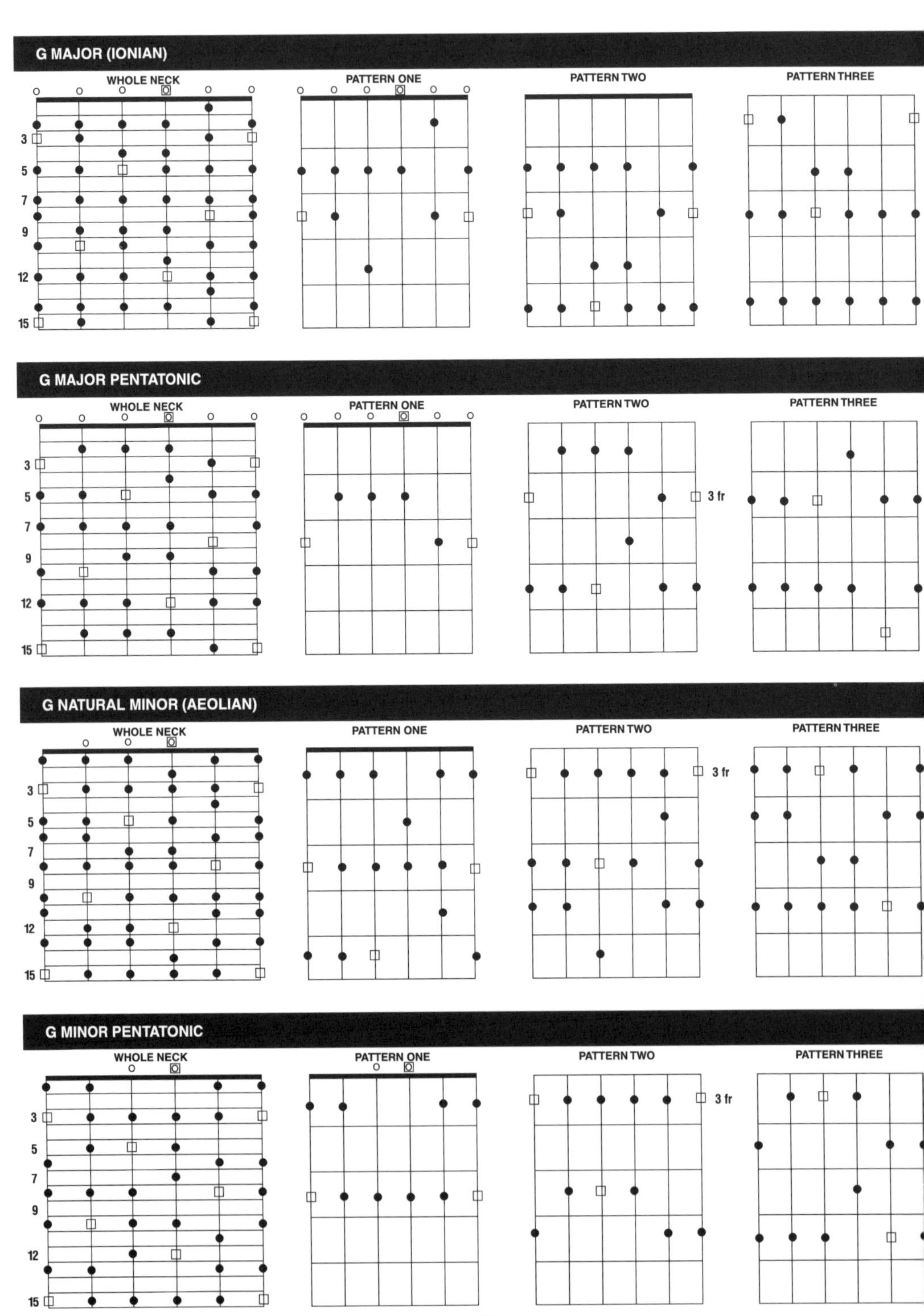

G MAJOR (IONIAN)
WHOLE NECK
PATTERN ONE
PATTERN TWO
PATTERN THREE

G MAJOR PENTATONIC
WHOLE NECK
PATTERN ONE
PATTERN TWO
PATTERN THREE
3 fr

G NATURAL MINOR (AEOLIAN)
WHOLE NECK
PATTERN ONE
PATTERN TWO
PATTERN THREE
3 fr

G MINOR PENTATONIC
WHOLE NECK
PATTERN ONE
PATTERN TWO
PATTERN THREE
3 fr

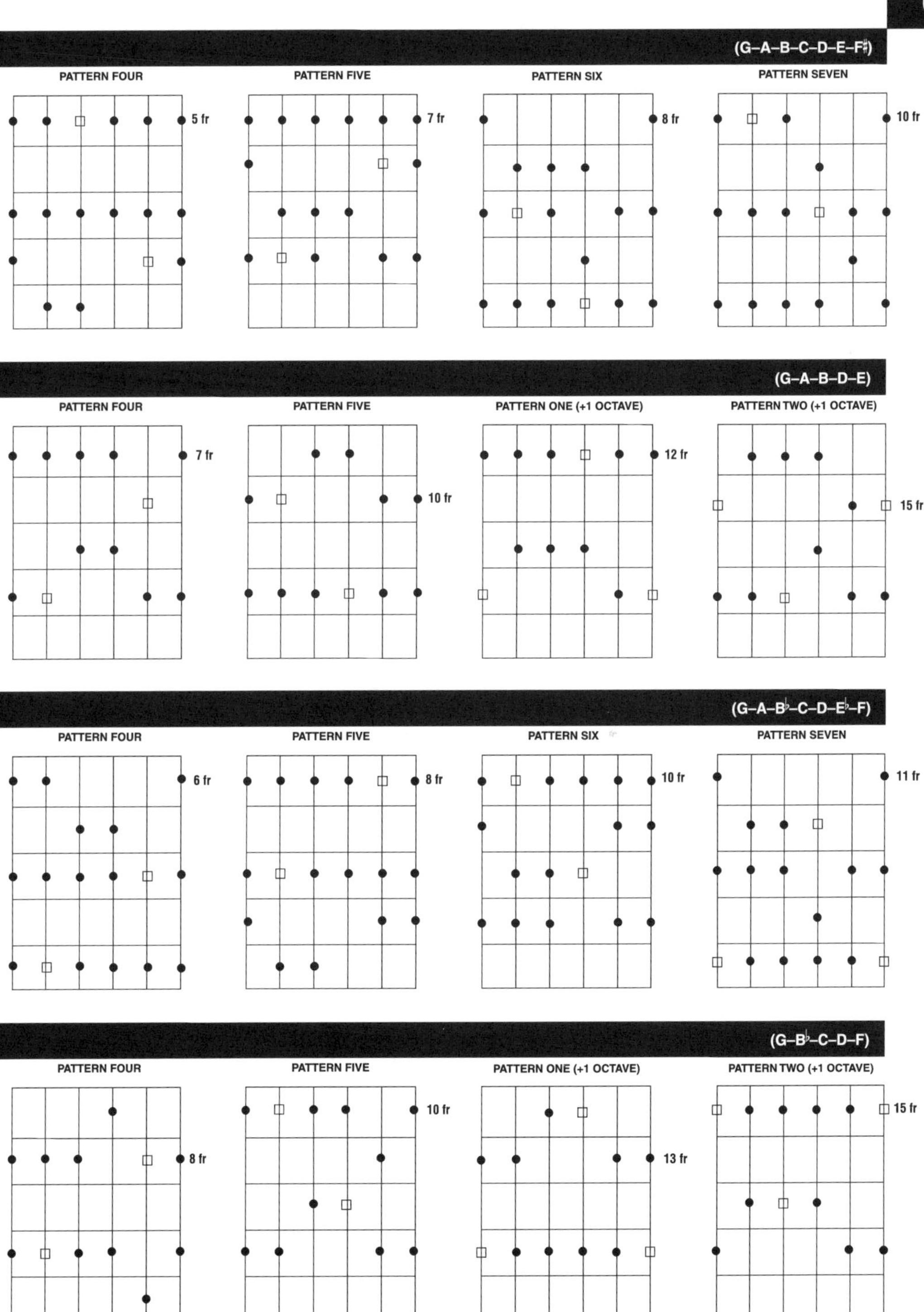
(G–A–B–C–D–E–F♯)
PATTERN FOUR
PATTERN FIVE
PATTERN SIX
PATTERN SEVEN
5 fr
7 fr
8 fr
10 fr
(G–A–B–D–E)
PATTERN FOUR
PATTERN FIVE
PATTERN ONE (+1 OCTAVE)
PATTERN TWO (+1 OCTAVE)
7 fr
10 fr
12 fr
15 fr
(G–A–B♭–C–D–E♭–F)
PATTERN FOUR
PATTERN FIVE
PATTERN SIX
PATTERN SEVEN
6 fr
8 fr
10 fr
11 fr
(G–B♭–C–D–F)
PATTERN FOUR
PATTERN FIVE
PATTERN ONE (+1 OCTAVE)
PATTERN TWO (+1 OCTAVE)
8 fr
10 fr
13 fr
15 fr

# G BLUES

|  | WHOLE NECK | PATTERN ONE | PATTERN TWO | PATTERN THREE |
|---|---|---|---|---|

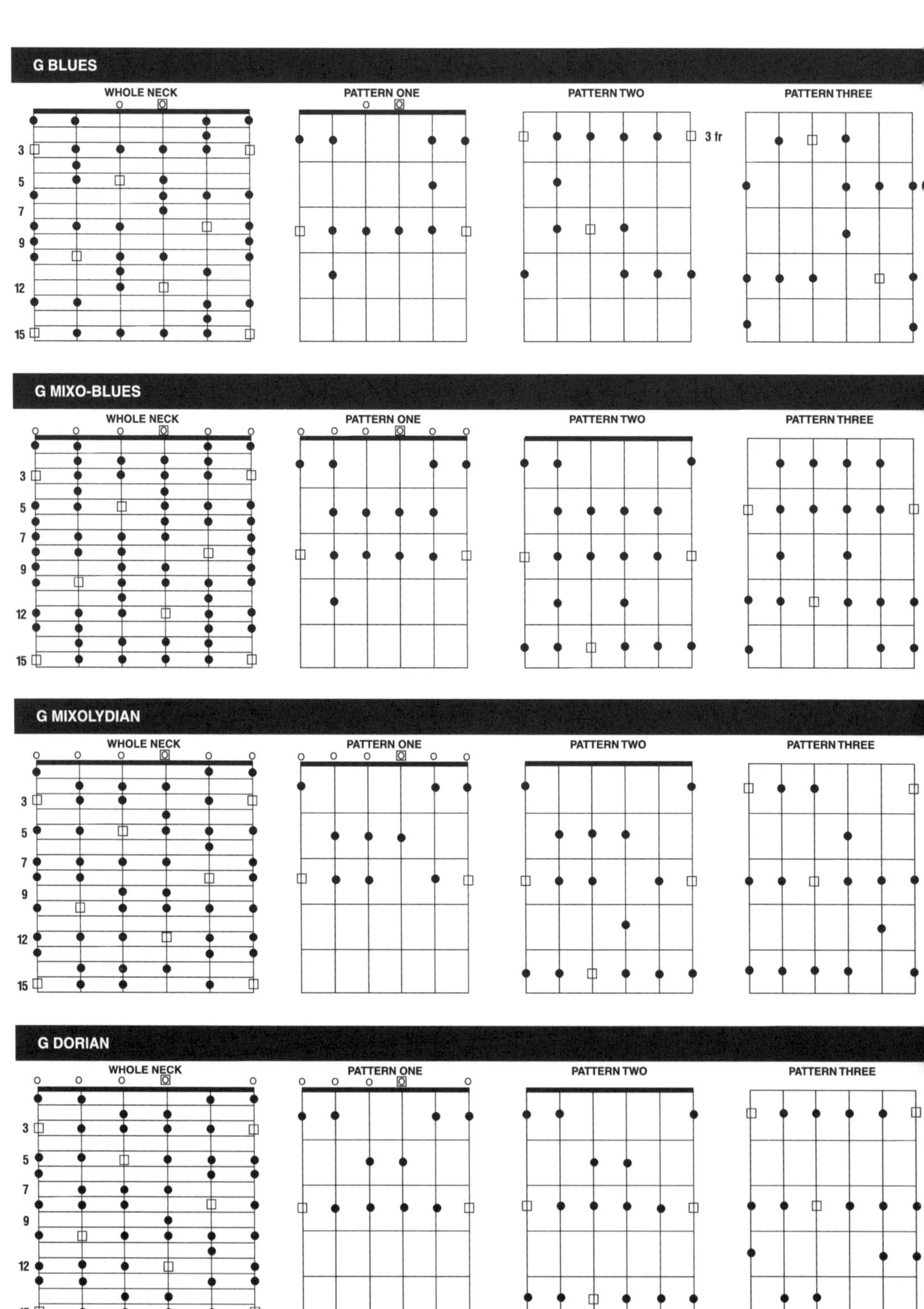


# G MIXO-BLUES

| WHOLE NECK | PATTERN ONE | PATTERN TWO | PATTERN THREE |
|---|---|---|---|

# G MIXOLYDIAN

| WHOLE NECK | PATTERN ONE | PATTERN TWO | PATTERN THREE |
|---|---|---|---|

# G DORIAN

| WHOLE NECK | PATTERN ONE | PATTERN TWO | PATTERN THREE |
|---|---|---|---|

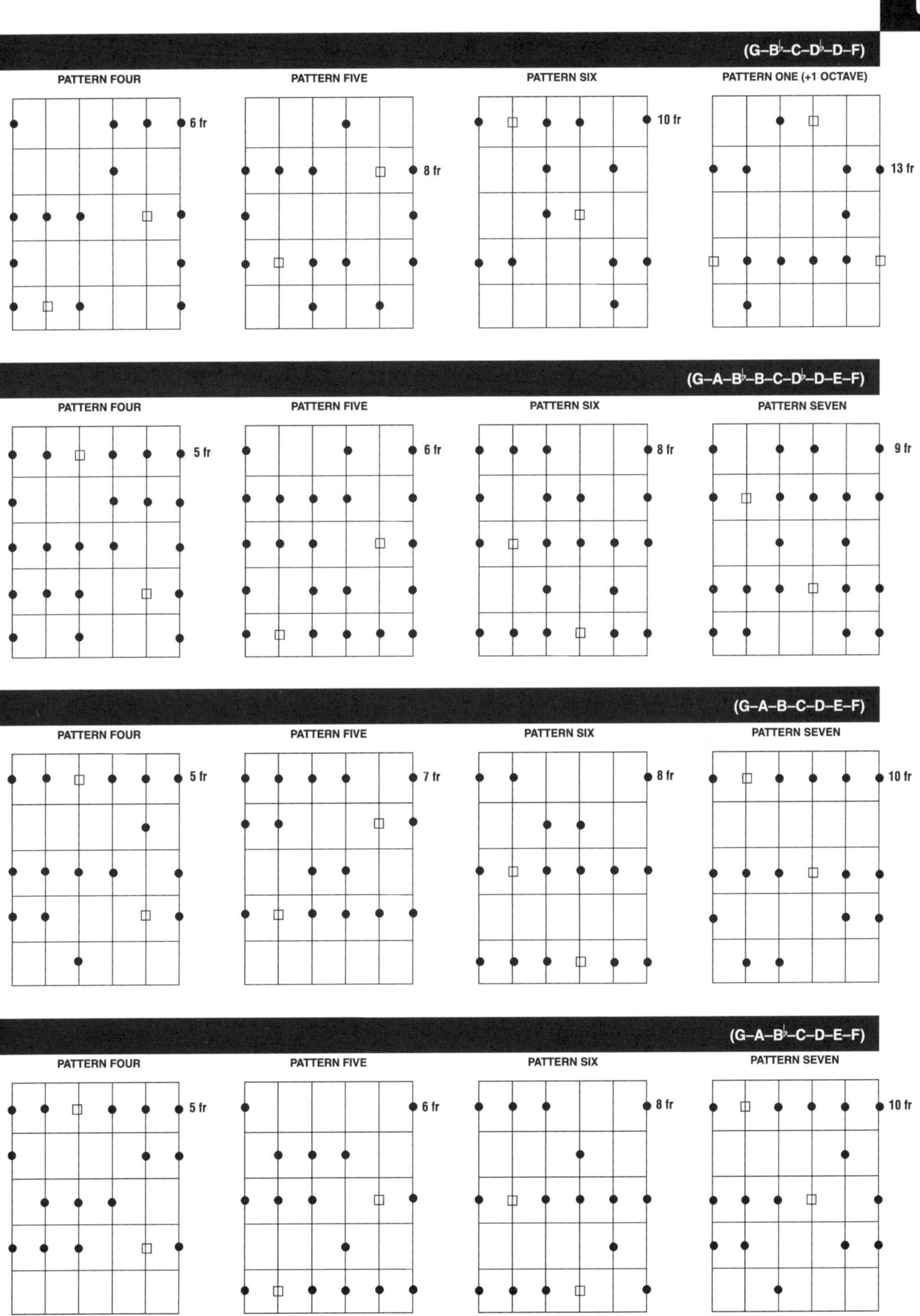


(G–B♭–C–D♭–D–F)
PATTERN FOUR
PATTERN FIVE
PATTERN SIX
PATTERN ONE (+1 OCTAVE)
6 fr
8 fr
10 fr
13 fr

(G–A–B♭–B–C–D♭–D–E–F)
PATTERN FOUR
PATTERN FIVE
PATTERN SIX
PATTERN SEVEN
5 fr
6 fr
8 fr
9 fr

(G–A–B–C–D–E–F)
PATTERN FOUR
PATTERN FIVE
PATTERN SIX
PATTERN SEVEN
5 fr
7 fr
8 fr
10 fr

(G–A–B♭–C–D–E–F)
PATTERN FOUR
PATTERN FIVE
PATTERN SIX
PATTERN SEVEN
5 fr
6 fr
8 fr
10 fr

# G MELODIC MINOR

WHOLE NECK | PATTERN ONE | PATTERN TWO | PATTERN THREE

# G HARMONIC MINOR

WHOLE NECK | PATTERN ONE | PATTERN TWO | PATTERN THREE

# G PHRYGIAN

WHOLE NECK | PATTERN ONE | PATTERN TWO | PATTERN THREE

# G LOCRIAN

WHOLE NECK | PATTERN ONE | PATTERN TWO | PATTERN THREE

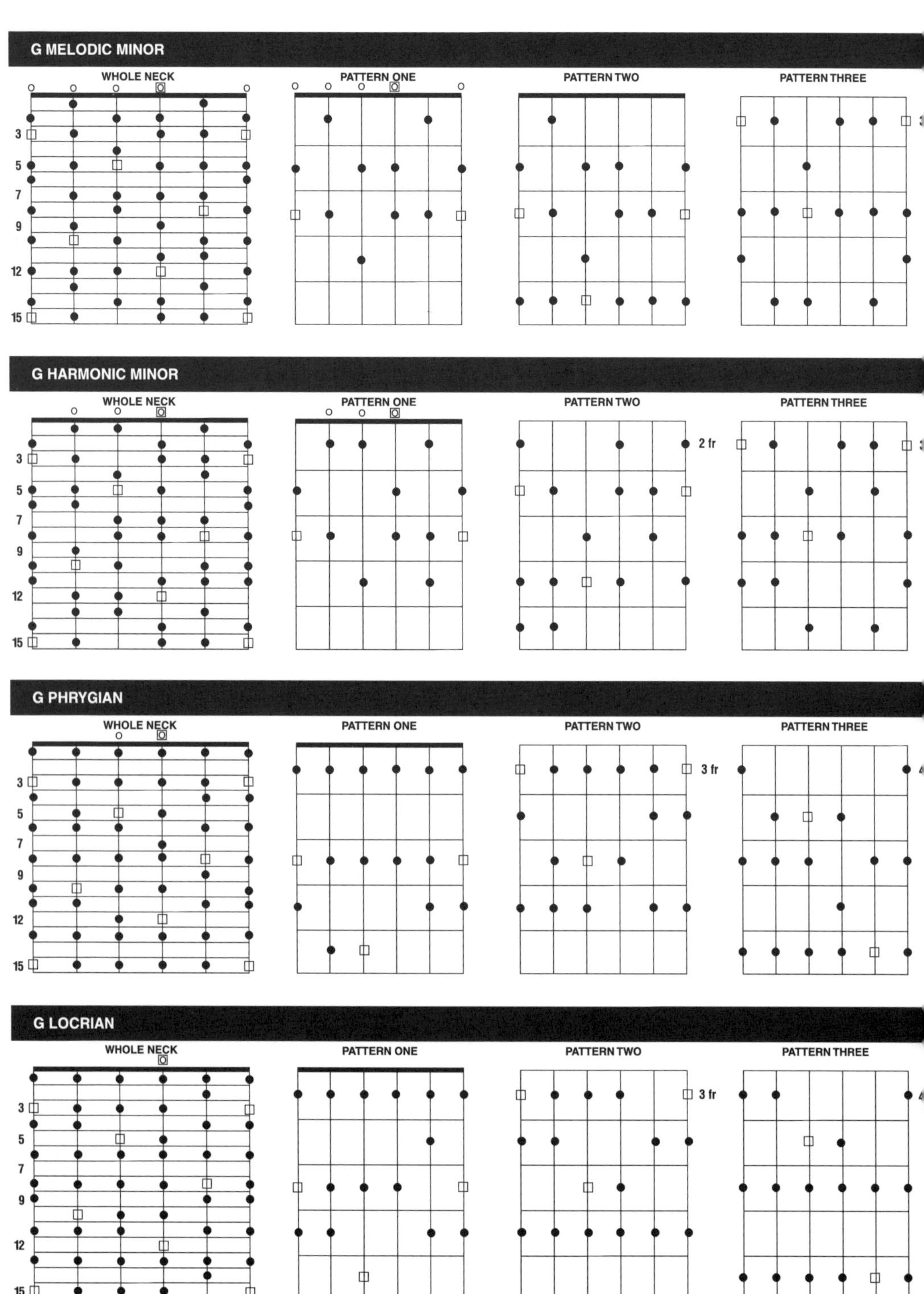

**(G–A–B♭–C–D–E–F♯)**

| PATTERN FOUR | PATTERN FIVE | PATTERN SIX | PATTERN SEVEN |
|---|---|---|---|

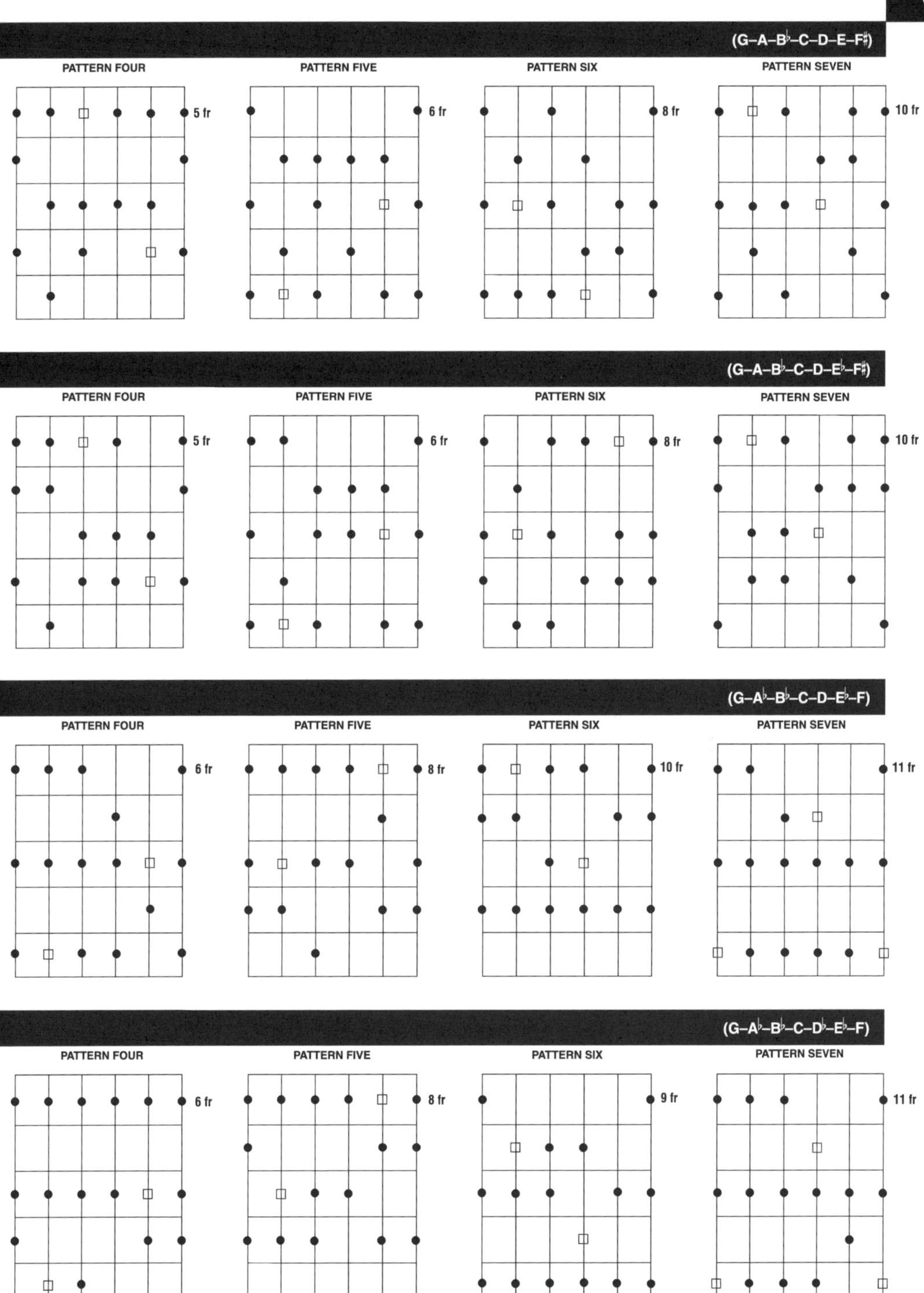

**(G–A–B♭–C–D–E♭–F♯)**

| PATTERN FOUR | PATTERN FIVE | PATTERN SIX | PATTERN SEVEN |
|---|---|---|---|

**(G–A♭–B♭–C–D–E♭–F)**

| PATTERN FOUR | PATTERN FIVE | PATTERN SIX | PATTERN SEVEN |
|---|---|---|---|

**(G–A♭–B♭–C–D♭–E♭–F)**

| PATTERN FOUR | PATTERN FIVE | PATTERN SIX | PATTERN SEVEN |
|---|---|---|---|

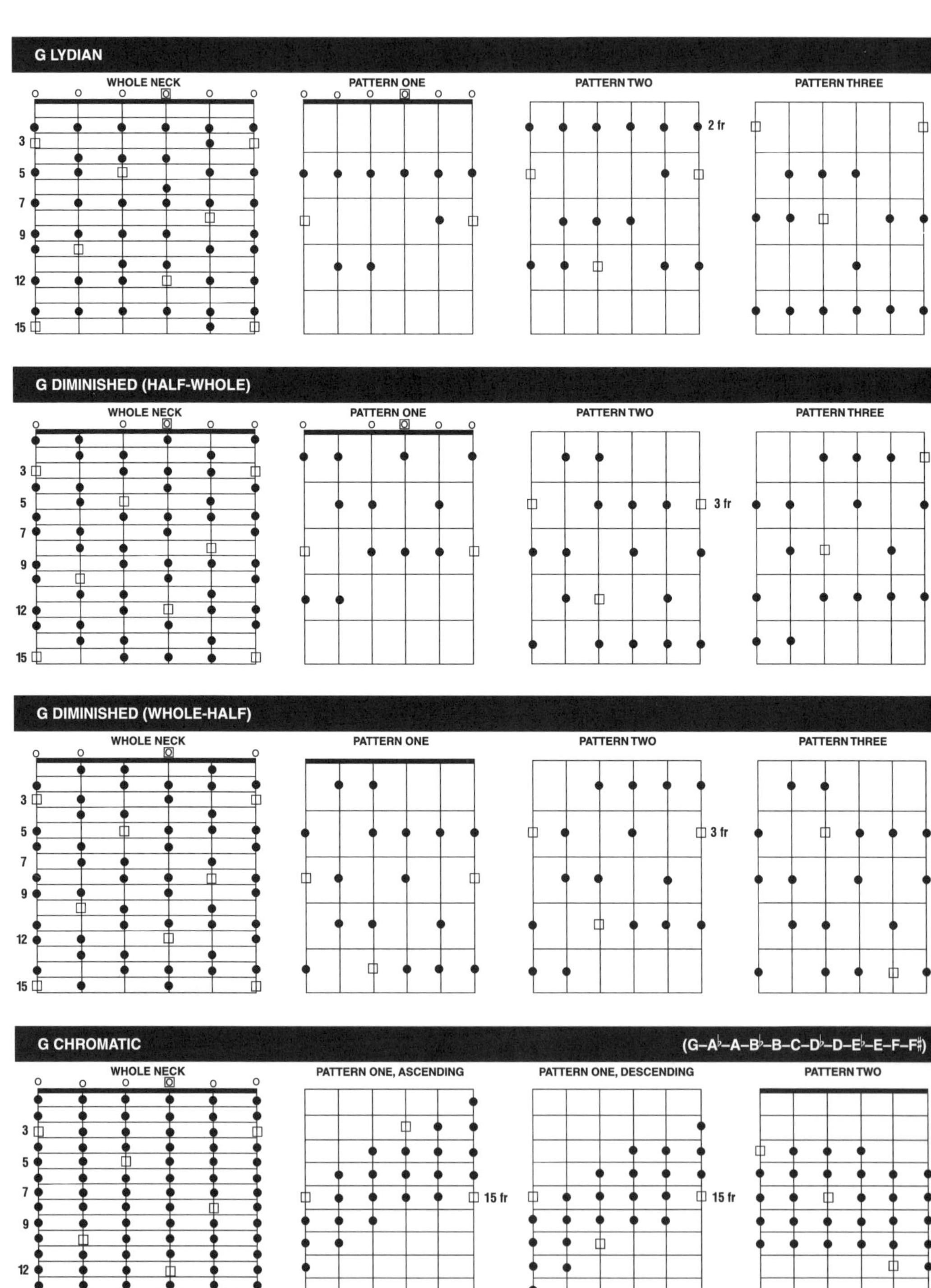


G LYDIAN
WHOLE NECK
PATTERN ONE
PATTERN TWO
PATTERN THREE
2 fr
G DIMINISHED (HALF-WHOLE)
WHOLE NECK
PATTERN ONE
PATTERN TWO
PATTERN THREE
3 fr
G DIMINISHED (WHOLE-HALF)
WHOLE NECK
PATTERN ONE
PATTERN TWO
PATTERN THREE
3 fr
G CHROMATIC
(G–A♭–A–B♭–B–C–D♭–D–E♭–E–F–F♯)
WHOLE NECK
PATTERN ONE, ASCENDING
PATTERN ONE, DESCENDING
PATTERN TWO
15 fr
15 fr

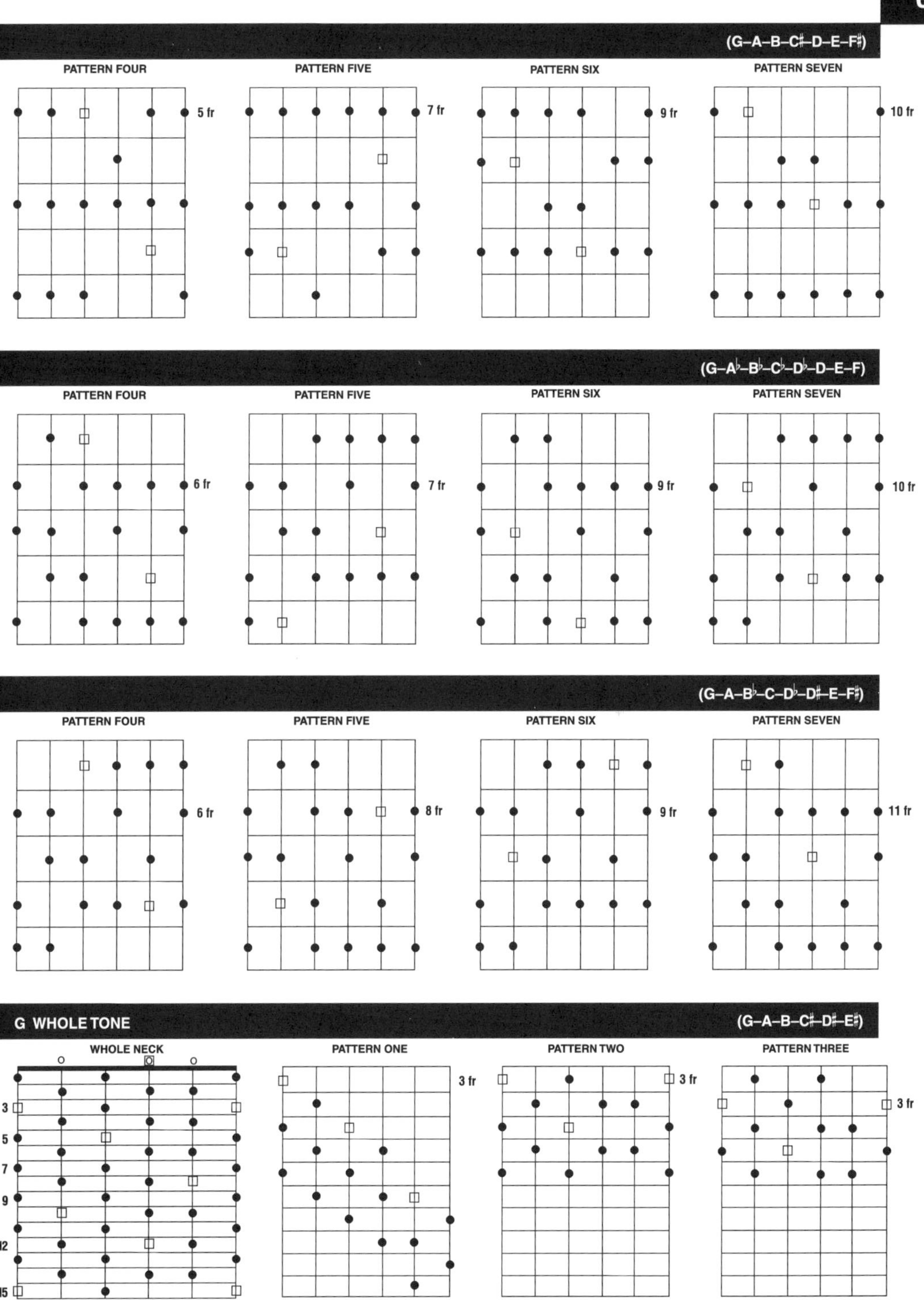G

(G–A–B–C#–D–E–F#)
PATTERN FOUR
PATTERN FIVE
PATTERN SIX
PATTERN SEVEN
5 fr
7 fr
9 fr
10 fr

(G–A♭–B♭–C♭–D♭–D–E–F)
PATTERN FOUR
PATTERN FIVE
PATTERN SIX
PATTERN SEVEN
6 fr
7 fr
9 fr
10 fr

(G–A–B♭–C–D♭–D#–E–F#)
PATTERN FOUR
PATTERN FIVE
PATTERN SIX
PATTERN SEVEN
6 fr
8 fr
9 fr
11 fr

G WHOLE TONE
(G–A–B–C#–D#–E#)
WHOLE NECK
PATTERN ONE
PATTERN TWO
PATTERN THREE
3
5
7
9
12
15
3 fr
3 fr
3 fr
3 fr

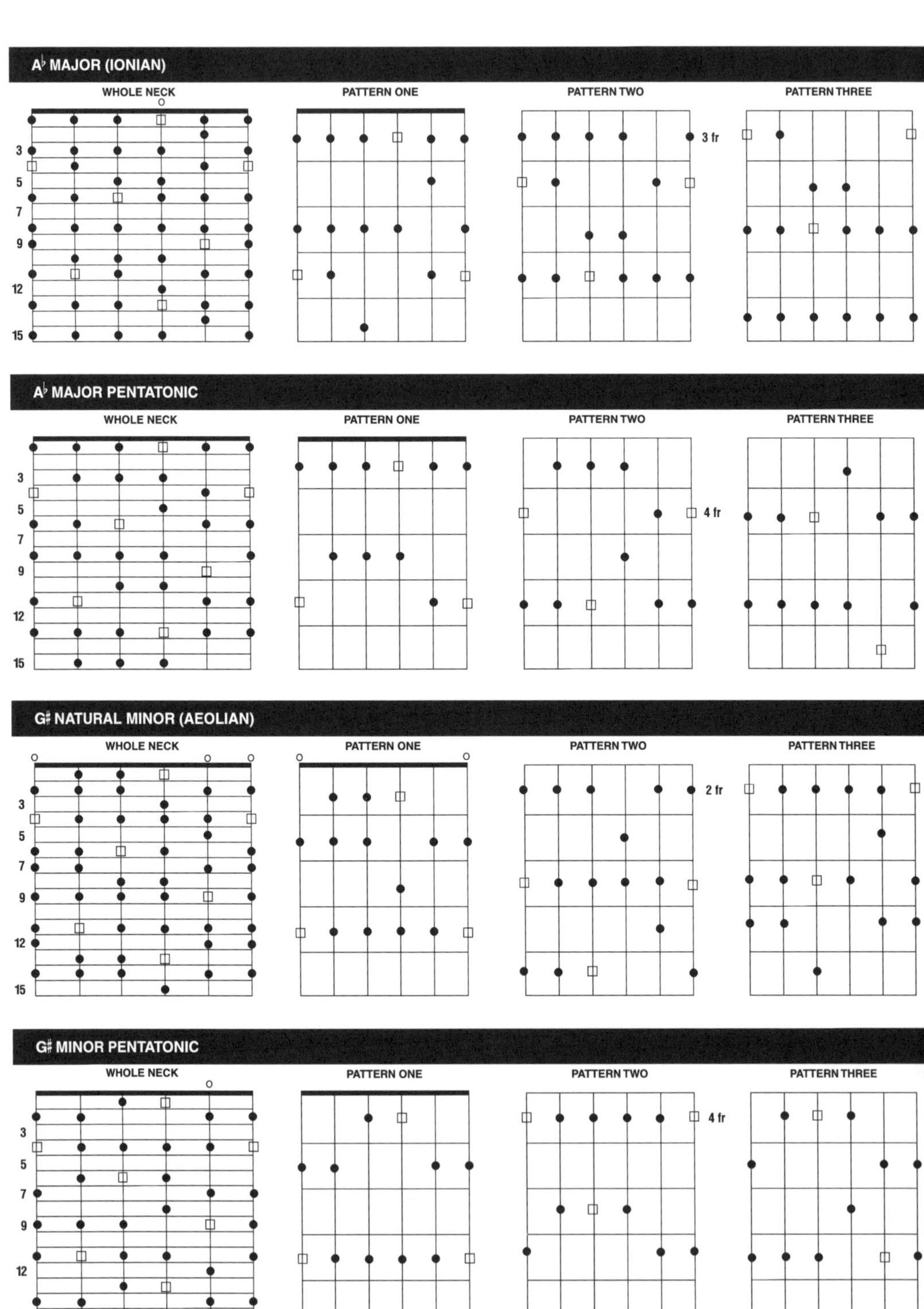

A♭ MAJOR (IONIAN)
WHOLE NECK
PATTERN ONE
PATTERN TWO
3 fr
PATTERN THREE
A♭ MAJOR PENTATONIC
WHOLE NECK
PATTERN ONE
PATTERN TWO
4 fr
PATTERN THREE
G♯ NATURAL MINOR (AEOLIAN)
WHOLE NECK
PATTERN ONE
PATTERN TWO
2 fr
PATTERN THREE
G♯ MINOR PENTATONIC
WHOLE NECK
PATTERN ONE
PATTERN TWO
4 fr
PATTERN THREE

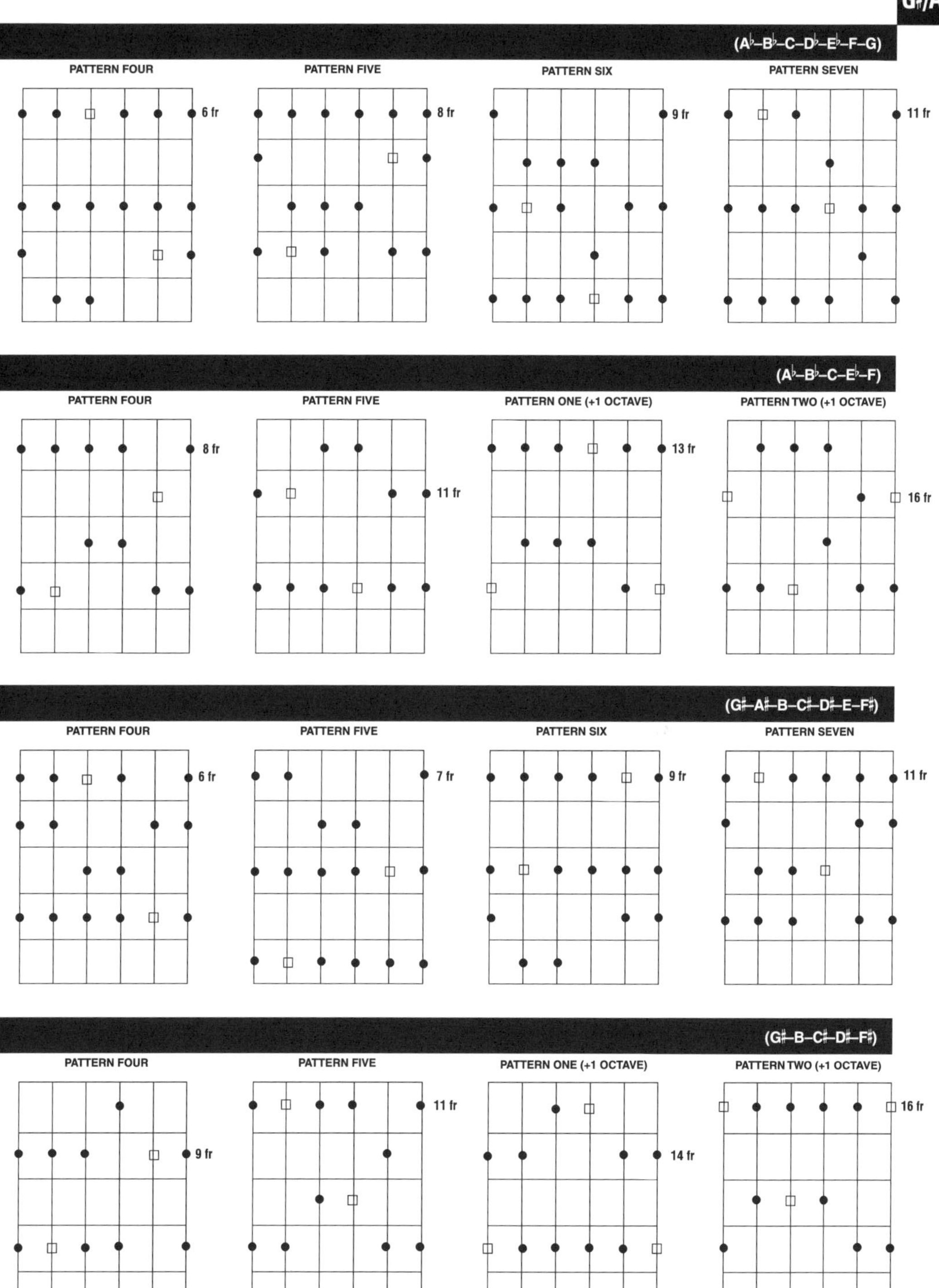
(A♭–B♭–C–D♭–E♭–F–G)
PATTERN FOUR
PATTERN FIVE
PATTERN SIX
PATTERN SEVEN
6 fr
8 fr
9 fr
11 fr
(A♭–B♭–C–E♭–F)
PATTERN FOUR
PATTERN FIVE
PATTERN ONE (+1 OCTAVE)
PATTERN TWO (+1 OCTAVE)
8 fr
11 fr
13 fr
16 fr
(G♯–A♯–B–C♯–D♯–E–F♯)
PATTERN FOUR
PATTERN FIVE
PATTERN SIX
PATTERN SEVEN
6 fr
7 fr
9 fr
11 fr
(G♯–B–C♯–D♯–F♯)
PATTERN FOUR
PATTERN FIVE
PATTERN ONE (+1 OCTAVE)
PATTERN TWO (+1 OCTAVE)
9 fr
11 fr
14 fr
16 fr

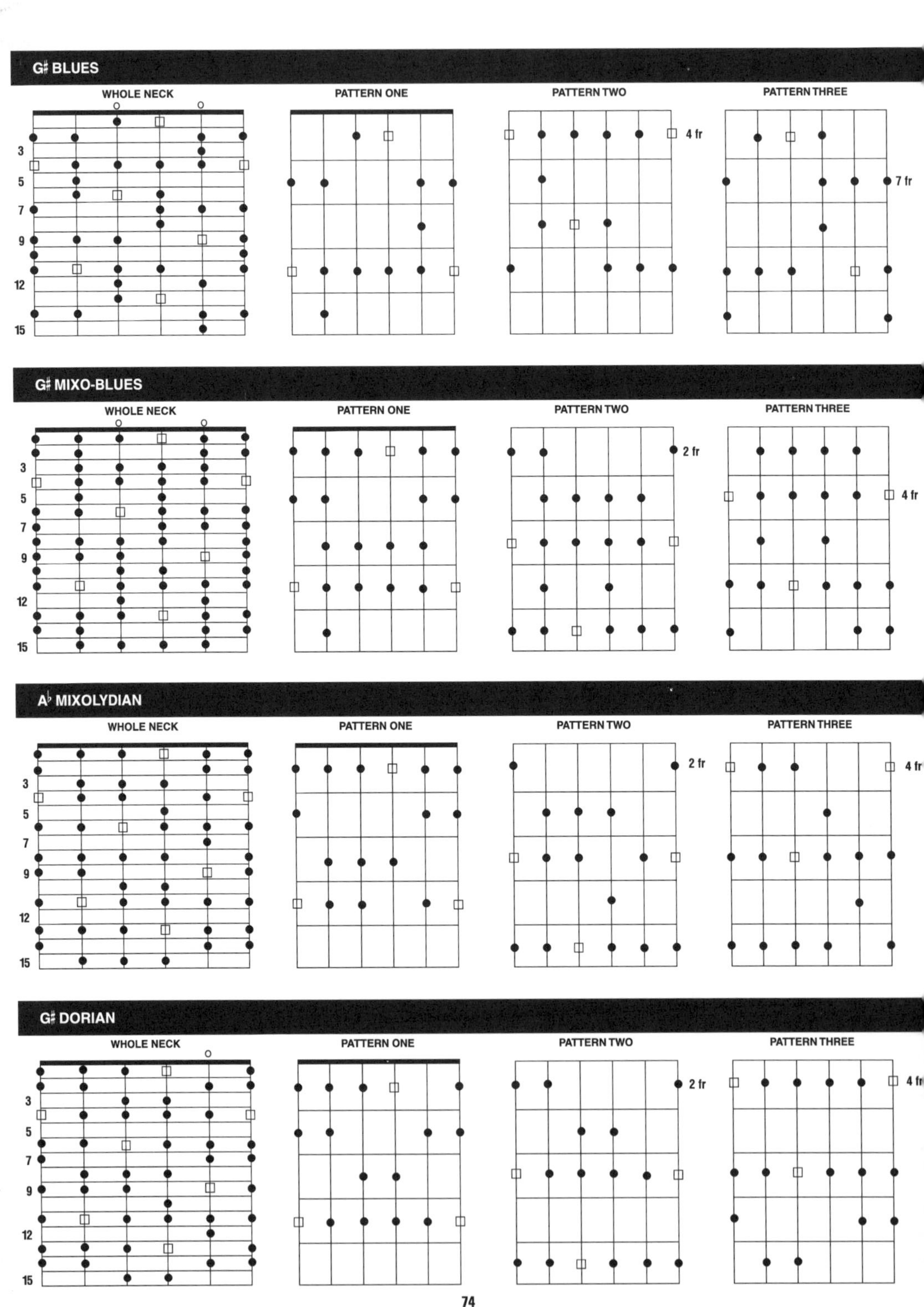

G# BLUES
WHOLE NECK
PATTERN ONE
PATTERN TWO
4 fr
PATTERN THREE
7 fr

G# MIXO-BLUES
WHOLE NECK
PATTERN ONE
PATTERN TWO
2 fr
PATTERN THREE
4 fr

A♭ MIXOLYDIAN
WHOLE NECK
PATTERN ONE
PATTERN TWO
2 fr
PATTERN THREE
4 fr

G# DORIAN
WHOLE NECK
PATTERN ONE
PATTERN TWO
2 fr
PATTERN THREE
4 fr

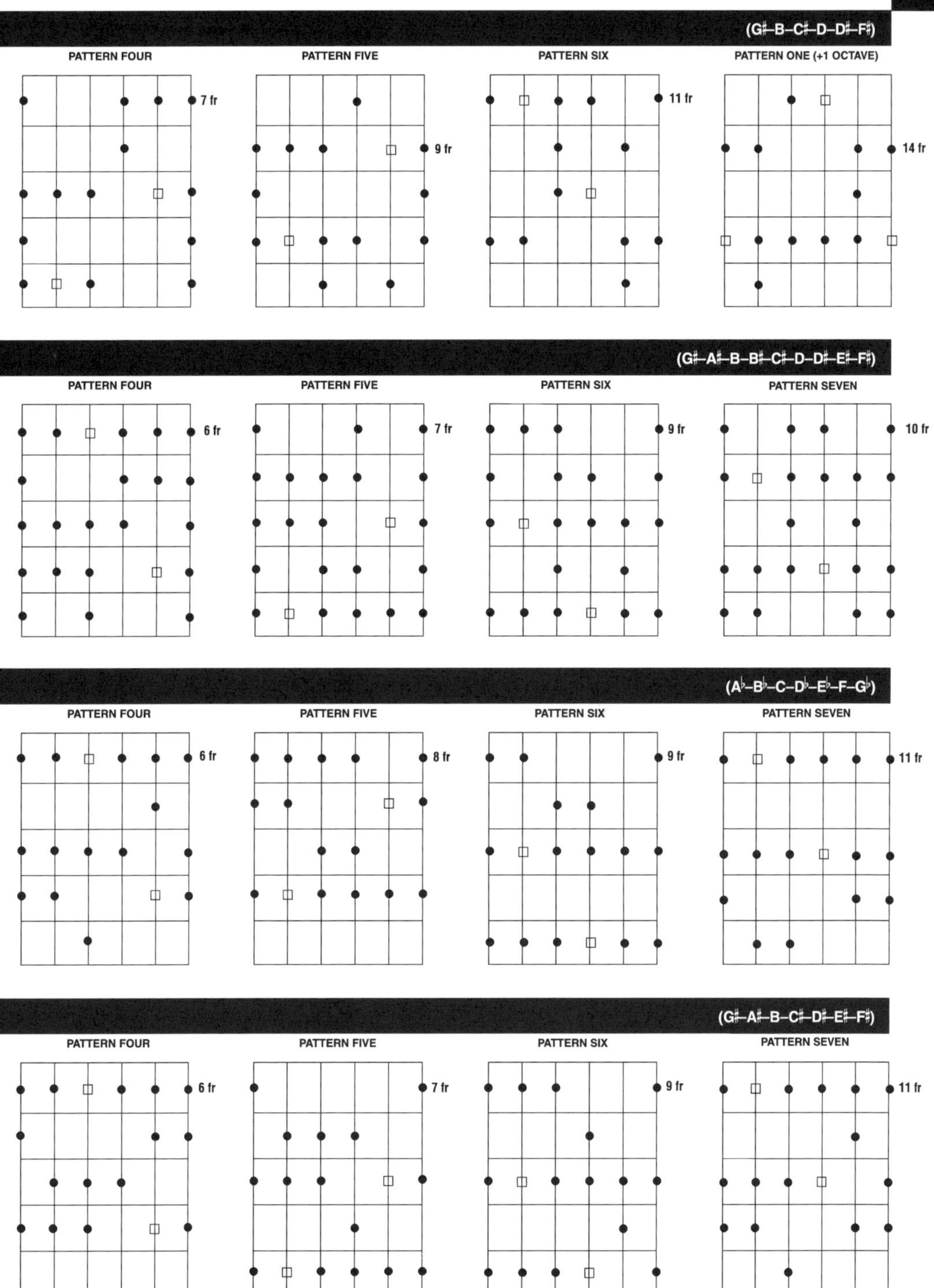
(G#–B–C#–D–D#–F#)
PATTERN FOUR
PATTERN FIVE
PATTERN SIX
PATTERN ONE (+1 OCTAVE)
7 fr
9 fr
11 fr
14 fr
(G#–A#–B–B#–C#–D–D#–E#–F#)
PATTERN FOUR
PATTERN FIVE
PATTERN SIX
PATTERN SEVEN
6 fr
7 fr
9 fr
10 fr
(A♭–B♭–C–D♭–E♭–F–G♭)
PATTERN FOUR
PATTERN FIVE
PATTERN SIX
PATTERN SEVEN
6 fr
8 fr
9 fr
11 fr
(G#–A#–B–C#–D#–E#–F#)
PATTERN FOUR
PATTERN FIVE
PATTERN SIX
PATTERN SEVEN
6 fr
7 fr
9 fr
11 fr

# A♭ MELODIC MINOR

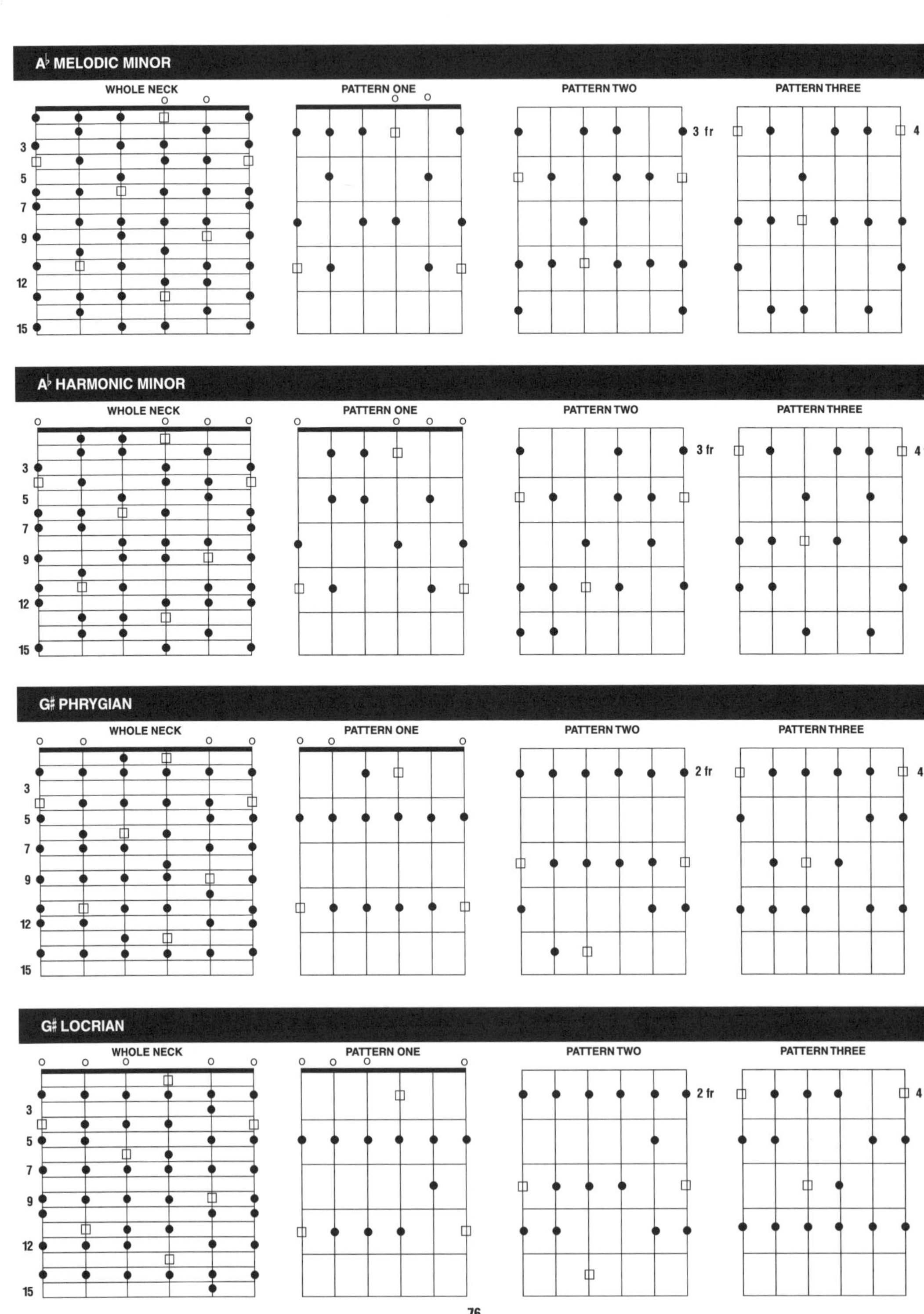

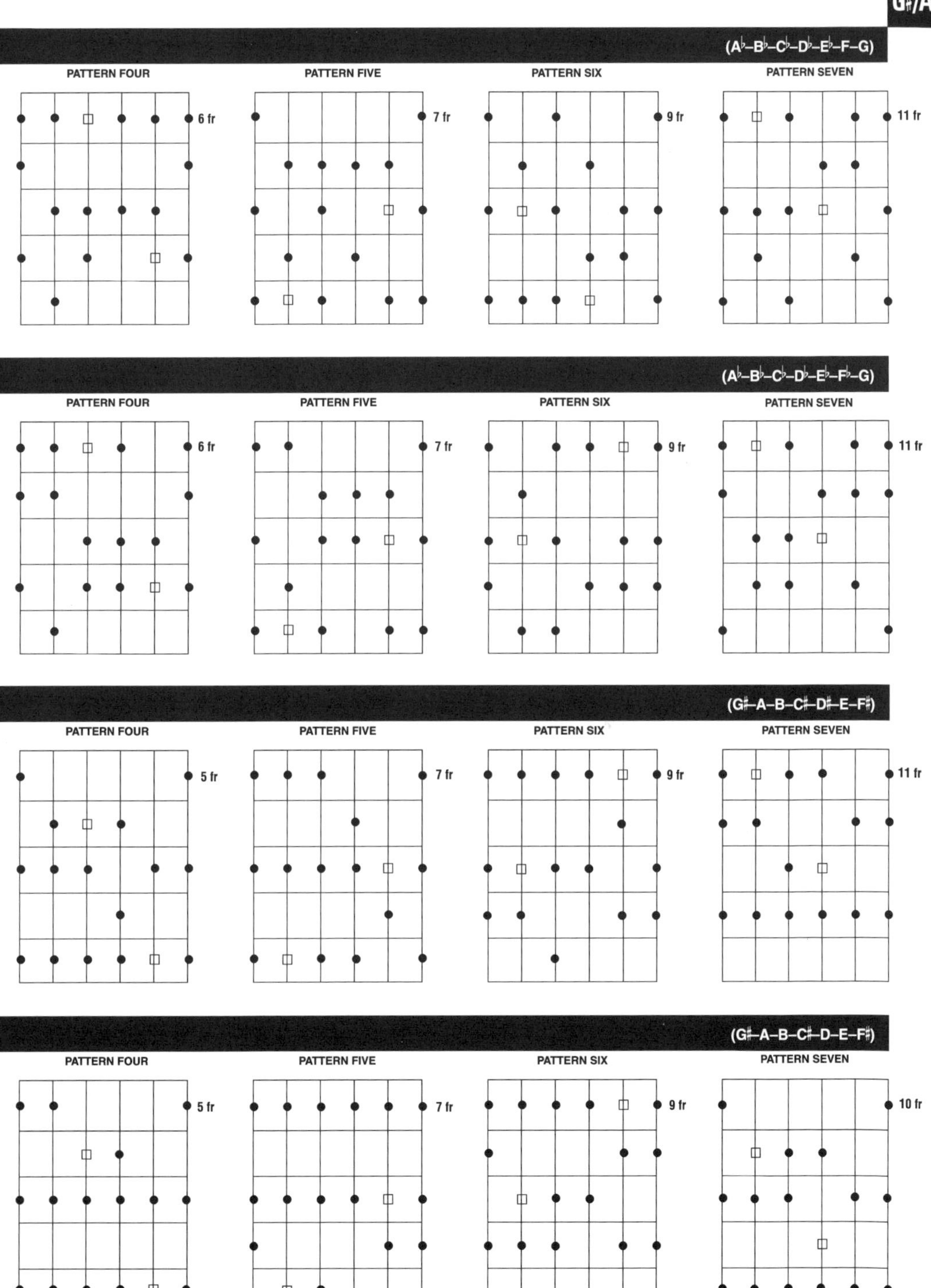
(A♭–B♭–C♭–D♭–E♭–F–G)
PATTERN FOUR
PATTERN FIVE
PATTERN SIX
PATTERN SEVEN
6 fr
7 fr
9 fr
11 fr

(A♭–B♭–C♭–D♭–E♭–F♭–G)
PATTERN FOUR
PATTERN FIVE
PATTERN SIX
PATTERN SEVEN
6 fr
7 fr
9 fr
11 fr

(G#–A–B–C#–D#–E–F#)
PATTERN FOUR
PATTERN FIVE
PATTERN SIX
PATTERN SEVEN
5 fr
7 fr
9 fr
11 fr

(G#–A–B–C#–D–E–F#)
PATTERN FOUR
PATTERN FIVE
PATTERN SIX
PATTERN SEVEN
5 fr
7 fr
9 fr
10 fr

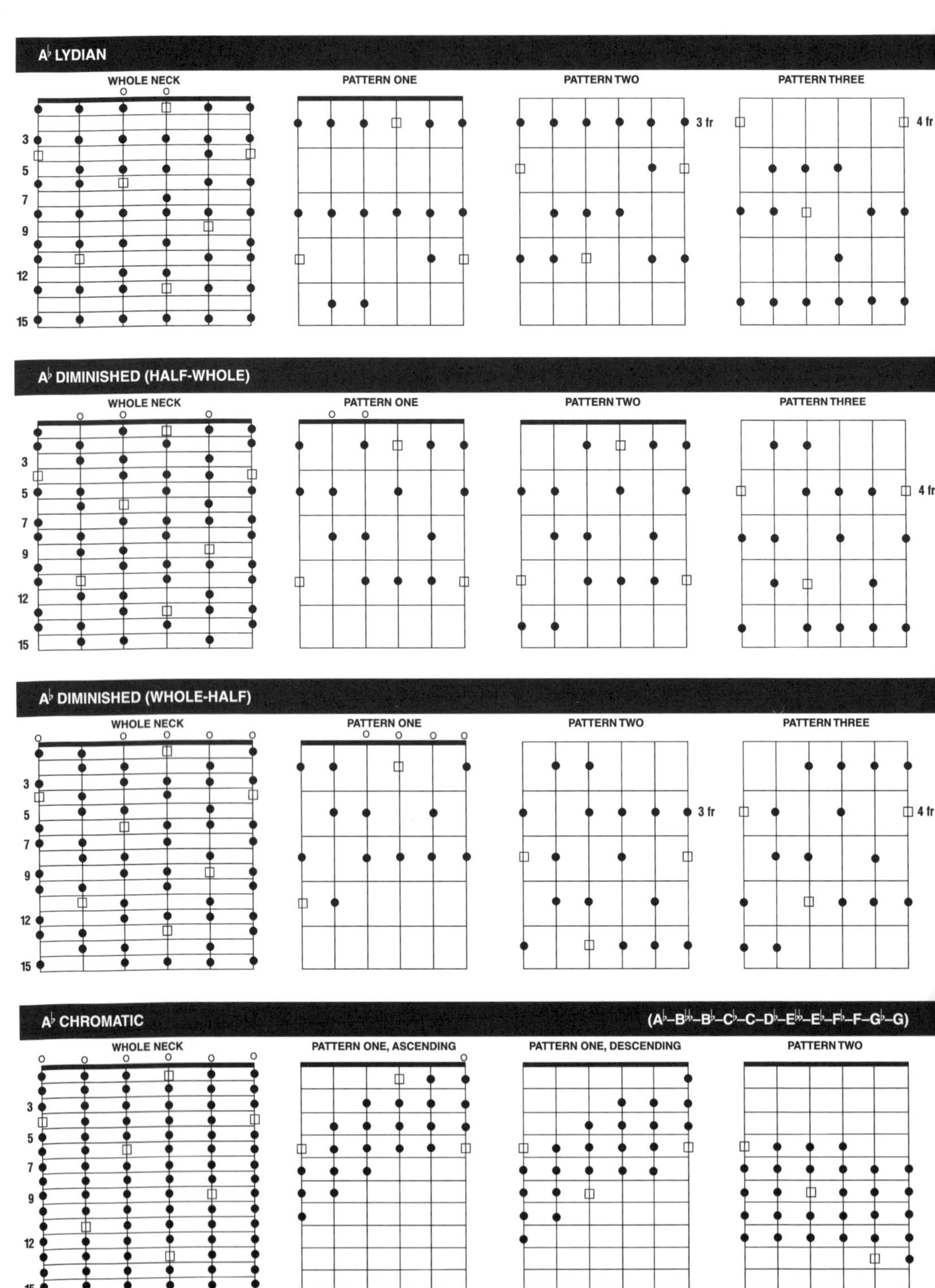


A♭ LYDIAN
WHOLE NECK
PATTERN ONE
PATTERN TWO
3 fr
PATTERN THREE
4 fr

A♭ DIMINISHED (HALF-WHOLE)
WHOLE NECK
PATTERN ONE
PATTERN TWO
PATTERN THREE
4 fr

A♭ DIMINISHED (WHOLE-HALF)
WHOLE NECK
PATTERN ONE
PATTERN TWO
3 fr
PATTERN THREE
4 fr

A♭ CHROMATIC
(A♭–B♭♭–B♭–C♭–C–D♭–E♭♭–E♭–F♭–F–G♭–G)
WHOLE NECK
PATTERN ONE, ASCENDING
PATTERN ONE, DESCENDING
PATTERN TWO

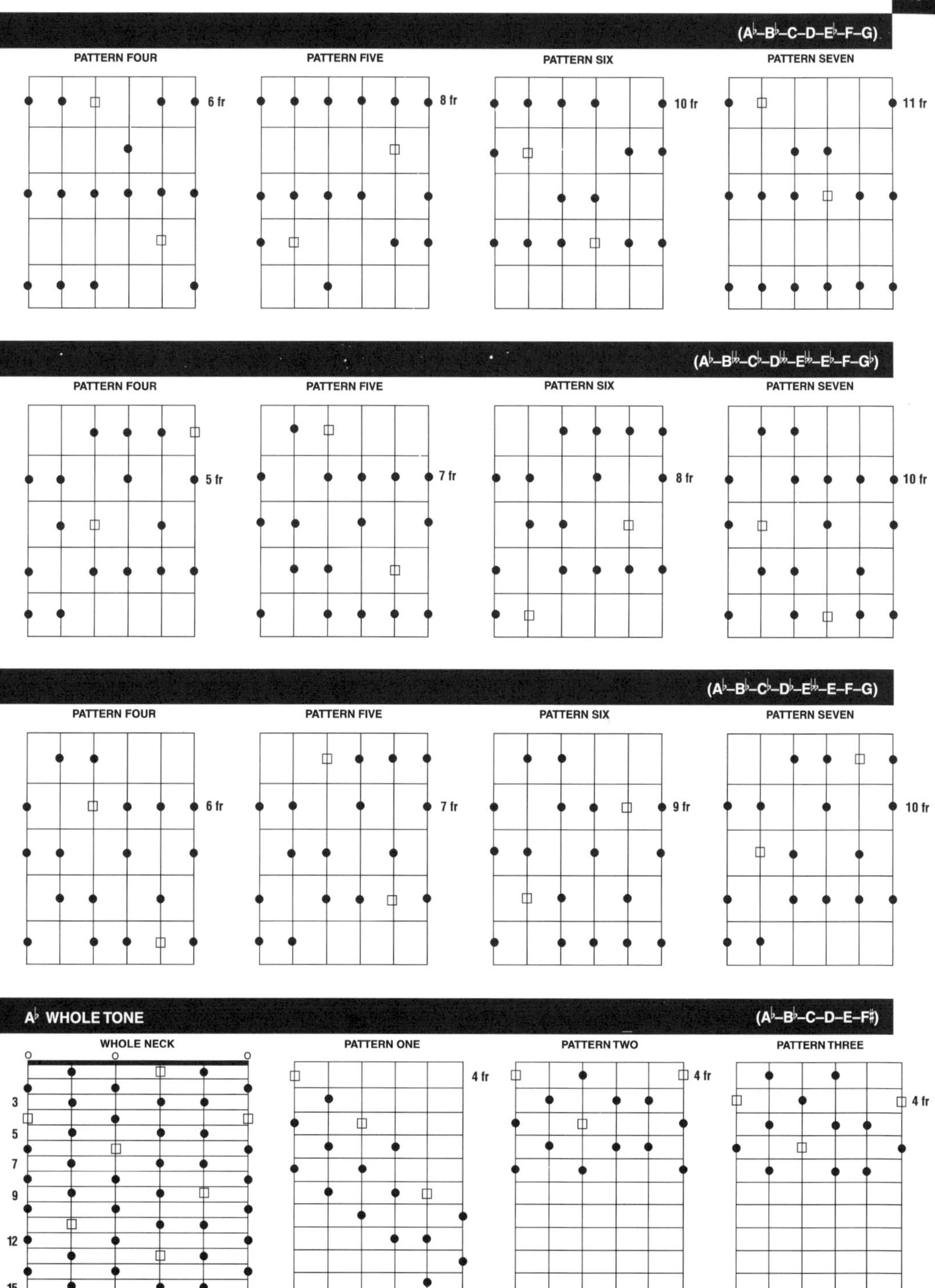
(A♭–B♭–C–D–E♭–F–G)
PATTERN FOUR
PATTERN FIVE
PATTERN SIX
PATTERN SEVEN
6 fr
8 fr
10 fr
11 fr

(A♭–B♭♭–C♭–D♭♭–E♭♭–E♭–F–G♭)
PATTERN FOUR
PATTERN FIVE
PATTERN SIX
PATTERN SEVEN
5 fr
7 fr
8 fr
10 fr

(A♭–B♭–C–D♭–E♭♭–E–F–G)
PATTERN FOUR
PATTERN FIVE
PATTERN SIX
PATTERN SEVEN
6 fr
7 fr
9 fr
10 fr

A♭ WHOLE TONE
(A♭–B♭–C–D–E–F#)
WHOLE NECK
PATTERN ONE
PATTERN TWO
PATTERN THREE
3
5
7
9
12
15
4 fr
4 fr
4 fr

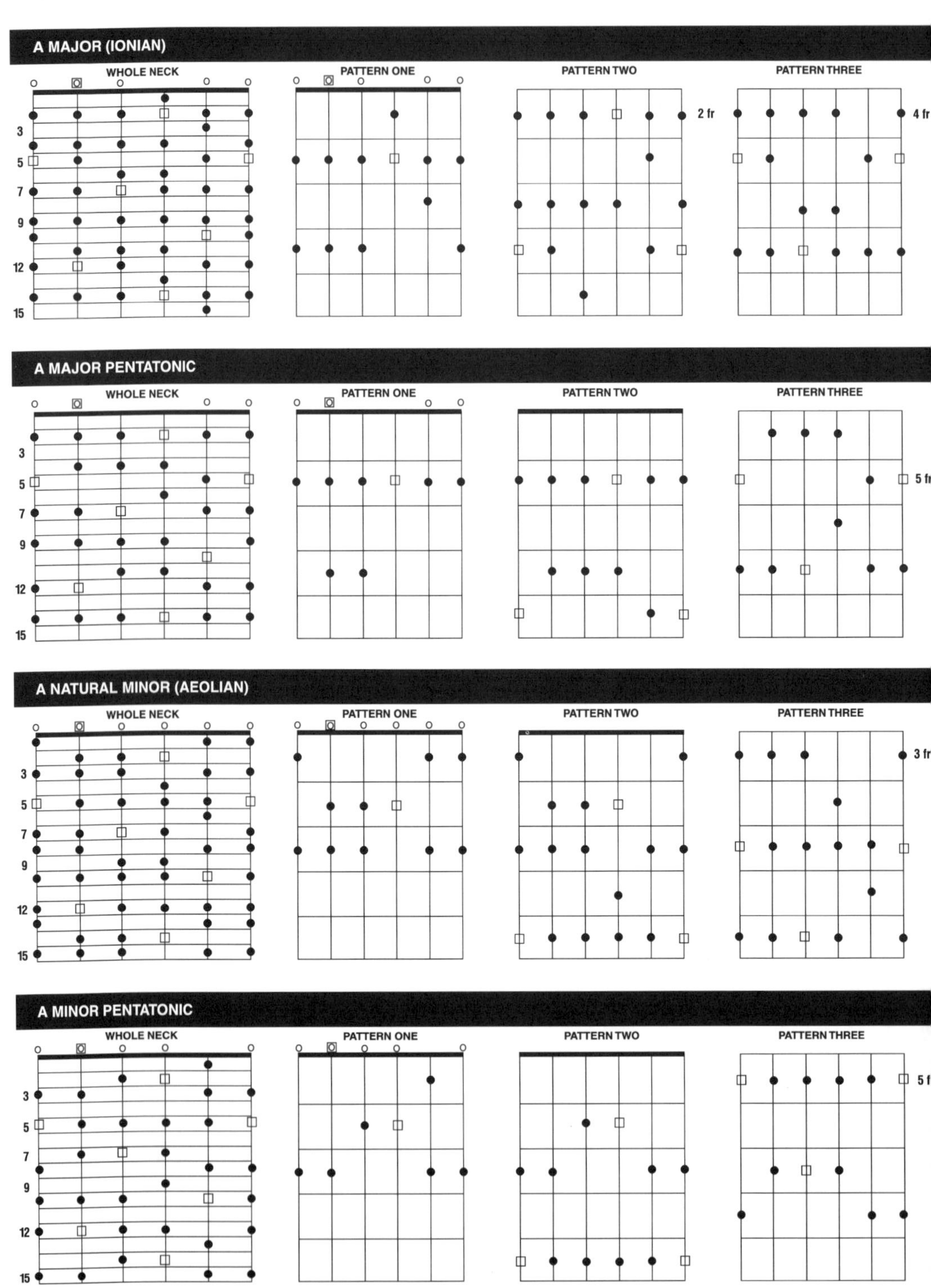


A MAJOR (IONIAN)
WHOLE NECK
PATTERN ONE
PATTERN TWO
PATTERN THREE
2 fr
4 fr

A MAJOR PENTATONIC
WHOLE NECK
PATTERN ONE
PATTERN TWO
PATTERN THREE
5 fr

A NATURAL MINOR (AEOLIAN)
WHOLE NECK
PATTERN ONE
PATTERN TWO
PATTERN THREE
3 fr

A MINOR PENTATONIC
WHOLE NECK
PATTERN ONE
PATTERN TWO
PATTERN THREE
5 fr

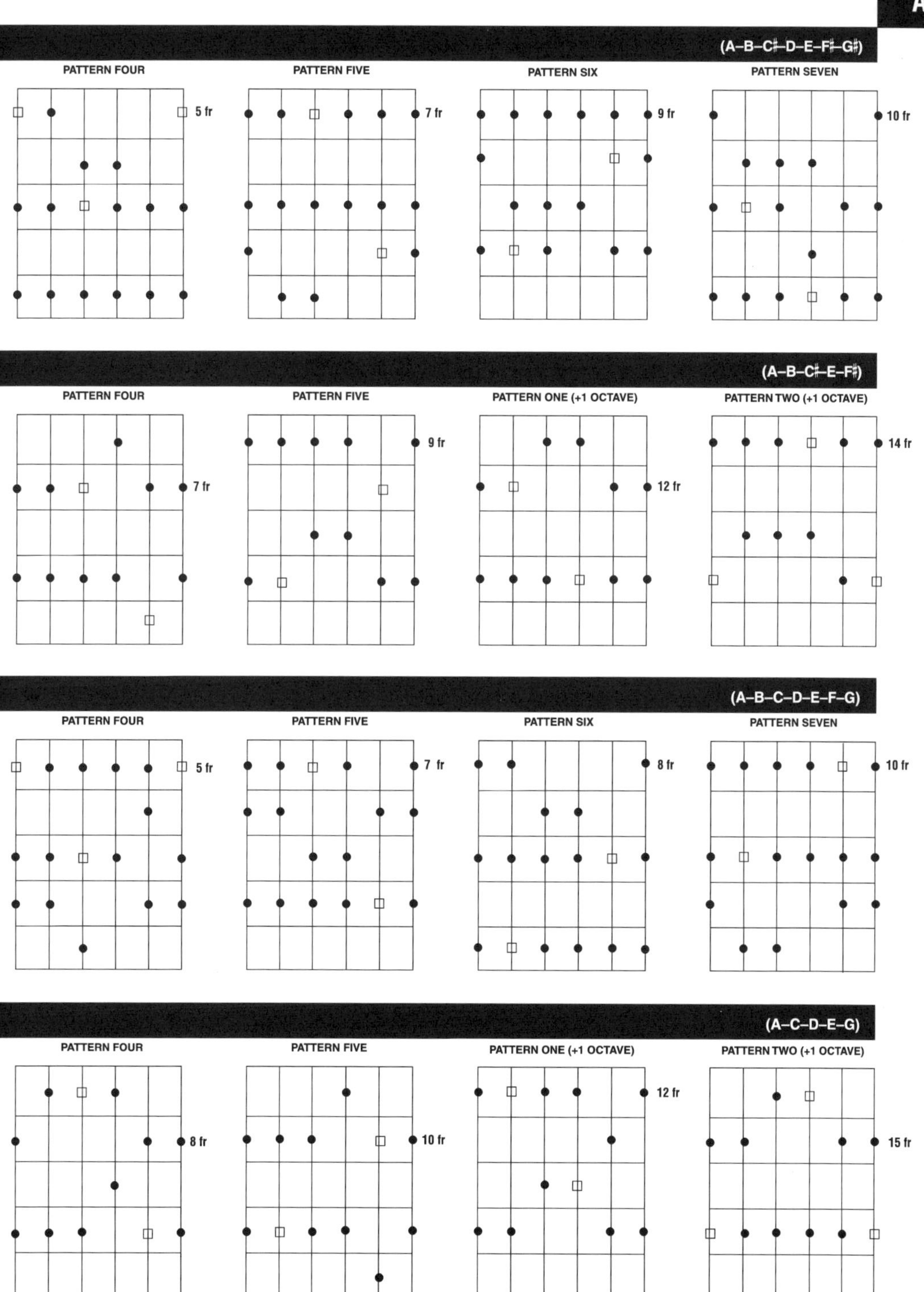
(A–B–C#–D–E–F#–G#)
PATTERN FOUR
PATTERN FIVE
PATTERN SIX
PATTERN SEVEN
5 fr
7 fr
9 fr
10 fr
(A–B–C#–E–F#)
PATTERN FOUR
PATTERN FIVE
PATTERN ONE (+1 OCTAVE)
PATTERN TWO (+1 OCTAVE)
7 fr
9 fr
12 fr
14 fr
(A–B–C–D–E–F–G)
PATTERN FOUR
PATTERN FIVE
PATTERN SIX
PATTERN SEVEN
5 fr
7 fr
8 fr
10 fr
(A–C–D–E–G)
PATTERN FOUR
PATTERN FIVE
PATTERN ONE (+1 OCTAVE)
PATTERN TWO (+1 OCTAVE)
8 fr
10 fr
12 fr
15 fr

## A BLUES

**WHOLE NECK**    **PATTERN ONE**    **PATTERN TWO**    **PATTERN THREE**

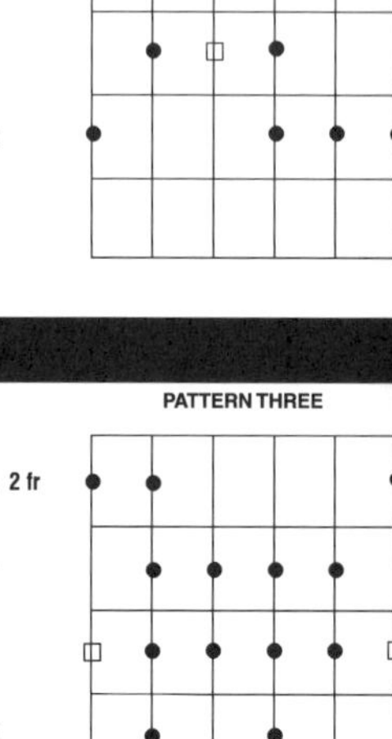

## A MIXO-BLUES

**WHOLE NECK**    **PATTERN ONE**    **PATTERN TWO**    **PATTERN THREE**

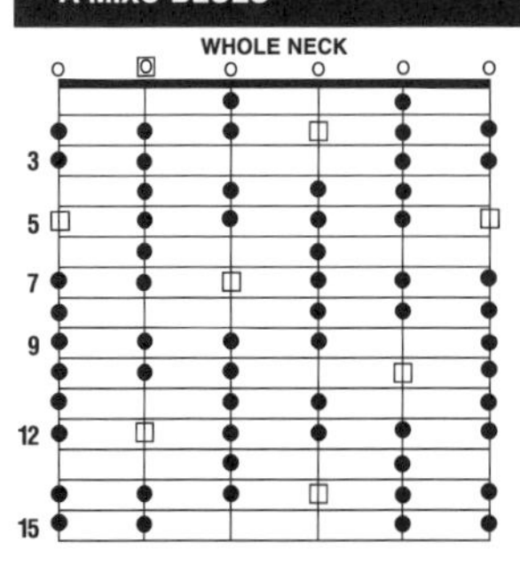 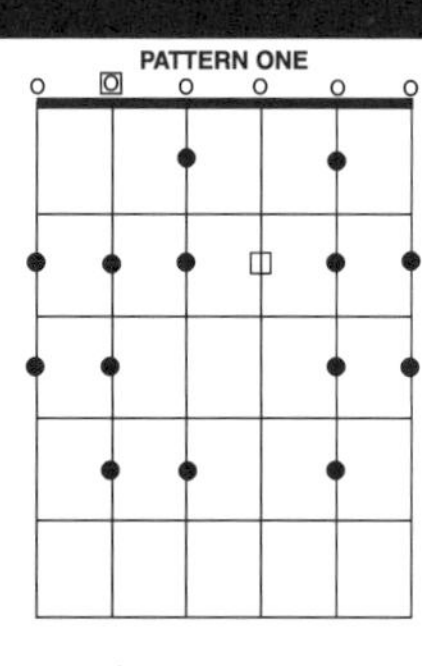

## A MIXOLYDIAN

**WHOLE NECK**    **PATTERN ONE**    **PATTERN TWO**    **PATTERN THREE**

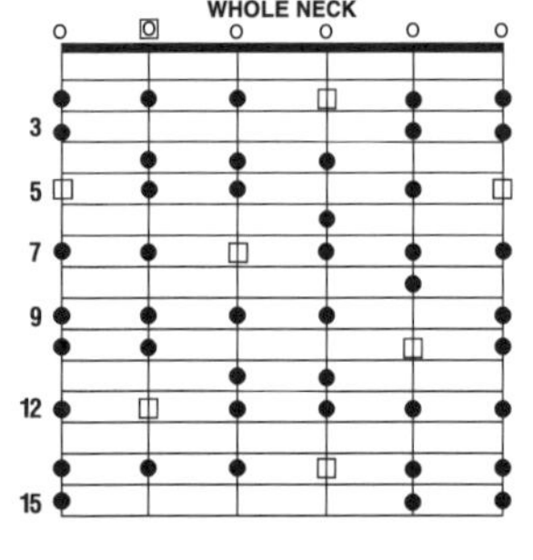 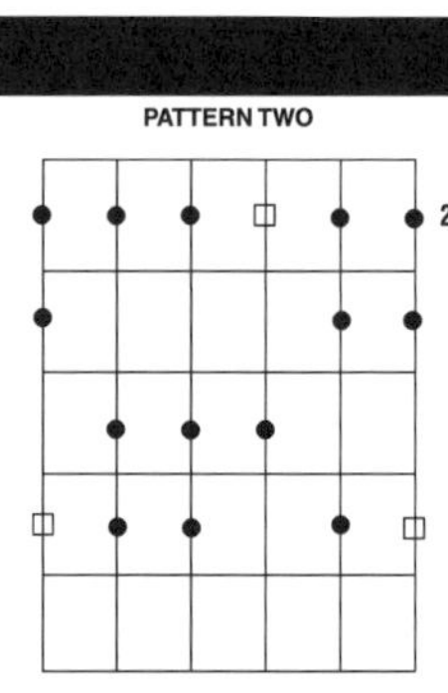 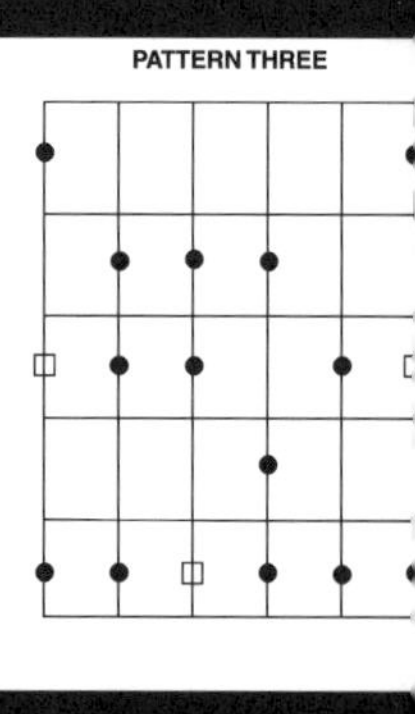

## A DORIAN

**WHOLE NECK**    **PATTERN ONE**    **PATTERN TWO**    **PATTERN THREE**

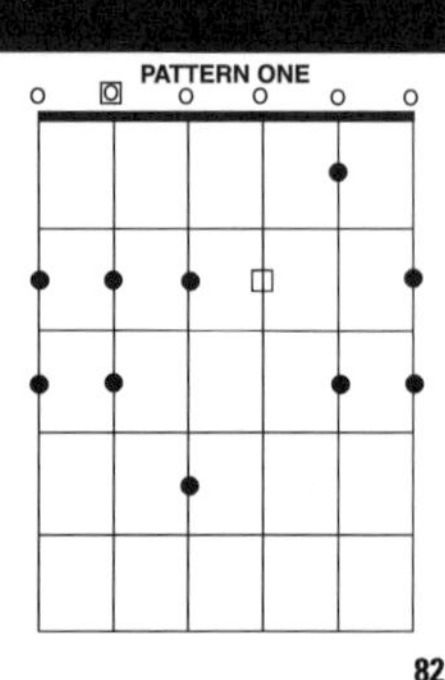 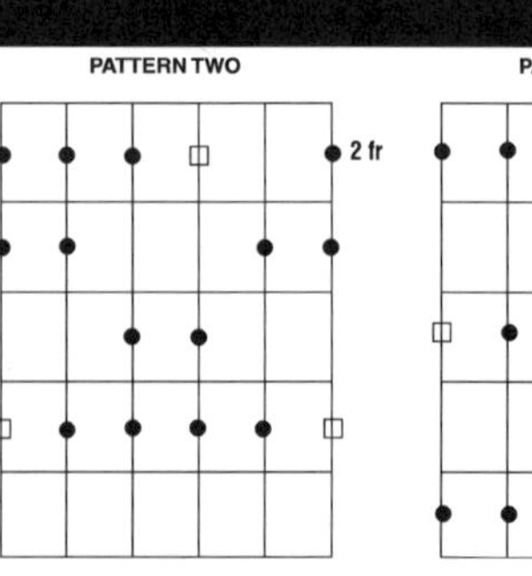

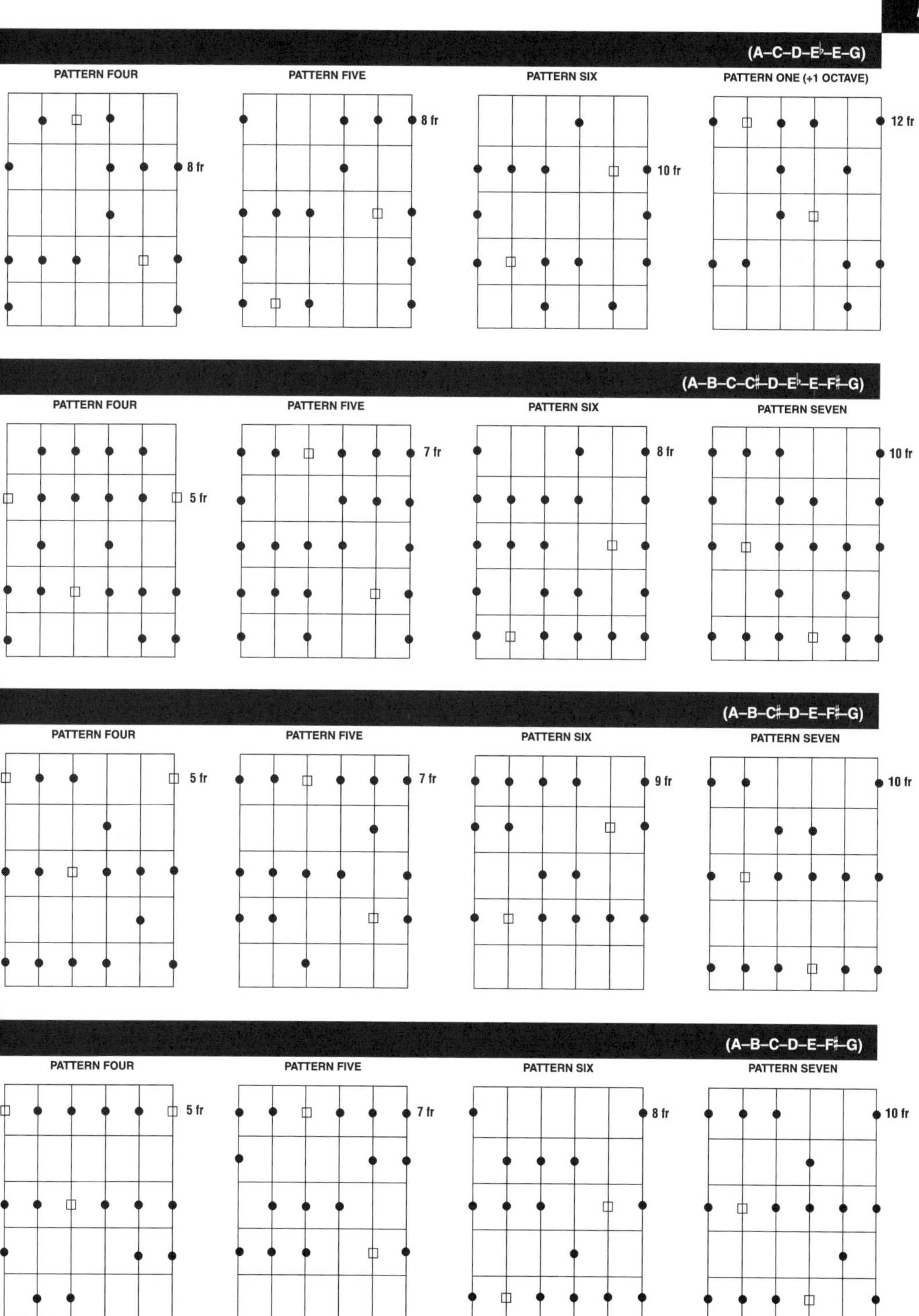

**(A–C–D–E♭–E–G)**

PATTERN FOUR | PATTERN FIVE | PATTERN SIX | PATTERN ONE (+1 OCTAVE)

**(A–B–C–C♯–D–E♭–E–F♯–G)**

PATTERN FOUR | PATTERN FIVE | PATTERN SIX | PATTERN SEVEN

**(A–B–C♯–D–E–F♯–G)**

PATTERN FOUR | PATTERN FIVE | PATTERN SIX | PATTERN SEVEN

**(A–B–C–D–E–F♯–G)**

PATTERN FOUR | PATTERN FIVE | PATTERN SIX | PATTERN SEVEN

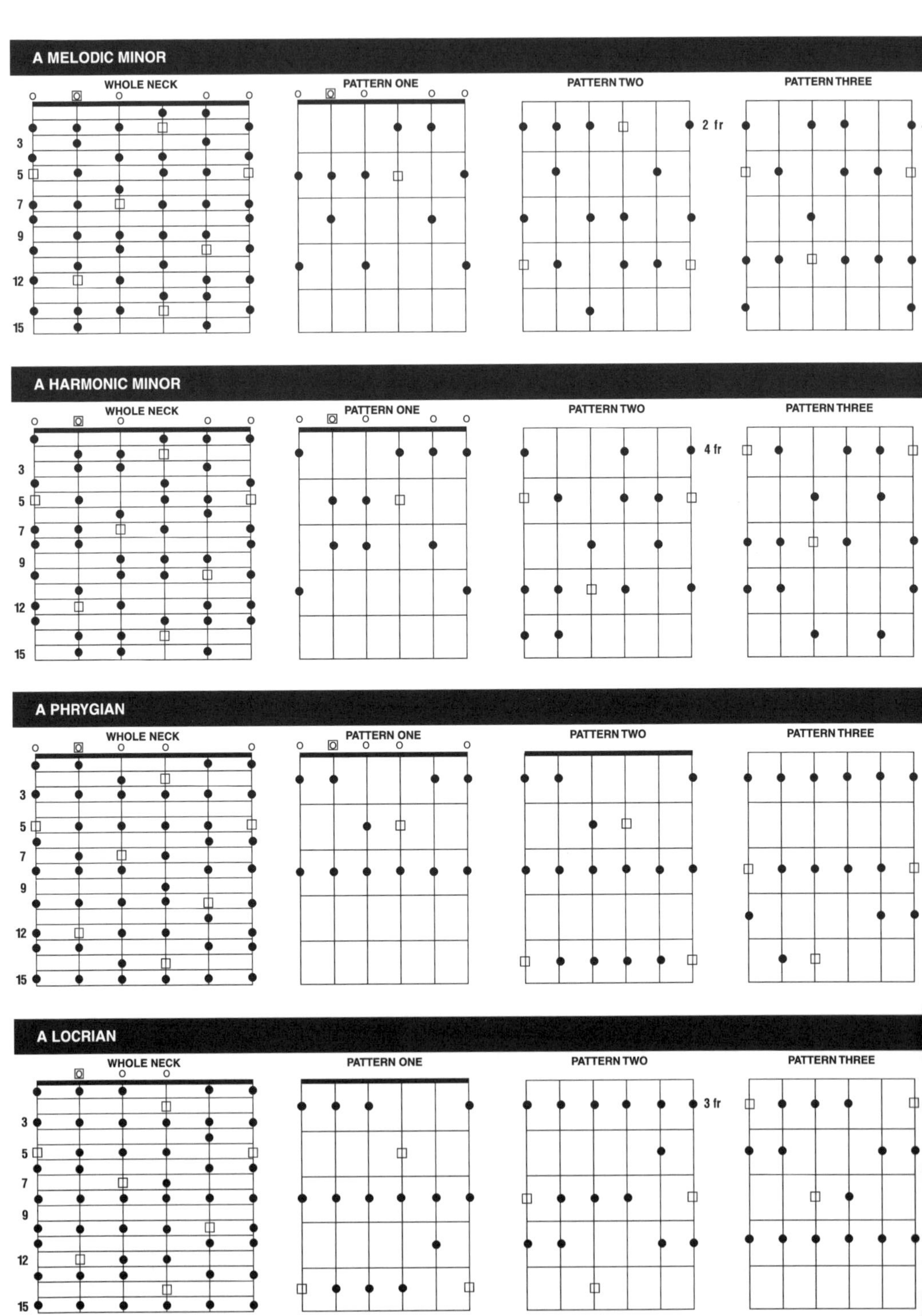

A MELODIC MINOR
WHOLE NECK
PATTERN ONE
PATTERN TWO
PATTERN THREE

A HARMONIC MINOR
WHOLE NECK
PATTERN ONE
PATTERN TWO
PATTERN THREE

A PHRYGIAN
WHOLE NECK
PATTERN ONE
PATTERN TWO
PATTERN THREE

A LOCRIAN
WHOLE NECK
PATTERN ONE
PATTERN TWO
PATTERN THREE

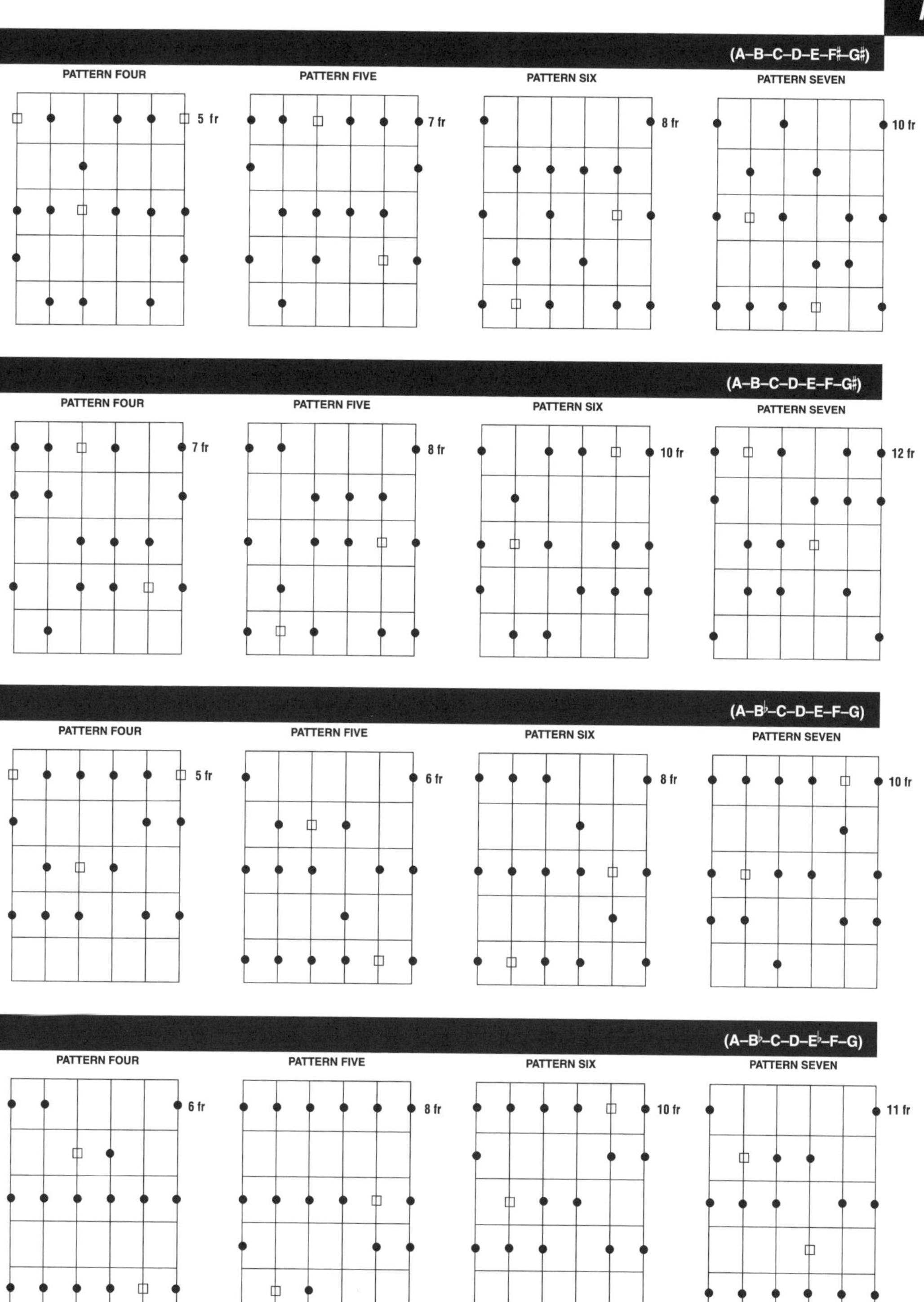
(A–B–C–D–E–F#–G#)
PATTERN FOUR
PATTERN FIVE
PATTERN SIX
PATTERN SEVEN
5 fr
7 fr
8 fr
10 fr
(A–B–C–D–E–F–G#)
PATTERN FOUR
PATTERN FIVE
PATTERN SIX
PATTERN SEVEN
7 fr
8 fr
10 fr
12 fr
(A–Bb–C–D–E–F–G)
PATTERN FOUR
PATTERN FIVE
PATTERN SIX
PATTERN SEVEN
5 fr
6 fr
8 fr
10 fr
(A–Bb–C–D–Eb–F–G)
PATTERN FOUR
PATTERN FIVE
PATTERN SIX
PATTERN SEVEN
6 fr
8 fr
10 fr
11 fr

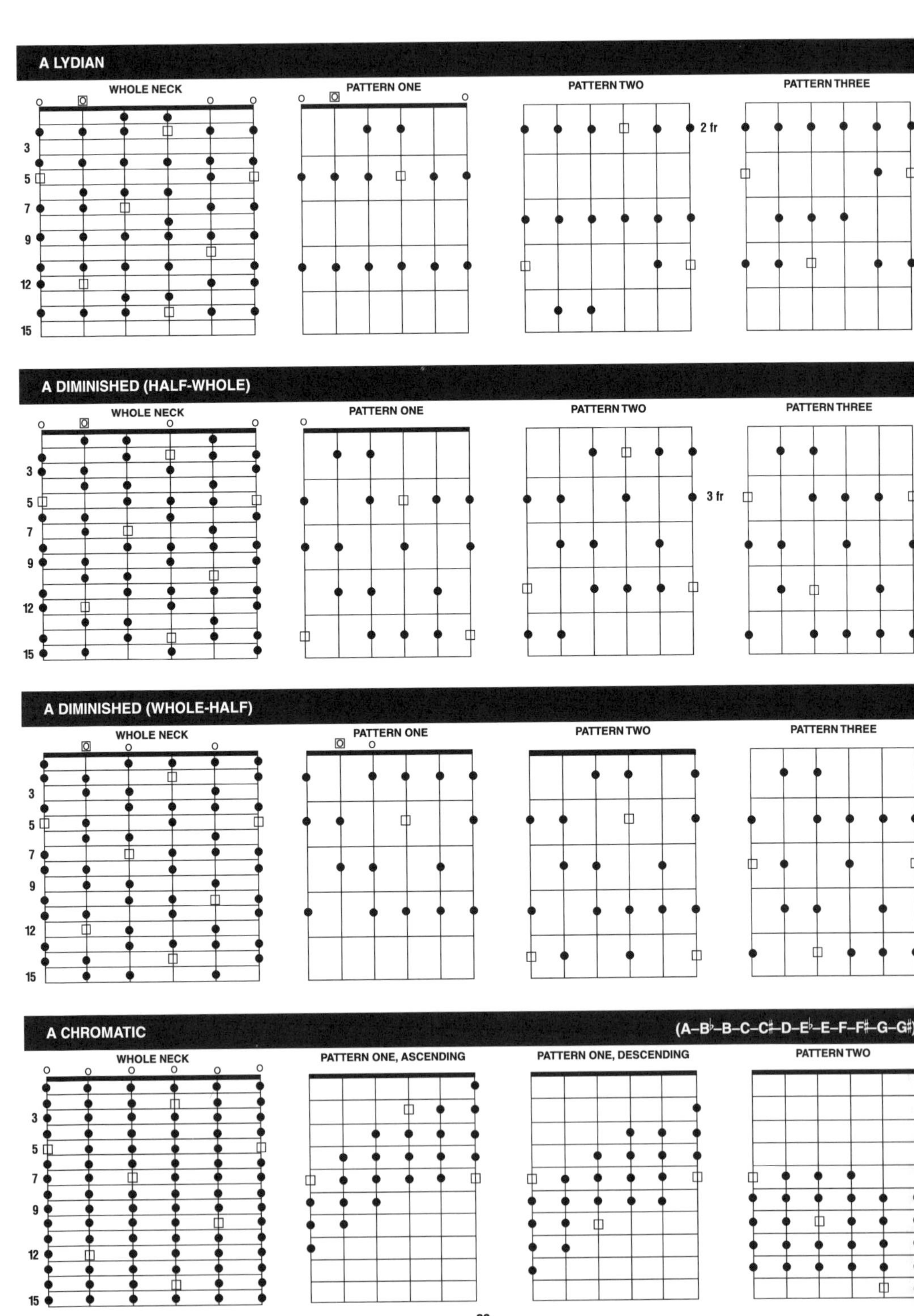

A LYDIAN
WHOLE NECK
PATTERN ONE
PATTERN TWO
PATTERN THREE
2 fr

A DIMINISHED (HALF-WHOLE)
WHOLE NECK
PATTERN ONE
PATTERN TWO
PATTERN THREE
3 fr

A DIMINISHED (WHOLE-HALF)
WHOLE NECK
PATTERN ONE
PATTERN TWO
PATTERN THREE

A CHROMATIC
(A–B♭–B–C–C♯–D–E♭–E–F–F♯–G–G♯)
WHOLE NECK
PATTERN ONE, ASCENDING
PATTERN ONE, DESCENDING
PATTERN TWO

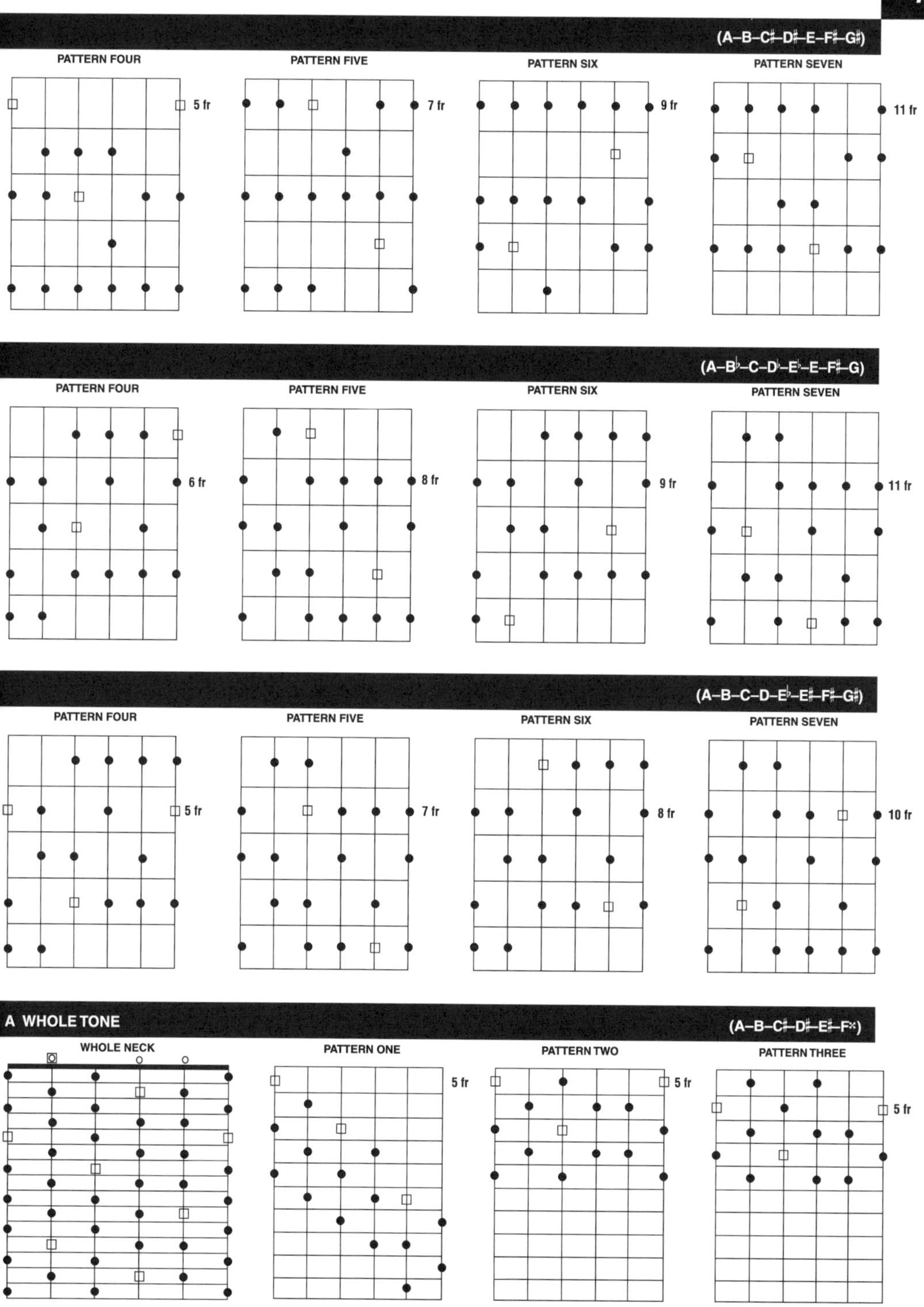
(A–B–C#–D#–E–F#–G#)
PATTERN FOUR
PATTERN FIVE
PATTERN SIX
PATTERN SEVEN
5 fr
7 fr
9 fr
11 fr
(A–Bb–C–D–Eb–E–F#–G)
PATTERN FOUR
PATTERN FIVE
PATTERN SIX
PATTERN SEVEN
6 fr
8 fr
9 fr
11 fr
(A–B–C–D–Eb–E#–F#–G#)
PATTERN FOUR
PATTERN FIVE
PATTERN SIX
PATTERN SEVEN
5 fr
7 fr
8 fr
10 fr
A WHOLE TONE
(A–B–C#–D#–E#–F×)
WHOLE NECK
PATTERN ONE
PATTERN TWO
PATTERN THREE
5 fr
5 fr
5 fr

# B♭ MAJOR (IONIAN)

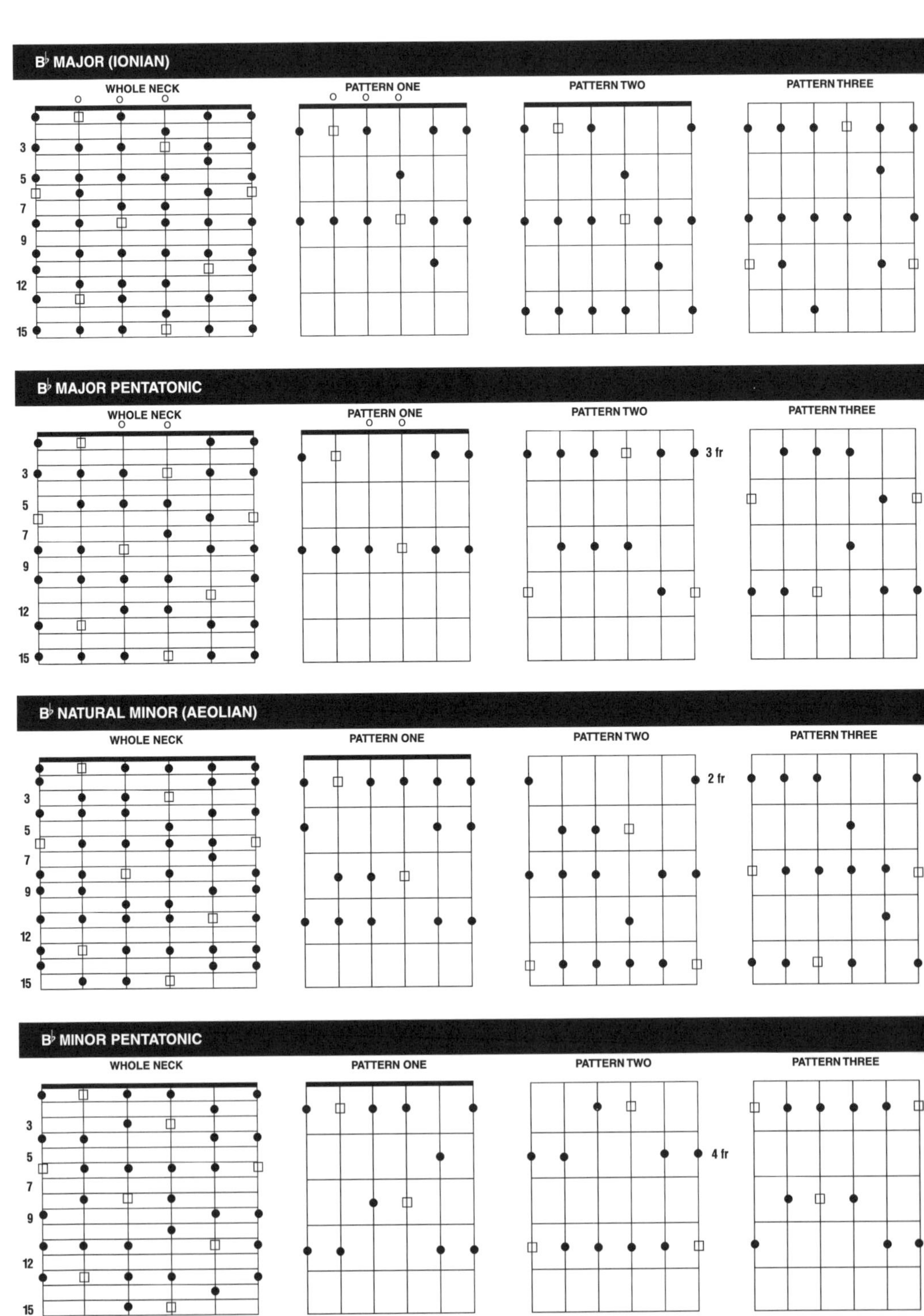

(B♭–C–D–E♭–F–G–A)

| PATTERN FOUR | PATTERN FIVE | PATTERN SIX | PATTERN SEVEN |
| --- | --- | --- | --- |

(B♭–C–D–F–G)

| PATTERN FOUR | PATTERN FIVE | PATTERN ONE (+1 OCTAVE) | PATTERN TWO (+1 OCTAVE) |
| --- | --- | --- | --- |

(B♭–C–D♭–E♭–F–G♭–A♭)

| PATTERN FOUR | PATTERN FIVE | PATTERN SIX | PATTERN SEVEN |
| --- | --- | --- | --- |

(B♭–D♭–E♭–F–A♭)

| PATTERN FOUR | PATTERN FIVE | PATTERN ONE (+1 OCTAVE) | PATTERN TWO (+1 OCTAVE) |
| --- | --- | --- | --- |

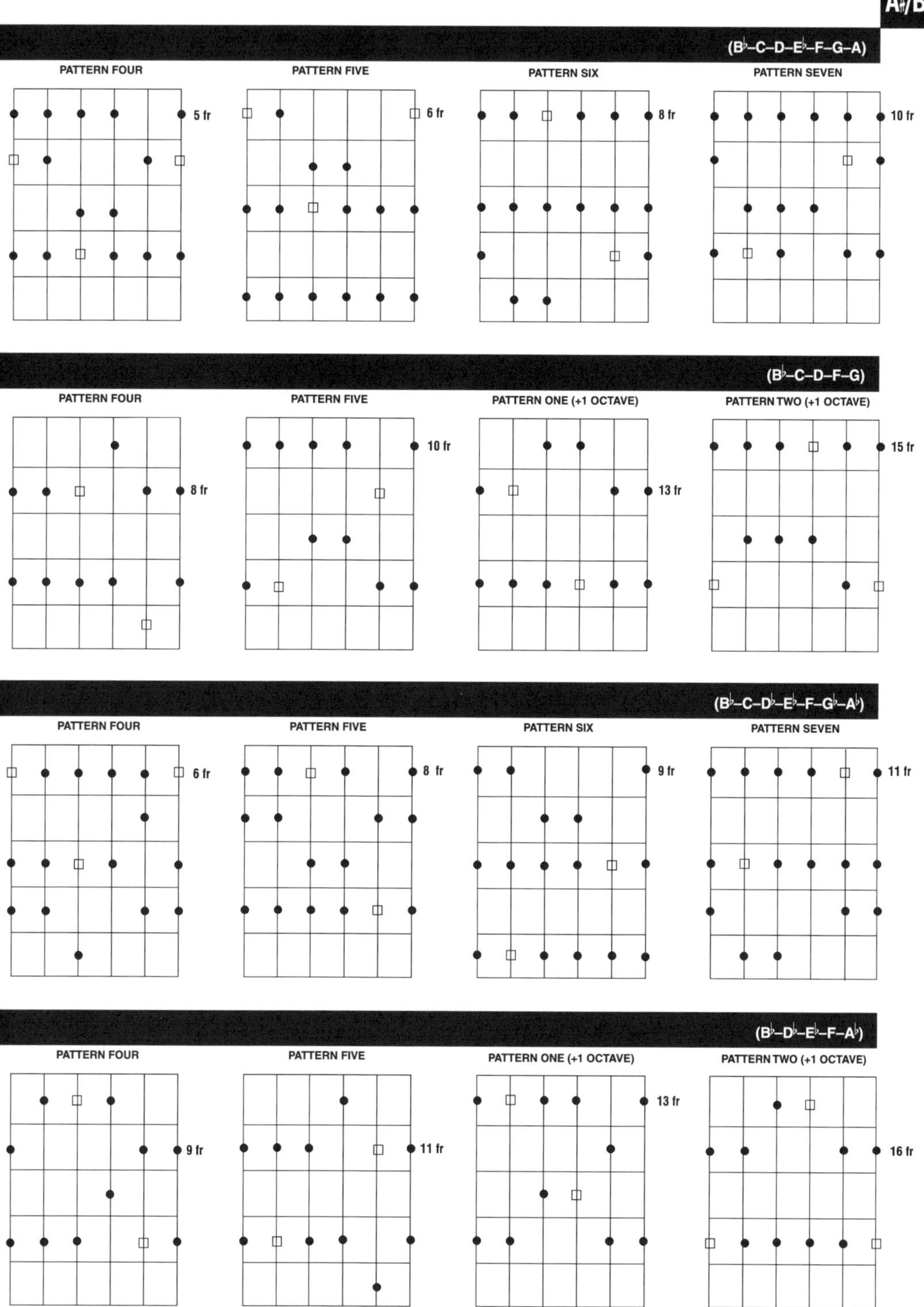

# B♭ BLUES

| WHOLE NECK | PATTERN ONE | PATTERN TWO | PATTERN THREE |

# B♭ MIXO-BLUES

| WHOLE NECK | PATTERN ONE | PATTERN TWO | PATTERN THREE |

# B♭ MIXOLYDIAN

| WHOLE NECK | PATTERN ONE | PATTERN TWO | PATTERN THREE |

# B♭ DORIAN

| WHOLE NECK | PATTERN ONE | PATTERN TWO | PATTERN THREE |

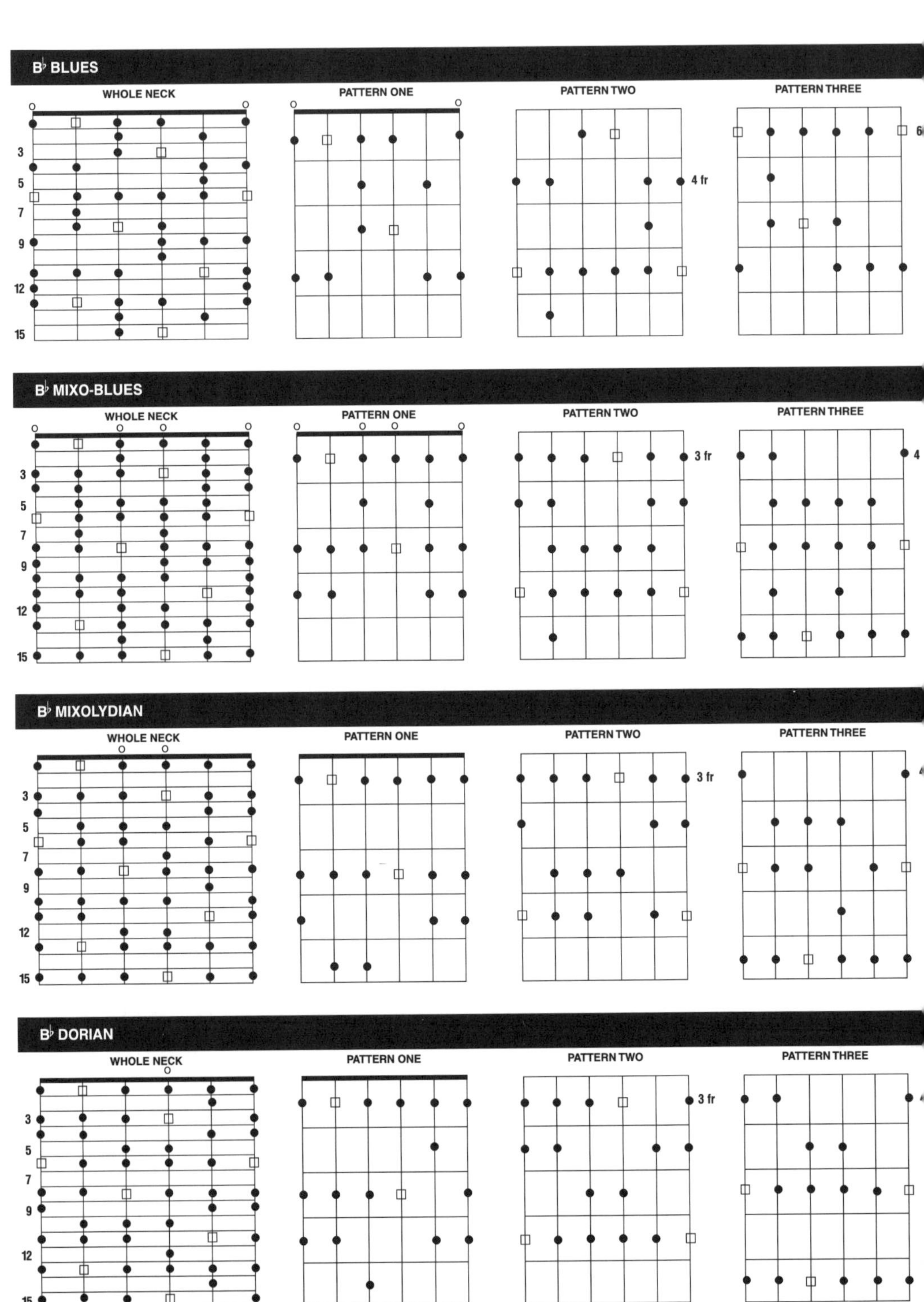

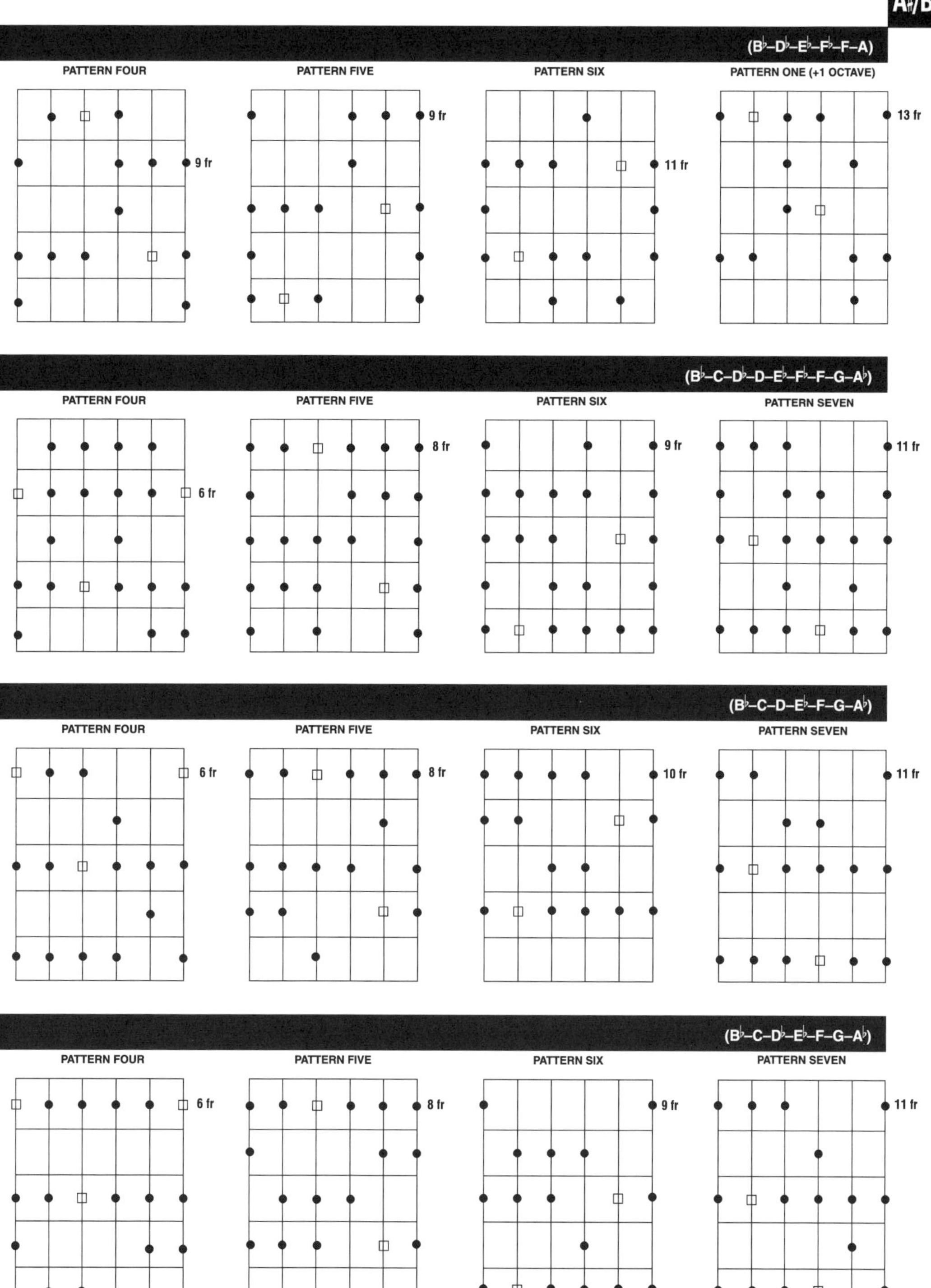
(B♭–D♭–E♭–F♭–F–A)
PATTERN FOUR
PATTERN FIVE
9 fr
PATTERN SIX
11 fr
PATTERN ONE (+1 OCTAVE)
13 fr
9 fr

(B♭–C–D♭–D–E♭–F♭–F–G–A♭)
PATTERN FOUR
6 fr
PATTERN FIVE
8 fr
PATTERN SIX
9 fr
PATTERN SEVEN
11 fr

(B♭–C–D–E♭–F–G–A♭)
PATTERN FOUR
6 fr
PATTERN FIVE
8 fr
PATTERN SIX
10 fr
PATTERN SEVEN
11 fr

(B♭–C–D–E♭–F–G–A♭)
PATTERN FOUR
6 fr
PATTERN FIVE
8 fr
PATTERN SIX
9 fr
PATTERN SEVEN
11 fr

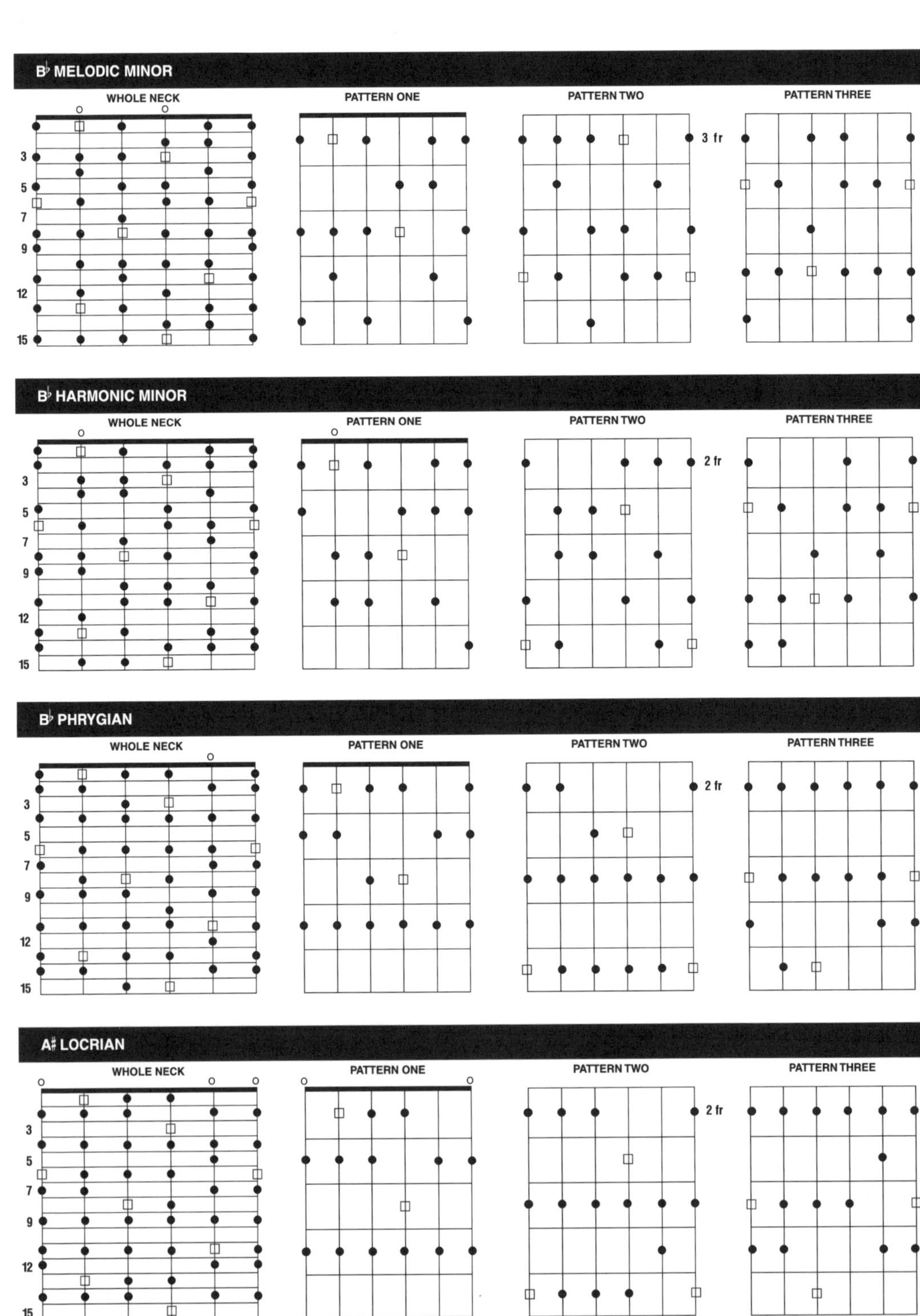

B♭ MELODIC MINOR
WHOLE NECK
PATTERN ONE
PATTERN TWO
PATTERN THREE
3 fr
5
B♭ HARMONIC MINOR
WHOLE NECK
PATTERN ONE
PATTERN TWO
PATTERN THREE
2 fr
B♭ PHRYGIAN
WHOLE NECK
PATTERN ONE
PATTERN TWO
PATTERN THREE
2 fr
A♯ LOCRIAN
WHOLE NECK
PATTERN ONE
PATTERN TWO
PATTERN THREE
2 fr
3 fr

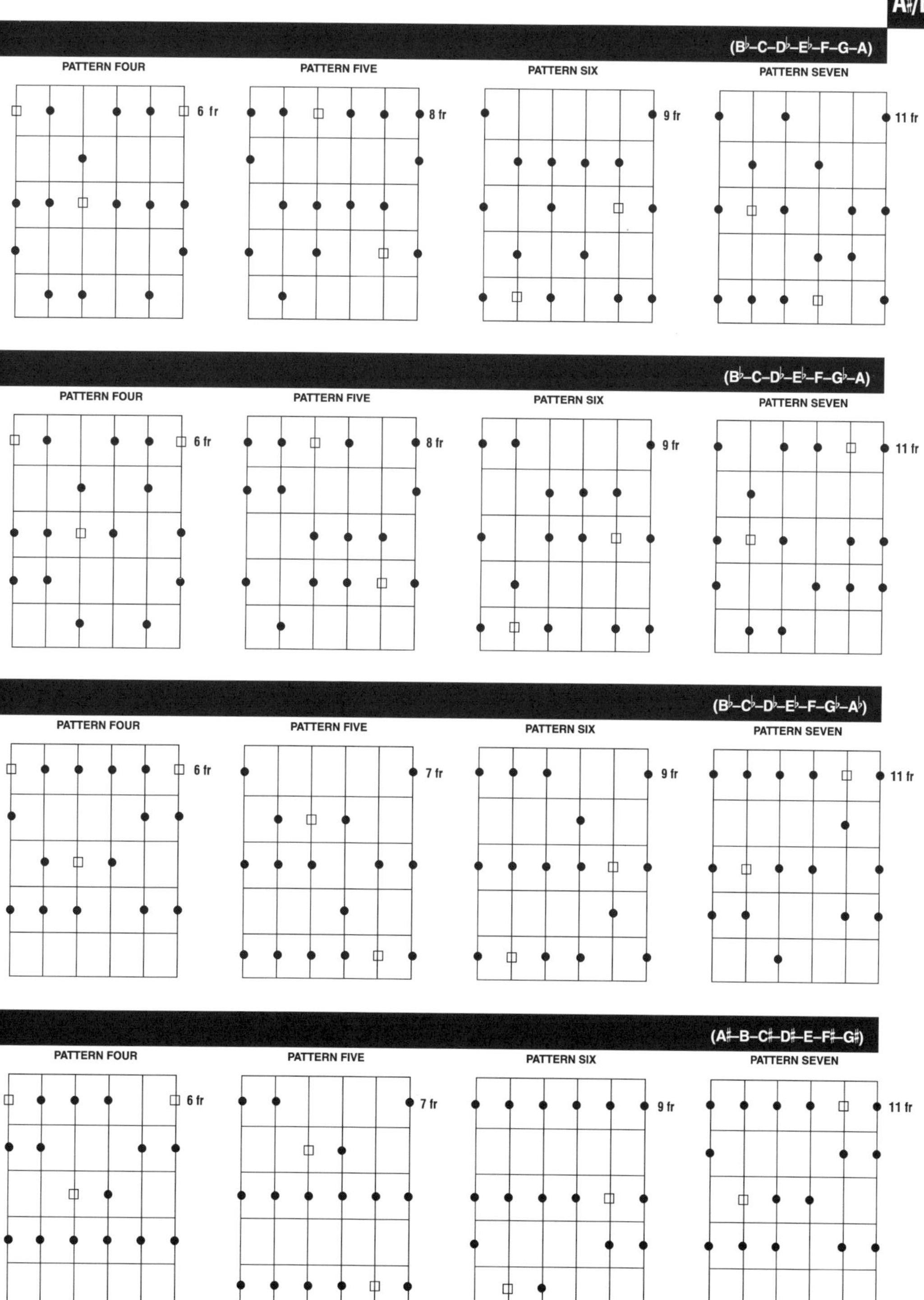
(B♭–C–D♭–E♭–F–G–A)
PATTERN FOUR
6 fr
PATTERN FIVE
8 fr
PATTERN SIX
9 fr
PATTERN SEVEN
11 fr
(B♭–C–D♭–E♭–F–G♭–A)
PATTERN FOUR
6 fr
PATTERN FIVE
8 fr
PATTERN SIX
9 fr
PATTERN SEVEN
11 fr
(B♭–C♭–D♭–E♭–F–G♭–A♭)
PATTERN FOUR
6 fr
PATTERN FIVE
7 fr
PATTERN SIX
9 fr
PATTERN SEVEN
11 fr
(A#–B–C#–D#–E–F#–G#)
PATTERN FOUR
6 fr
PATTERN FIVE
7 fr
PATTERN SIX
9 fr
PATTERN SEVEN
11 fr

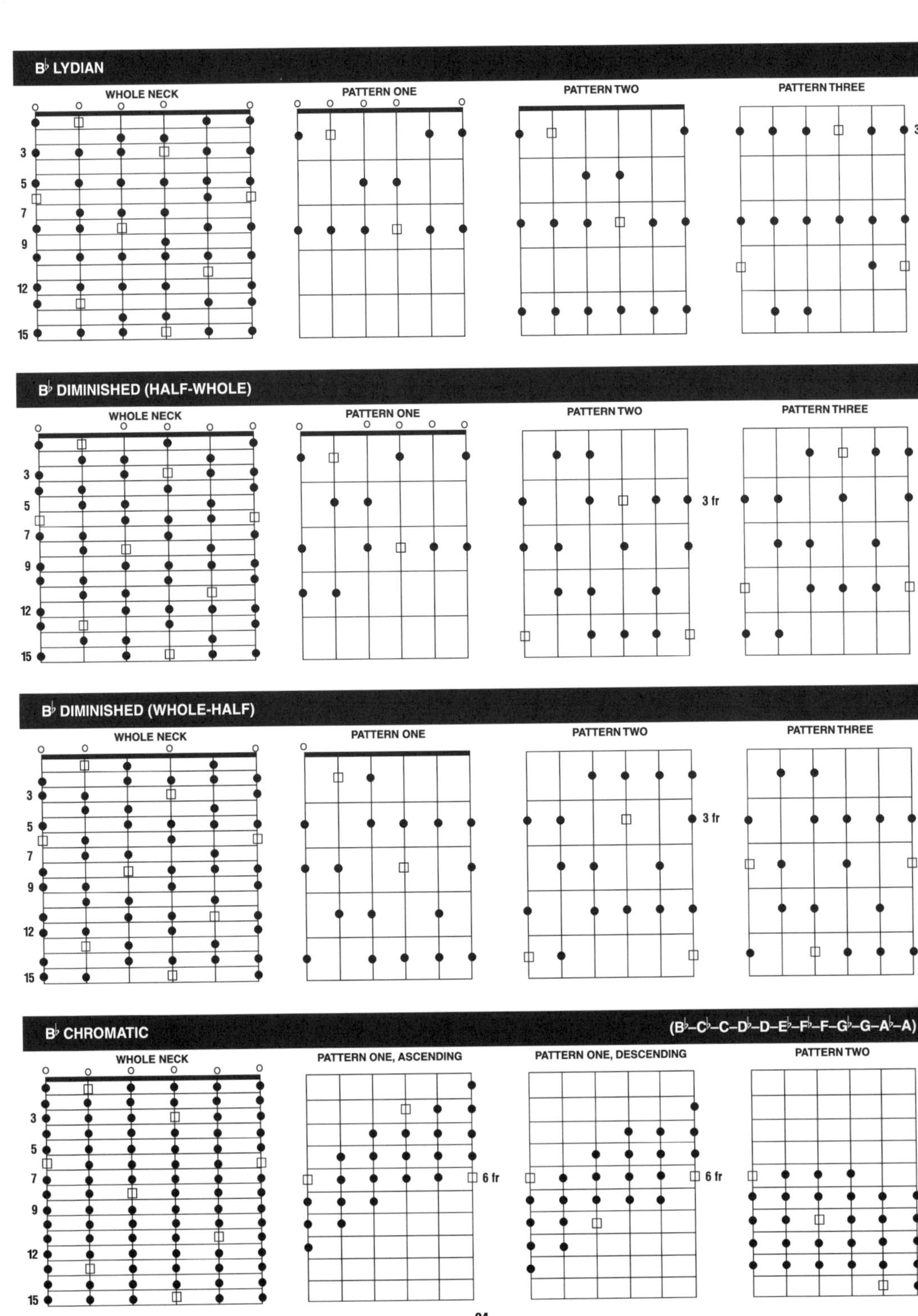
B♭ LYDIAN
WHOLE NECK
PATTERN ONE
PATTERN TWO
PATTERN THREE
B♭ DIMINISHED (HALF-WHOLE)
WHOLE NECK
PATTERN ONE
PATTERN TWO
PATTERN THREE
B♭ DIMINISHED (WHOLE-HALF)
WHOLE NECK
PATTERN ONE
PATTERN TWO
PATTERN THREE
B♭ CHROMATIC
(B♭–C♭–C–D♭–D–E♭–F♭–F–G♭–G–A♭–A)
WHOLE NECK
PATTERN ONE, ASCENDING
PATTERN ONE, DESCENDING
PATTERN TWO
3 fr
6 fr

**(B♭–C–D–E–F–G–A)**

| PATTERN FOUR | PATTERN FIVE | PATTERN SIX | PATTERN SEVEN |
|---|---|---|---|

**(B♭–C–D♭–E♭–F♭–F–G–A♭)**

| PATTERN FOUR | PATTERN FIVE | PATTERN SIX | PATTERN SEVEN |
|---|---|---|---|

**(B♭–C–D♭–E♭–F♭–F♯–G–A)**

| PATTERN FOUR | PATTERN FIVE | PATTERN SIX | PATTERN SEVEN |
|---|---|---|---|

## B♭ WHOLE TONE

**(B♭–C–D–E–F♯–G♯)**

| WHOLE NECK | PATTERN ONE | PATTERN TWO | PATTERN THREE |
|---|---|---|---|

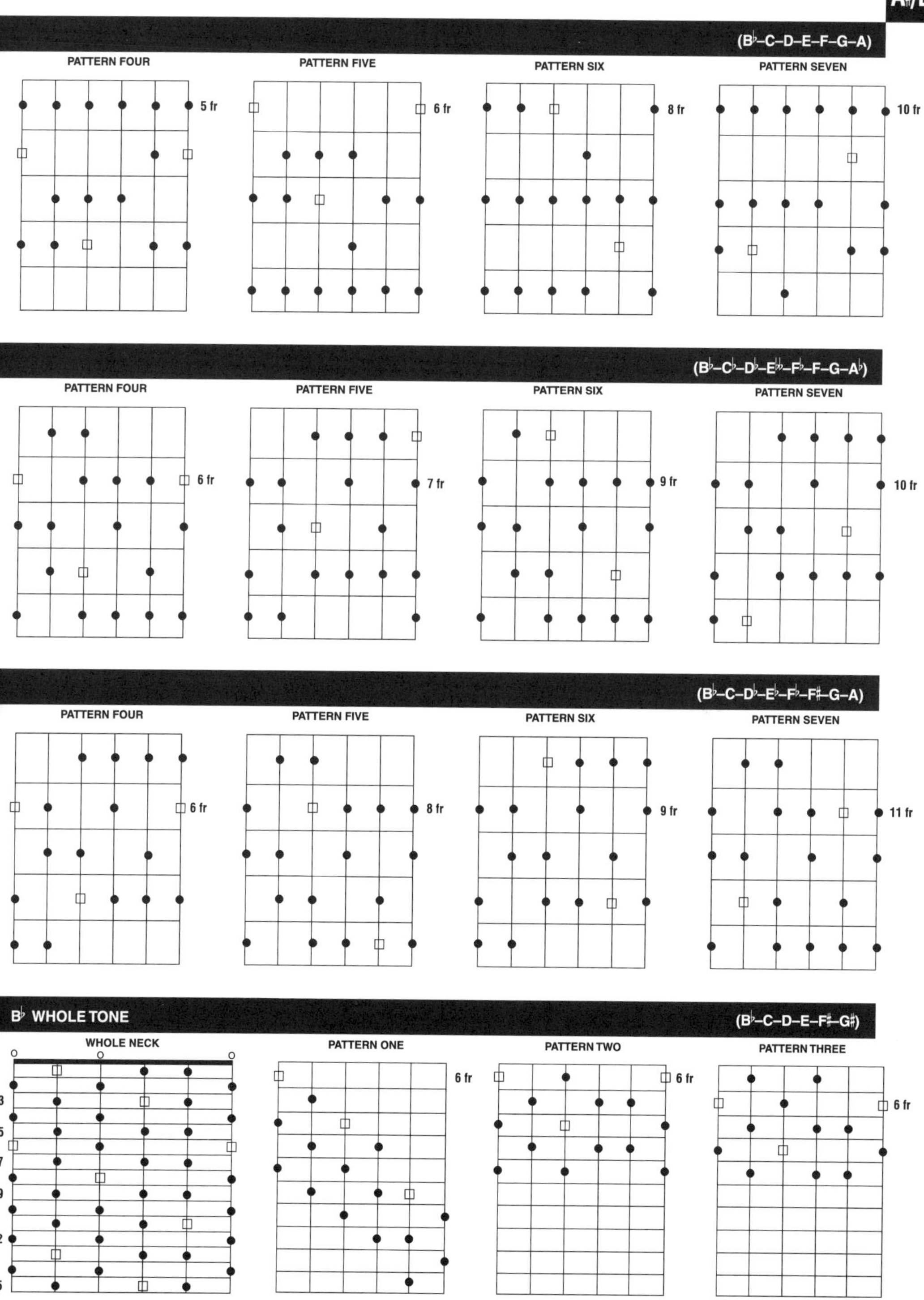

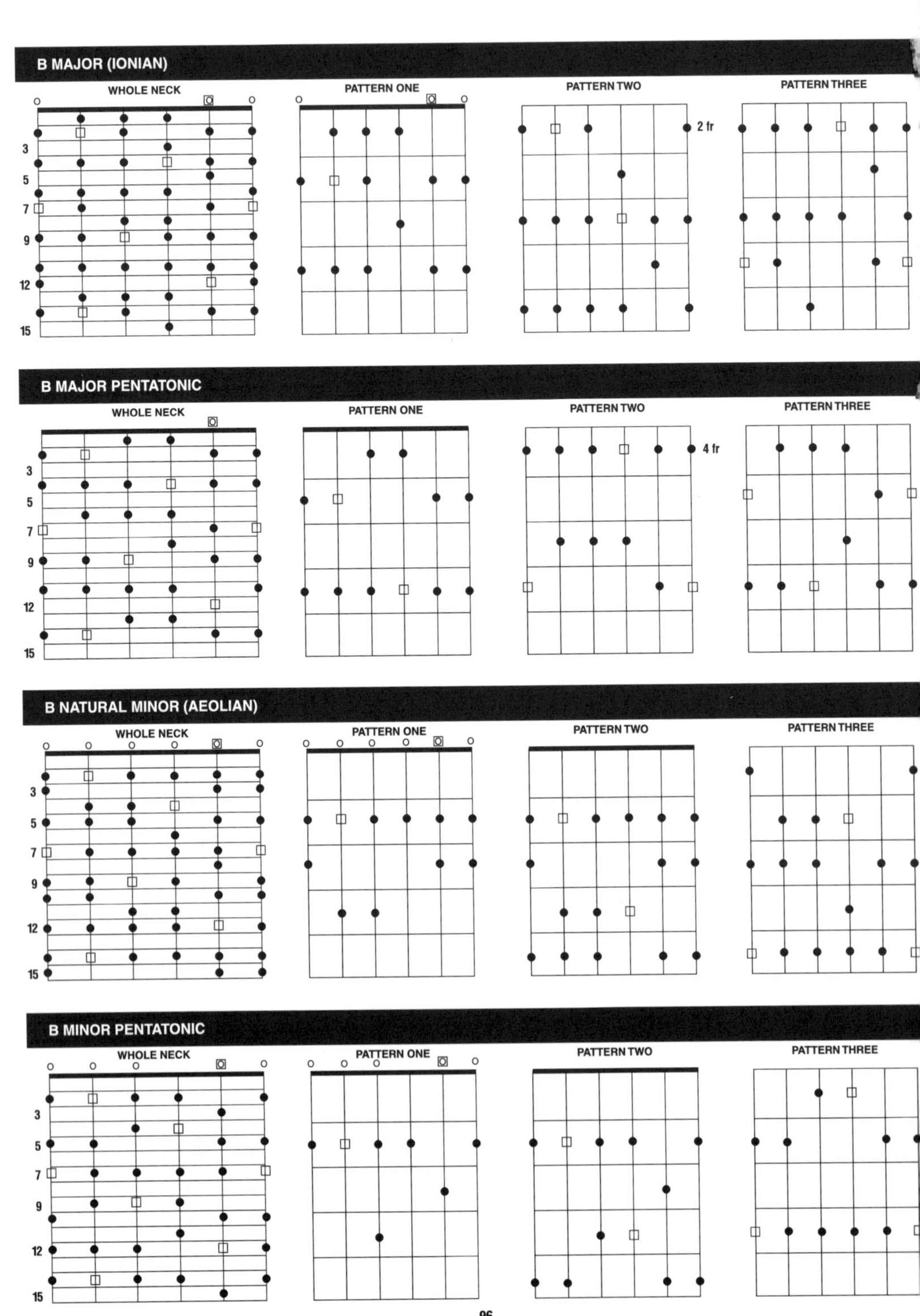

B MAJOR (IONIAN)
WHOLE NECK
PATTERN ONE
PATTERN TWO
2 fr
PATTERN THREE

B MAJOR PENTATONIC
WHOLE NECK
PATTERN ONE
PATTERN TWO
4 fr
PATTERN THREE

B NATURAL MINOR (AEOLIAN)
WHOLE NECK
PATTERN ONE
PATTERN TWO
PATTERN THREE

B MINOR PENTATONIC
WHOLE NECK
PATTERN ONE
PATTERN TWO
PATTERN THREE

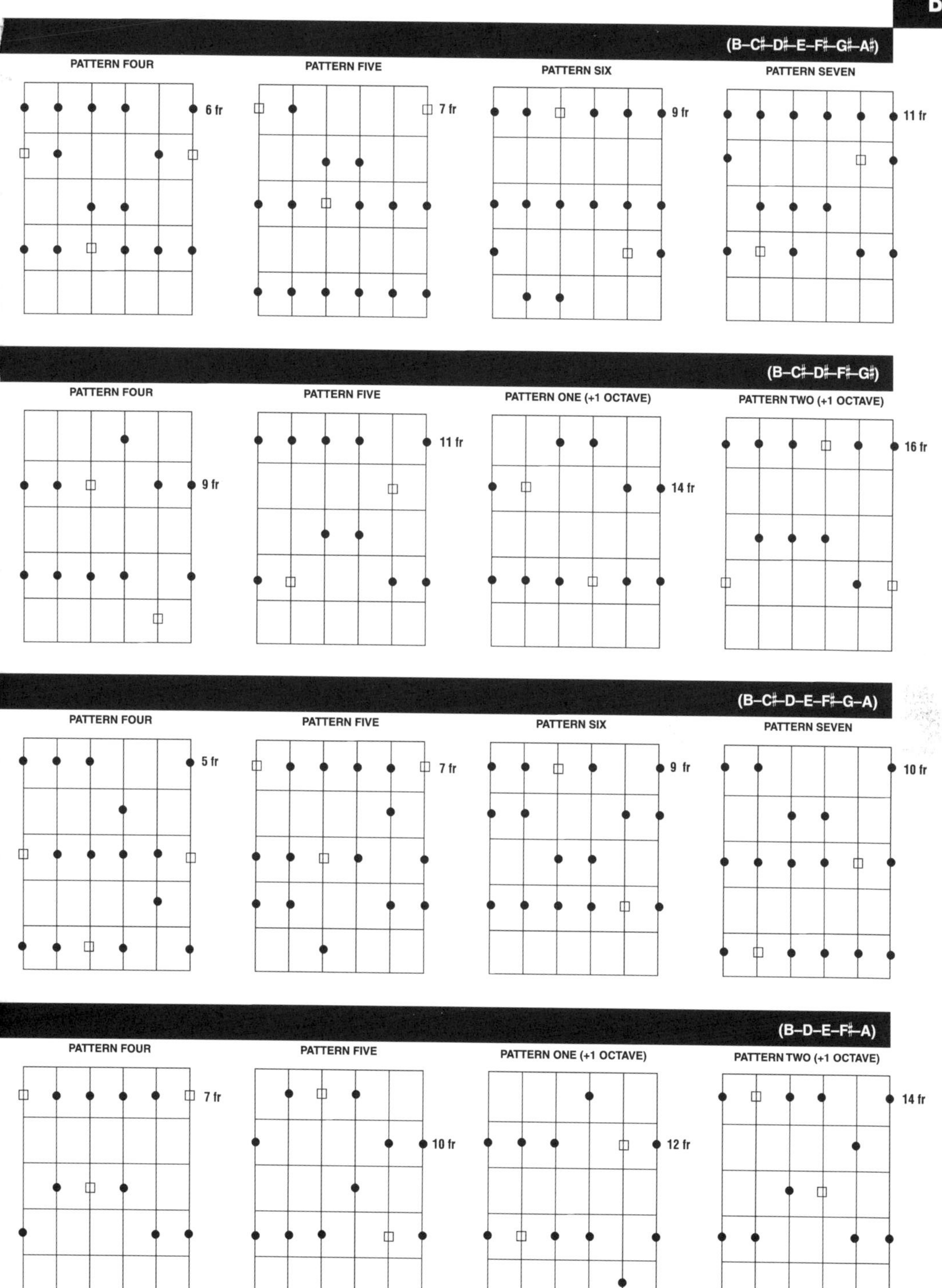

(B–C#–D#–E–F#–G#–A#)
PATTERN FOUR
PATTERN FIVE
PATTERN SIX
PATTERN SEVEN
6 fr
7 fr
9 fr
11 fr
(B–C#–D#–F#–G#)
PATTERN FOUR
PATTERN FIVE
PATTERN ONE (+1 OCTAVE)
PATTERN TWO (+1 OCTAVE)
9 fr
11 fr
14 fr
16 fr
(B–C#–D–E–F#–G–A)
PATTERN FOUR
PATTERN FIVE
PATTERN SIX
PATTERN SEVEN
5 fr
7 fr
9 fr
10 fr
(B–D–E–F#–A)
PATTERN FOUR
PATTERN FIVE
PATTERN ONE (+1 OCTAVE)
PATTERN TWO (+1 OCTAVE)
7 fr
10 fr
12 fr
14 fr

# B BLUES

| WHOLE NECK | PATTERN ONE | PATTERN TWO | PATTERN THREE |

# B MIXO-BLUES

| WHOLE NECK | PATTERN ONE | PATTERN TWO | PATTERN THREE |

# B MIXOLYDIAN

| WHOLE NECK | PATTERN ONE | PATTERN TWO | PATTERN THREE |

# B DORIAN

| WHOLE NECK | PATTERN ONE | PATTERN TWO | PATTERN THREE |

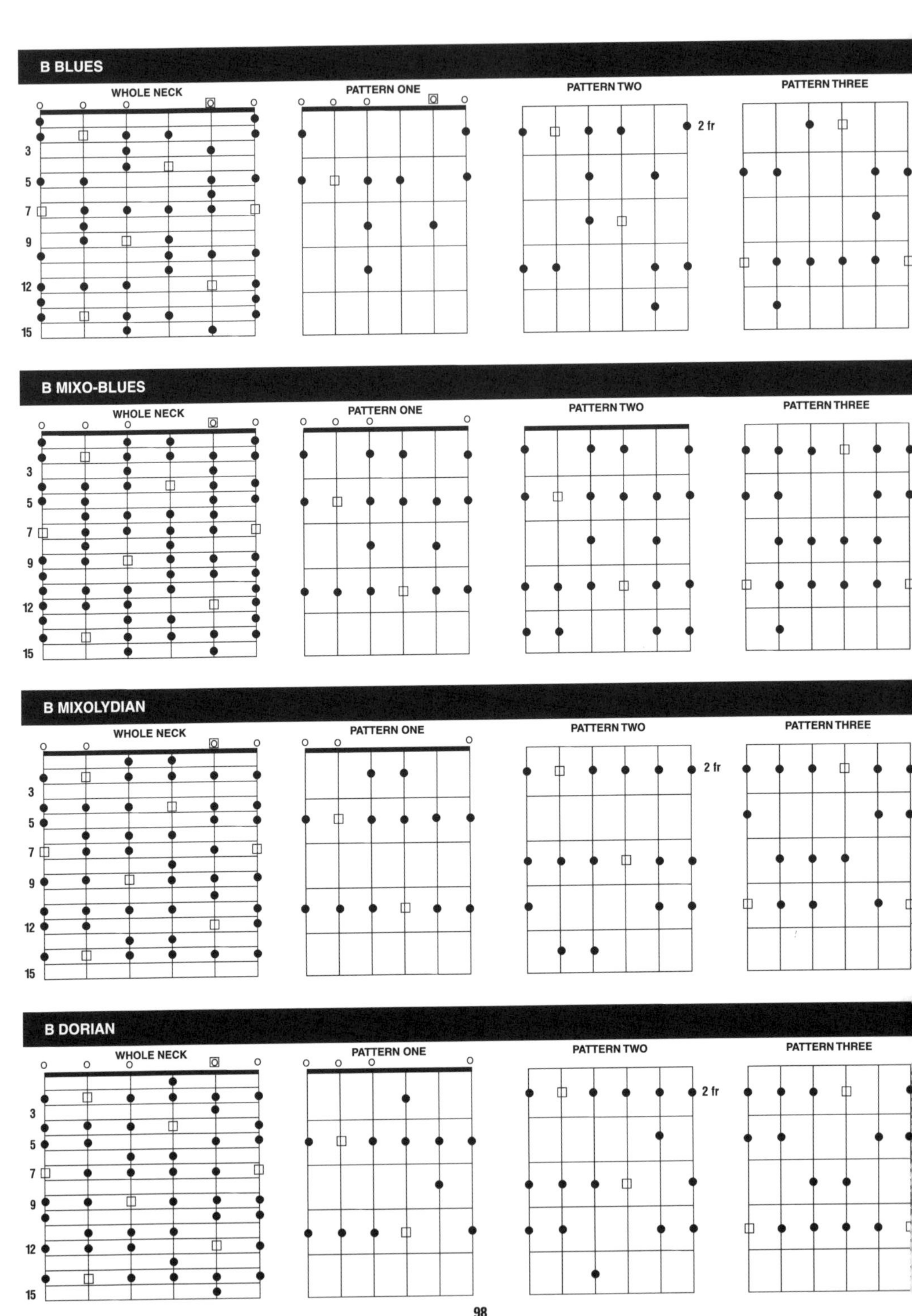

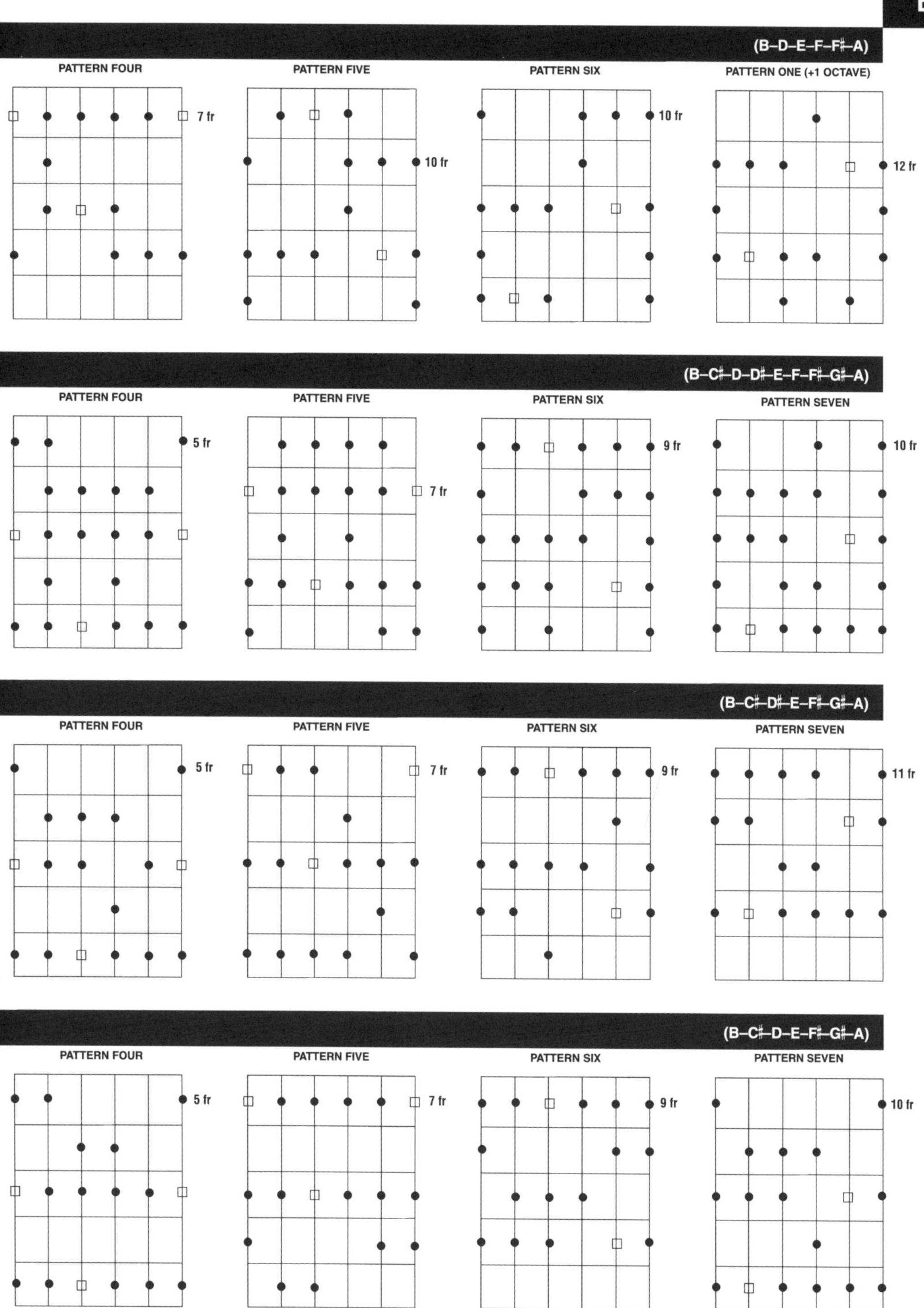

(B–D–E–F–F#–A)
PATTERN FOUR
PATTERN FIVE
PATTERN SIX
PATTERN ONE (+1 OCTAVE)
7 fr
10 fr
10 fr
12 fr
(B–C#–D–D#–E–F–F#–G#–A)
PATTERN FOUR
PATTERN FIVE
PATTERN SIX
PATTERN SEVEN
5 fr
7 fr
9 fr
10 fr
(B–C#–D#–E–F#–G#–A)
PATTERN FOUR
PATTERN FIVE
PATTERN SIX
PATTERN SEVEN
5 fr
7 fr
9 fr
11 fr
(B–C#–D–E–F#–G#–A)
PATTERN FOUR
PATTERN FIVE
PATTERN SIX
PATTERN SEVEN
5 fr
7 fr
9 fr
10 fr

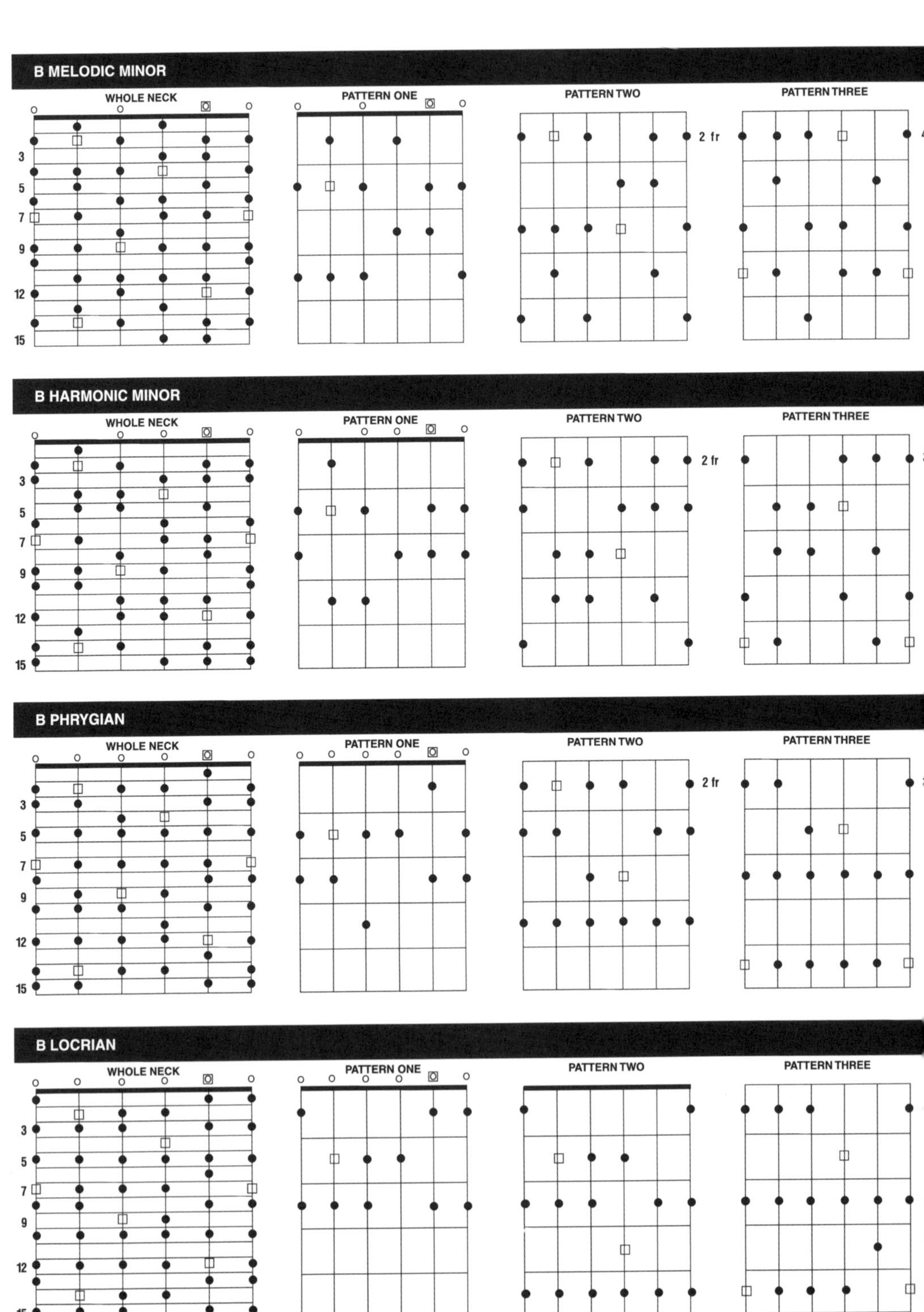

B MELODIC MINOR
WHOLE NECK
PATTERN ONE
PATTERN TWO
2 fr
PATTERN THREE

B HARMONIC MINOR
WHOLE NECK
PATTERN ONE
PATTERN TWO
2 fr
PATTERN THREE

B PHRYGIAN
WHOLE NECK
PATTERN ONE
PATTERN TWO
2 fr
PATTERN THREE

B LOCRIAN
WHOLE NECK
PATTERN ONE
PATTERN TWO
PATTERN THREE

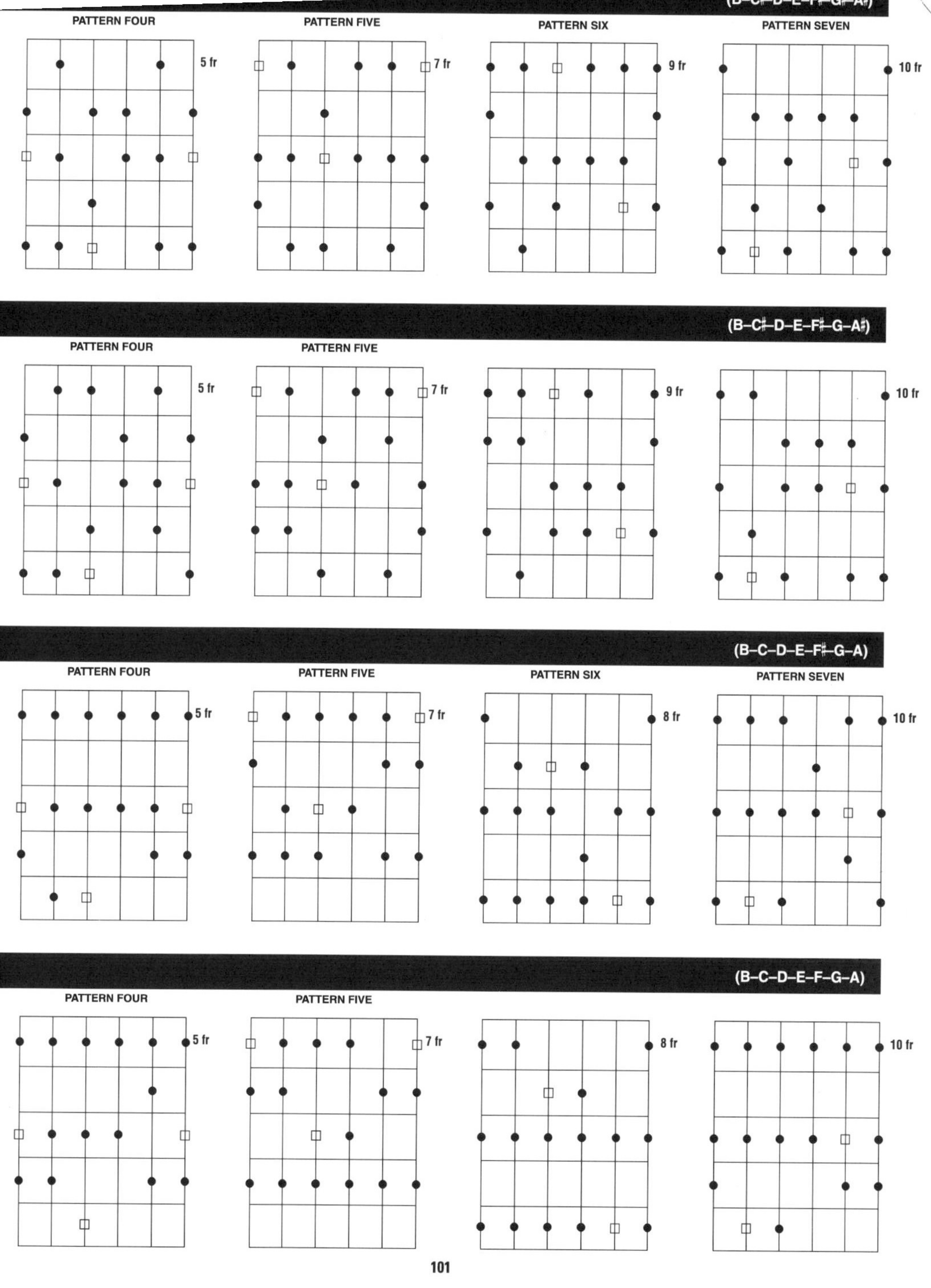

(B–C♯–D–E–F♯–G♯–A♯)
PATTERN FOUR
PATTERN FIVE
PATTERN SIX
PATTERN SEVEN
5 fr
7 fr
9 fr
10 fr
(B–C♯–D–E–F♯–G–A♯)
PATTERN FOUR
PATTERN FIVE
5 fr
7 fr
9 fr
10 fr
(B–C–D–E–F♯–G–A)
PATTERN FOUR
PATTERN FIVE
PATTERN SIX
PATTERN SEVEN
5 fr
7 fr
8 fr
10 fr
(B–C–D–E–F–G–A)
PATTERN FOUR
PATTERN FIVE
5 fr
7 fr
8 fr
10 fr

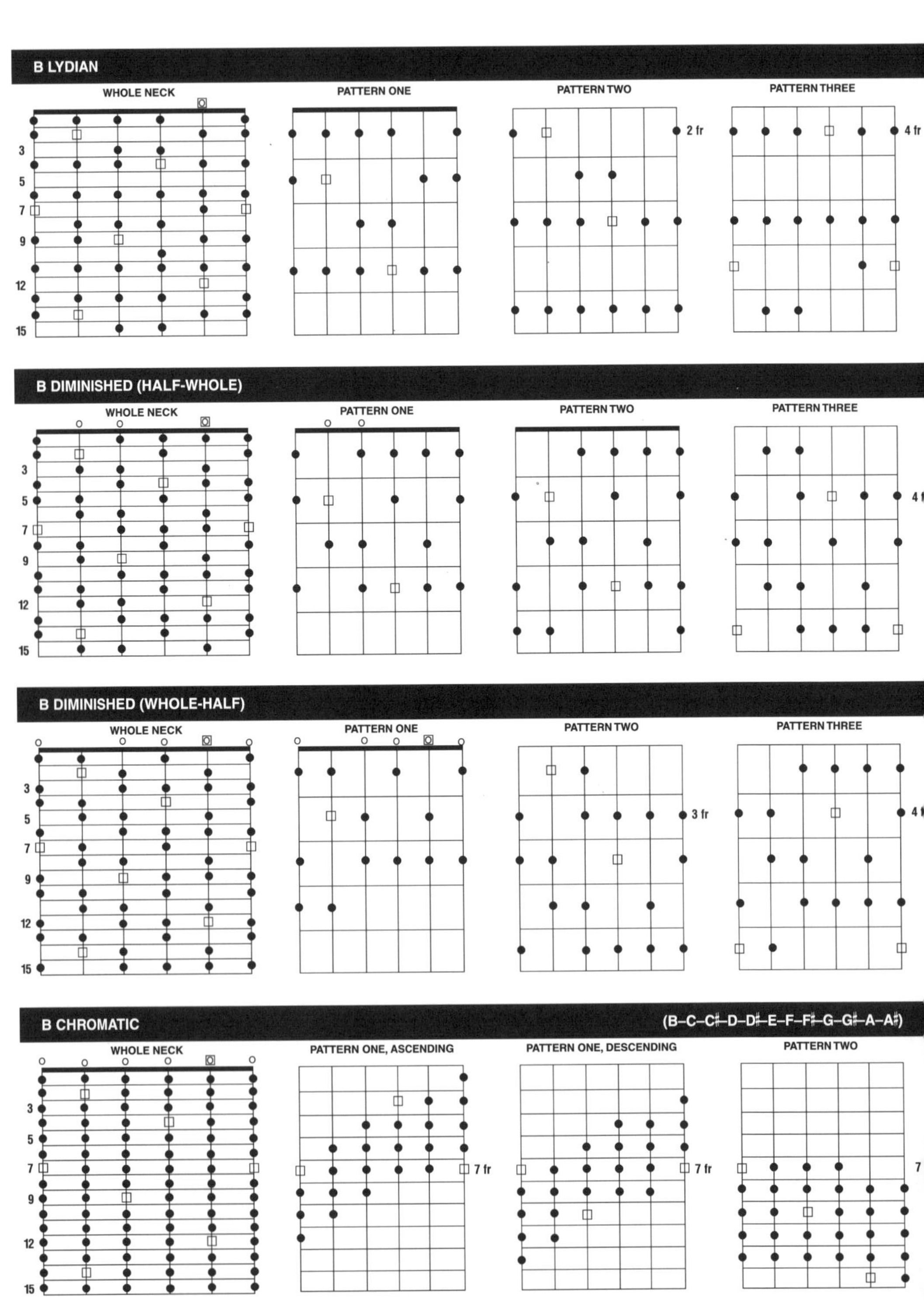

B LYDIAN
WHOLE NECK
PATTERN ONE
PATTERN TWO
2 fr
PATTERN THREE
4 fr
3
5
7
9
12
15
B DIMINISHED (HALF-WHOLE)
WHOLE NECK
PATTERN ONE
PATTERN TWO
PATTERN THREE
4
3
5
7
9
12
15
B DIMINISHED (WHOLE-HALF)
WHOLE NECK
PATTERN ONE
PATTERN TWO
3 fr
PATTERN THREE
4
3
5
7
9
12
15
B CHROMATIC
(B–C–C♯–D–D♯–E–F–F♯–G–G♯–A–A♯)
WHOLE NECK
PATTERN ONE, ASCENDING
7 fr
PATTERN ONE, DESCENDING
7 fr
PATTERN TWO
7
3
5
7
9
12
15

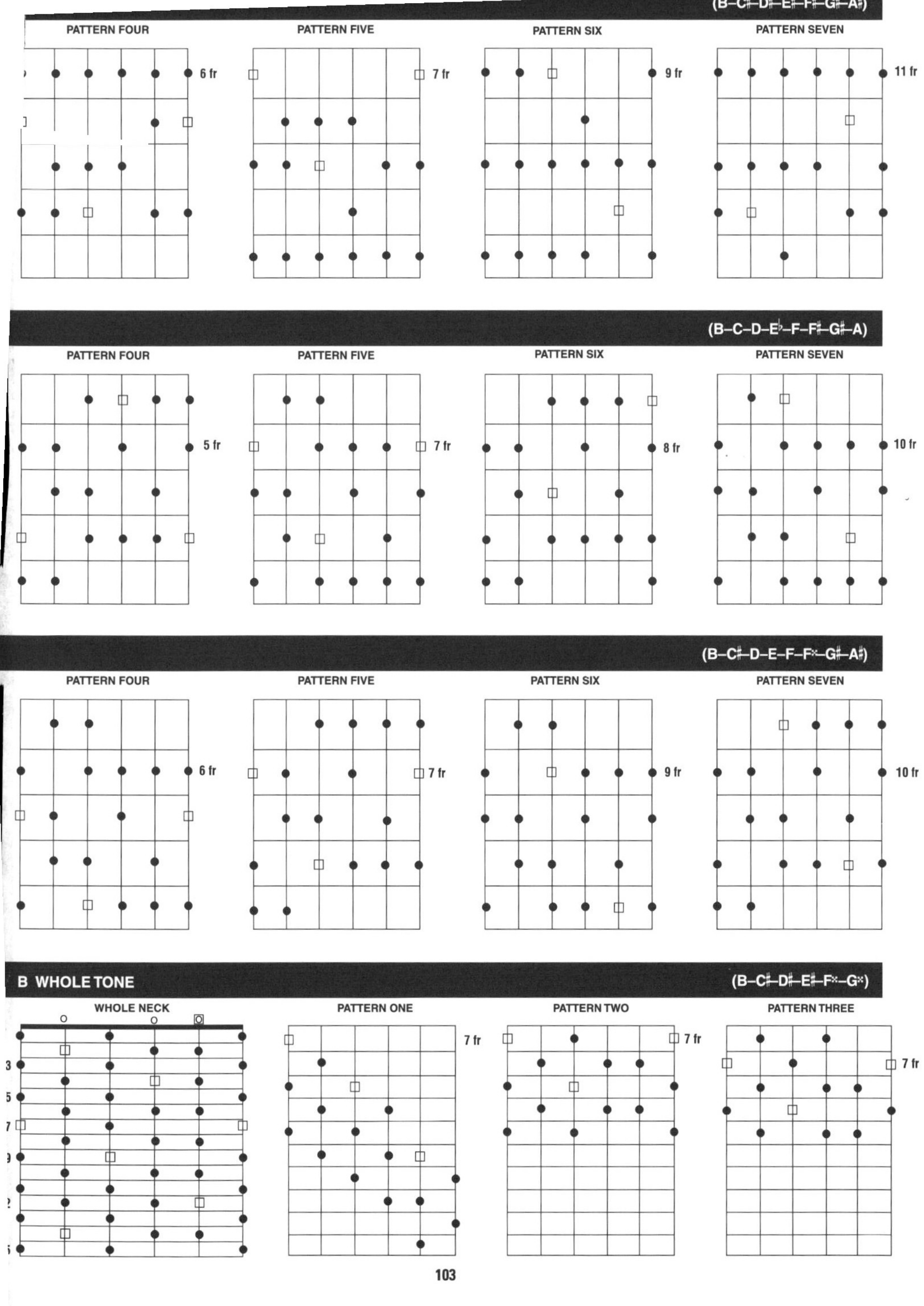

# HOW TO USE THIS BOOK

The *Incredible Scale Finder* is a fast and fun way to gain instant access to over 1,300 essential scale patterns. Just look up a scale, and you can easily find out how and where to play it on your guitar.

## Finding a Scale

To find a scale, first determine the *root* you're looking for (C, D, E, etc.) and then the scale type or *quality* (major, natural minor, etc.).

### Scale Spelling
The scale spelling (e.g., C–D–E–F–G–A–B) tells you the notes of the scale.

### Whole Neck Diagram
A whole neck diagram shows the scale across the entire fretboard. Use it to help you connect the patterns or practice single-string scale improvisation.

### Fretboard Patterns
Fretboard patterns show you how to play the scale in different positions along the neck, from low to high. Each scale has as many as seven patterns—each in a different position on the fretboard.

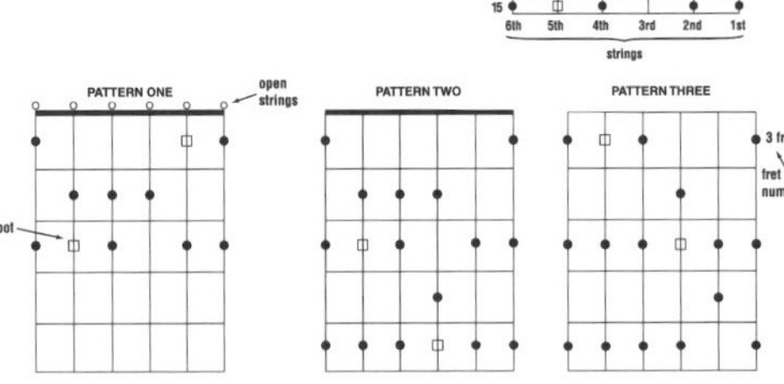

## Playing the Patterns

In general, when playing a scale pattern, keep your hand in one position, and follow the **"one-finger-per-fret" rule**—that is, 1st finger on the 1st fret, 2nd finger on the 2nd fret, 3rd finger on the 3rd fret, and 4th finger on the 4th fret. (A darkened **nut** line or a **fret number** shows you where to position your hand on the fretboard to start the pattern.)

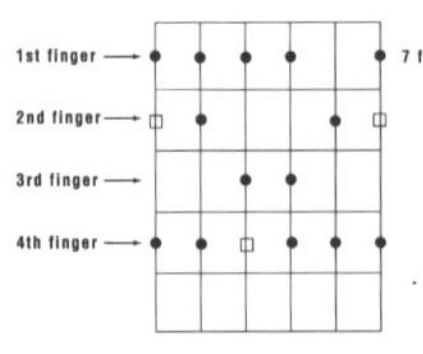


However, if a scale covers more than four frets, you'll need to modify the "one-finger-per-fret" rule. To play these patterns, you must either:

- **stretch** your hand
  to cover the wider distance, or
- **shift** your hand up (or down)
  the fretboard.

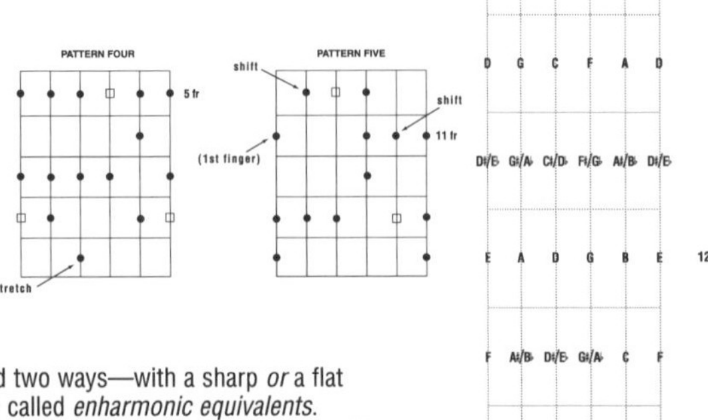


NOTE: Many notes on the guitar can be spelled two ways—with a sharp *or* a flat (e.g., C#/Db, D#/Eb, F#/Gb, etc.). These notes are called *enharmonic equivalents*. Refer to the fretboard chart at right if you need to determine the enharmonic spelling of a scale, or to better understand the component notes of a given fingering.